Beneath
The Southern Cross

(Dreamers and Doers, Part II)

Arlene Galisky

SCRIPTOR HOUSE
THE EPITOME OF GREATNESS

Scriptor House LLC

2810 N Church St Wilmington, Delaware, 19802

www.scriptorhouse.com

Phone: +1302-205-2043

Published by Scriptor House LLC

Paperback: 979-8-88692-098-7
eBook: 979-8-88692-090-1

Waltzing Matilda
Old Australian slang for
traveling on foot and carrying
a swag or bedroll.

CONTENTS

PROLOGUE

Dave and I have just made landfall in Brisbane, Australia, after sailing across the Pacific Ocean. Seventeen months earlier, we'd departed from Victoria, Canada, in a forty-foot sailboat. Our route took us from the west coast of Canada to Hawaii, then south through the Doldrums and across the equator to American Samoa, Tonga, and New Zealand. After spending cyclone season there, we continued on to Fiji, Vanuatu, New Caledonia, and Australia. In that time, we spent 110 days at sea and sailed 10,300 nautical miles (19.075 km).

A year and a half before that, we'd lived 500 miles from the ocean, and neither of us had ever been on a sailboat. Dave then retired at age 55 and we pursued his dream. The learning curve had been steep, events tumultuous, and our lives were transformed. Sharing responsibility for the safety of the boat, for our very survival really, I'd had to overcome many fears. But ultimately, we both enjoyed the lifestyle and reveled in our newly found freedom. (*Crossing the Pacific, Dreamers and Doers, Part 1*).

We now look for a safe haven for *Windy Lady* in a marina near Brisbane, as we plan to explore Australia. We never discuss returning to Canada or selling the boat, and she is our home for another thirteen years. Dave is now 58 years old and I'm 51.

CHAPTER 1
The Adventure Continues

Brisbane is a beautiful city, and as we drive through the suburbs, clouds of delicate, mauve flowers float around the jacaranda trees lining the sidewalks. We've joined forces with another cruising couple and are checking out local marinas. After looking for two days, we settle on a clean, quiet, secure facility run by the Moreton Bay Boat Club on picturesque Redcliffe Peninsula.

We now spend hours searching out shopping areas and walking along nearby beaches. On our first Sunday, we join members of the club on their annual outing to Moreton Island, boarding a flat-bottomed barge to cross the bay. It loads/offloads vehicles directly onto the beach near a huge cement structure that turns out to be a WW II gun emplacement. It's the first of many reminders we will see of the war's impact on this country.

Two days later, we are introduced to the Melbourne Cup, a traditional thoroughbred horse race that is celebrated throughout the land. Members arrive at the club early, prepared to party the day away; some are dressed to the nines and drink champagne, others have a pint and place a bet.

A mass of tropical air then moves down the east coast, bringing forty-degree-plus temperatures and high humidity. The days are brutal as we don't have air conditioning and cannot use our large fans because we don't have the transformer necessary to step down the Aussie 220-240-

volt system to the 110 system on the boat. But we have chores that have to be done before we can leave *Windy Lady*, and as the temperature climbs, our tempers grow shorter. Fortunately, small computer fans in the berths that run off the boat's battery bank get us through the nights.

Dave buys a white 1987 Ford Falcon station wagon, and we scour the city for camping equipment. I can't help but notice the plethora of *NO* signs that we pass: *NO entrance, NO exit, NO passing, NO parking, NO stopping, NO bicycles*; a sign on the beach even threatens a $1,200 fine if a dog isn't on a leash. Canada is no different, I'm sure, but after seventeen months of living on the hook, I'm struck by how restrictive our free societies have become.

When we tell our new acquaintances that we plan to drive up to Darwin and around to Perth, most are not encouraging. We're warned, "Communities outback are few and far between and roads aren't very good. Make sure you take extra supplies, especially things like fan belts, radiator hoses, and spare tires."

Almost as often, we hear, "We'll soon be in the middle of *the Wet*, and rivers flood with the heavy rains, so make sure you don't get stranded! Rivers have been known to cut roads both in front and behind unwary travelers."

The responses become more animated when we reveal that we intend to camp along the way, and most are directed at me. "Arlene, do you know there are over 200 varieties of snakes in this country, and 195 of them are poisonous? They hang off the trees and will slither right through your campsite!"

Another favorite is, "Watch out for crocodiles! Most rivers and billabongs have them, and they just lie in wait for prey, including any foolish camper who happens to come along!"

In fact, the mass of tropical air sitting over Brisbane is a signal that the season is changing, and our research reveals that we have about a month to cross to the northwest coast before rain becomes a problem. So, on a hot, humid Monday morning in mid-November of 1997, we load camping gear and supplies into the back of the station wagon. With the sweat running down my face and back, I'm already having doubts as to how far we'll go.

We'll actually drive 18,700 km in the next ten weeks and spend sixty-five nights sleeping on the ground. We mostly stay in 'van parks, which are numerous and pleasant, as many Australians travel around the country in caravans (trailers). These facilities provide fresh water, toilets, showers, and large common areas for tenters; many also have laundry facilities and camp kitchens.

We experience the intense humidity that blankets the country at the start of the wet, and the tropical storms that follow, bringing torrents of rain. Passing through ancient landscapes, we see evidence of the immense richness of the many resources, and the nearby deep-water ports that make them easy to export. We meet many people, learn about early settlers, and see kangaroos, wallabies, emus, camels, cane toads, frogs, and fruit bats in the wild. We also become familiar with many varieties of birds, goannas, flies, and ants. Our only close encounters with crocodiles, snakes, wombats, cassowaries, and koalas are in the safety of a wildlife park.

CHAPTER 2
Stray Dogs, Crocodiles, and Box Jellyfish

Spending about four hours a day on the road, we take five days to drive the 1,700 km north to Cairns. The hot, humid weather continues, with clouds promising rain that seldom falls. Dave does the driving, as he grew comfortable occupying the left side of the road during our stay in New Zealand. He's also a very restless passenger.

Travel the first day is slow and boring, as we pass through built-up areas on a four-lane highway that's under construction. We spend the night at an oceanfront 'van park near Bundaberg, where a fresh sea breeze pushes waves up on large boulders that spill out from the edge of the property. The owner shows us around the empty campground, blaming the drought for the sparse yellow grass covering the ground.

The wind plays havoc as we set up the tent, and I finally lie down on it while Dave pegs the corners. We then fight to insert poles in sleeves and tie down the fly. When we're finished, a gust flattens the whole thing to the ground. I watch in dismay as it uncertainly wobbles upright, but he solves the problem by opening both doors and turning it a bit, allowing the wind to blow through.

A big 4x4 SUV pulls into the grounds as we work, and three people climb out. A white-haired gentleman is soon limping back and forth under the trees, while a young couple look for a camping spot. They then haul out a ton of gear, and as they're setting up a large three-room tent, the wind rips out one of the floor tabs.

Meanwhile, Dave attempts to speak to the older man but gets no response. Trying again, he volunteers, "I worked in Mount Isa for six months back in 1963, and we're going back to check out the place."

The old man's eyes instantly brighten and he responds in heavily accented English, "I work there seven years!" He then adds that his name is Adolph, and the two of them are soon chatting like old mates.

Dave explains, "I immigrated to Australia in December 1962 and had a choice of cutting sugarcane or working at the mine. I chose the mine, but soon knew that it wasn't something I wanted to do for the rest of my life. It took me six months to save enough money to buy a ticket back to Canada."

Adolph responds, "I go back to Austria in 1962. My wife and son stay here. I take only bad leg from motorcycle accident." He assures Dave, "I visit Isa five years ago and road is good; you have no trouble." Chuckling, he adds, "Not like before, when road follow dry wash. Very rough!"

Nodding his head in agreement, Dave remembers, "Yeah, the housekeeper in the barracks where I stayed, Mrs. 'Tosh, she lost her husband when a flashflood caught him on the road."

The young couple prove to be Adolph's son and daughter-in-law and live near Sydney. She isn't as confident about road conditions as he is and tells me, "We wouldn't go outback without a four-wheel drive." Frowning, she then looks around our campsite and asks, "How do you manage to get by with so little?"

"Practice," I assure her, "Just practice."

Bundaberg (pop. 33,000) is a processing and exporting center for the area's sugarcane, and the aroma of its most famous product, Bundaberg Rum, drifts through the streets when we drive into town next morning. We find a hardware store and buy spikes to replace the flimsy pegs that came with the tent, then visit with a few cruisers whose boats are moored in a marina on the Burnett River.

It's almost midday when we head north, and as grasslands replace subdivisions, the ripe odor of roadkill fouls the air. The toll is heavy, as kangaroos graze near the highway at dawn and dusk and are difficult to see. Many of the vehicles we meet have bull bars protecting the front ends, but we don't, so will try to stay off the road during those hours.

Brahman cows, with their distinctive shoulder humps, graze on the sparse, bleached grasses near the road, and we will see many thousands in the days to come. A large statue of a Brahman bull stands at the entrance to Rockhampton (pop. 62,000), and a sign proclaims it to be Australia's beef capital. We stay at a nearby ocean-side campsite, arriving late and leaving early, and see only extensive mud flats at low tide.

Next day, the countryside looks even drier, with stands of dead-looking trees scattered alongside the road. Mechanical harvesters work in sugarcane fields as we approach Mackay (pop. 60,000), and narrow-gauge railway tracks frequently cross the highway.

We follow a dead-end road to a beach north of town and find a 'van park tucked in behind low sand dunes. It's a beautiful, peaceful spot, and once we've organized our camp, we relax in lounge chairs in the shade of the trees. With a cool breeze stirring the warm air, it's bliss. Later, we walk down the beach and see boats high and dry in a nearby cove; the coast here has twenty-foot tides.

Light rain falls overnight, bringing somewhat cooler temperatures, and clouds sit low on the hills come morning. Welcoming the break in the heat and humidity, we hike down the wide, white-sand beach in misty rain, avoiding large pools of water trapped between sandbars by the low tide. After about thirty minutes, the clouds begin to break up. We now see two rows of tall posts on the beach ahead. They run for about 150 feet from the high-water line down to the ocean. Closer inspection reveals wire mesh stretching around the perimeter. It turns out to be a swimming pen used when box jellyfish invade the bay.

Although no one else is around, two dogs race exuberantly up and down the shoreline, stopping occasionally to dig furiously in the sand or tussle with each other. They both wear collars but appear to be strays, and we assume they've been abandoned. We keep our distance, but when we start back down the beach, the older animal takes up a position about twenty feet behind Dave. Although his mate soon disappears, he follows us for over a mile. (This empathy between Dave and dogs, and sometimes small boys, surfaces occasionally in the years to come. At a vineyard in Chile, I have to laugh when I turn and see both a boy and a dog trailing behind him.)

Dawg has a serious look about his eyes and a reserved manner that I find appealing. He's of medium-size, with a square head and muzzle, and the muscles ripple beneath his tawny coat. We half-heartedly try to send him away, but he follows us to the campsite and creeps under the picnic table. Placing his head on his paws, he keeps watch and later accompanies us when we walk to the corner store. Dave sneaks him a sausage or two at suppertime, and he creeps into the vestibule when we go to bed, throwing himself on the edge of the tent close to my head.

As we're finishing supper that night, a vehicle pulls in beside us and a young couple with a small boy climb out. The man immediately walks over to our picnic table and introduces himself as Todd; he's about thirty, of medium height, and quite muscular, with hair cropped short on top, a long ponytail hanging down his back, and straggly red hair covering his face and chest.

Sitting down across from Dave, Todd tells us that he owns *semis* and hauls freight across the country, then complains that fuel prices vary so much, he has to carry his own fuel. He also boasts that he owns several houses and half-a-million acres of ranch land, but doesn't pay any taxes. We take it all with a grain of salt.

His wife keeps busy unloading the car, organizing supper, and looking after the boy, who appears to be about four. When he later introduces her as Christine, she makes it plain that she's not happy with him. They seem an oddly matched couple, as she's slim and neatly dressed, with long brown hair and a refined manner of speaking. Next morning, I'm not surprised when Todd appears soon after breakfast and announces, "Christine says she's thinking of leaving me and going back to Sydney."

Frowning, he sits down at our picnic table and deals with the issue by demanding, "So, what can you tell me about the sailing life?" Giving himself a mental shake, Dave does his best to respond.

When we later pack up the car, Dawg watches our movements closely and I can't help but feel guilty. If it had been possible, we would have taken him, but we live on a boat and stay in 'van parks. Already, his presence had triggered a visit from the manager, who warned that pets were not allowed. With a somber look, Dawg watches the car pull away, then turns and heads back down the trail to the beach.

After a two-hour drive, we arrive at the resort town of Airlie Beach (pop. 3,000), which services the Whitsunday Islands on the Great Barrier Reef. The midday heat is oppressive and haze obscures the views across to the islands, so we check into a downtown 'van park and spend the afternoon visiting with overseas tourists. A carload of young Israeli women arrives after dark, and with headlights on and doors banging, they squeeze a tent into the middle of an already full tenting area, keeping everyone awake until nearly midnight.

We spend most of the next day at a wildlife park. Goannas, cassowaries, and other birds are housed in small buildings or pens, but kangaroos, wallabies, emus, peacocks, and ducks of all kinds roam freely in the grounds. Dave pauses as we're strolling down the path, and when I turn and follow his eyes, I see a big buck kangaroo bent over a much smaller female. The buck is already straightening and seems to be looking back at him, so I grab his arm, breaking any eye contact. I don't know anything about 'roos, but this one is bigger than even Dave's husky, six-foot-plus figure.

When we arrive at the snake house, Rob, the self-styled *Barefoot Bushman,* is lifting a poisonous snake out of a glass cage. He handles several while describing their habits and habitats and debunks many of the tales we've heard about snakes hanging off trees and lurking behind bushes. (It makes me feel a bit better about camping.) We then run through a downpour to the koala house and listen to his next spiel. I later pet one of these cuddly-looking creatures and am surprised to find the fur rough and hard.

We arrive early for the scheduled crocodile feeding and are disappointed to see only a small *saltie* lying beside a pond covered with green scum. Rob then enters the enclosure, pokes about in the water with a short, slender stick, and a huge saltwater crocodile lunges forward; Solomon is fifteen feet long and weighs 1,000 pounds. We are so impressed with what we see that we stay for the next show.

Rob explains that, as a rule of thumb, a croc doubles in weight for every foot in length. They can stay submerged for up to three hours, and like fish, don't waste energy chasing food, just lie in wait for it. He throws a bit of chicken four feet away from Solomon, who ignores it, but when a piece lands beside him, he grabs it with an incredibly quick twist of his head, and a loud, explosive *whump* as his jaw snaps shut. To prove some point, maybe just to give the audience a thrill, Rob also feeds him by hand, and the crocodile carefully takes the meat in his huge jaws.

Rather defensively, he now explains that Solomon badly mauled his niece a year earlier, putting her in hospital for nine weeks. She tripped during a show, falling beside the reptile, which grabbed her legs and pulled her into the water. Her dad was able to beat him off, and then did so a second time when she was grabbed again.

Several weeks later, we hear a radio interview with the young woman, the first since her accident. She explains that she fell into the croc's *kitchen*, so what happened wasn't Solomon's fault. She adds that she remained conscious throughout the attack and held her head out of the water, or might have drowned. After numerous operations, she still requires further surgery.

After leaving the wildlife park, we stumble across a National Parks Center and stop for a quick look. There's not much to see but what there is blows my mind. A model of a box jellyfish hangs overhead, showing a small, rectangular, diaphanous body, with tentacles attached to each of its four corners. The ribbon-like tentacles are over six feet long and stretch out in various directions. On a wall nearby, photographs show the injuries sustained by a woman when a tentacle wrapped itself around her thigh. Taken at two weeks, two months, and two years, the images of raw, inflamed sores caused by the suckers make me shudder; each is about an inch across and leaves an ugly scar. (As I recall, ten feet of tentacle wrapped around a child could deliver enough poison to cause death.)

That night, we have to acknowledge that there is much we don't know about camping in Australia. We do know, however, that we don't have time to waste recovering from such horrendous injuries. For the rest of the trip, we don't consider swimming or camping in areas posted with warning signs.

Next morning, the crazy laughter of several kookaburras echoes through the campground as we have breakfast. A sudden downpour sends us running to the camp kitchen, where we visit with two British couples until the rain stops, then everyone packs up and leaves.

We drive north to a range of hills that rises sharply above the coastal plain, then turn into Bowling Green Bay National Park, where we stop at the Alligator Creek campground. The vegetation is sparse and dry, save for a narrow strip of green alongside the dry creek bed, and I'm reminded of camping at home in the fall when half the leaves are off the trees. Now, however, cicadas whine shrilly in our ears, and bits and pieces of bark from gum trees litter the nearby meadow.

We set up the tent under a large tree near the meadow, and as soon as we've finished, big green ants are streaming up from the four corners of the fly. The darn things also drop off the trees as we relax in our lounge chairs, and they bite! Toward dusk, small kangaroos and wallabies appear in the meadow and graze between the tents. The young joeys are wary, and whenever one is startled, it jumps head first into mother's pouch, leaving two huge feet hanging out behind.

After supper, we talk to an American backpacker from Oregon, who reports on his adventures in Oz. Ivan has just hiked the trail we plan to do next day and tells me, "Yeah, I saw a tree snake when I was coming down the trail! It was just at eye level, watching me as I came toward it."

Upon learning that we're from British Columbia, he eagerly describes touring the province on a bicycle and cites the places that he visited. When we tell him that we sailed across the Pacific Ocean, he throws up his hands and moans, "You win! I can't compete with that!" As we talk, the sky grows darker, kangaroos and wallabies disappear into the bush, and large cane toads take over the meadow. When the hum of the cicadas reaches a final crescendo and falls silent, we go to bed.

We start Week 2 with our first hike in the Australian bush and are underway at 0630, hoping to beat the heat. We follow a power line through a very dry forest of whitish, poplar-sized gum trees, then work our way up a creek bottom, where a shallow trickle of water joins shady pools, and scattered mounds of gravel and large boulders reveal the extent of flooding during the rainy season. I constantly scan the path and trees for snakes but see none. Two hours later, we climb up a steep slope, work our way around huge rocks along the edge of a ravine, and arrive at a rock face over which Alligator Creek falls. While we rest, numerous small lizards dart about the rocks, and I see several large, brilliant blue dragonflies.

Dark clouds hang low over the hills when we start back, and a cloudburst catches us out in the open. With the first large, cold drops, I run for the trees but their long, slender leaves provide no shelter. We continue walking and are quickly soaked to the skin. Twenty minutes later, the rain passes, and our shirts dry quickly when the sun returns. We're back in camp at 1130, only to find we've left the tent fly open and have a pool of water on the floor and wet mattresses. Despite more showers, everything is dry before dark.

Next morning, we're disgusted to find the tent and car roof covered in bird droppings, but a park ranger informs us that cicadas are the culprits. He disappears for a few minutes and returns with a large insect, about two inches long, with a broad, blunt head. Pointing to a round, half-inch hole in the ground nearby, he explains, "They spend part of their life cycle underground and are now emerging from their old bodies." We've already seen complete shells of bodies, including legs and wings, stuck on tree trunks and our car tire.

We plan to spend the night in the resort city of Cairns, but as we draw closer, the sky grows darker and a rain shower partly obscures a nearby range of hills. Minutes later, gusts of wind buffet the car and driving rain bounces off the bitumen and floods the windshield. Travelers coming from the area have told us the heat was so uncomfortable they were happy to leave. It's our fate to arrive with the first good storm of the wet, which brings a widespread, cold rain.

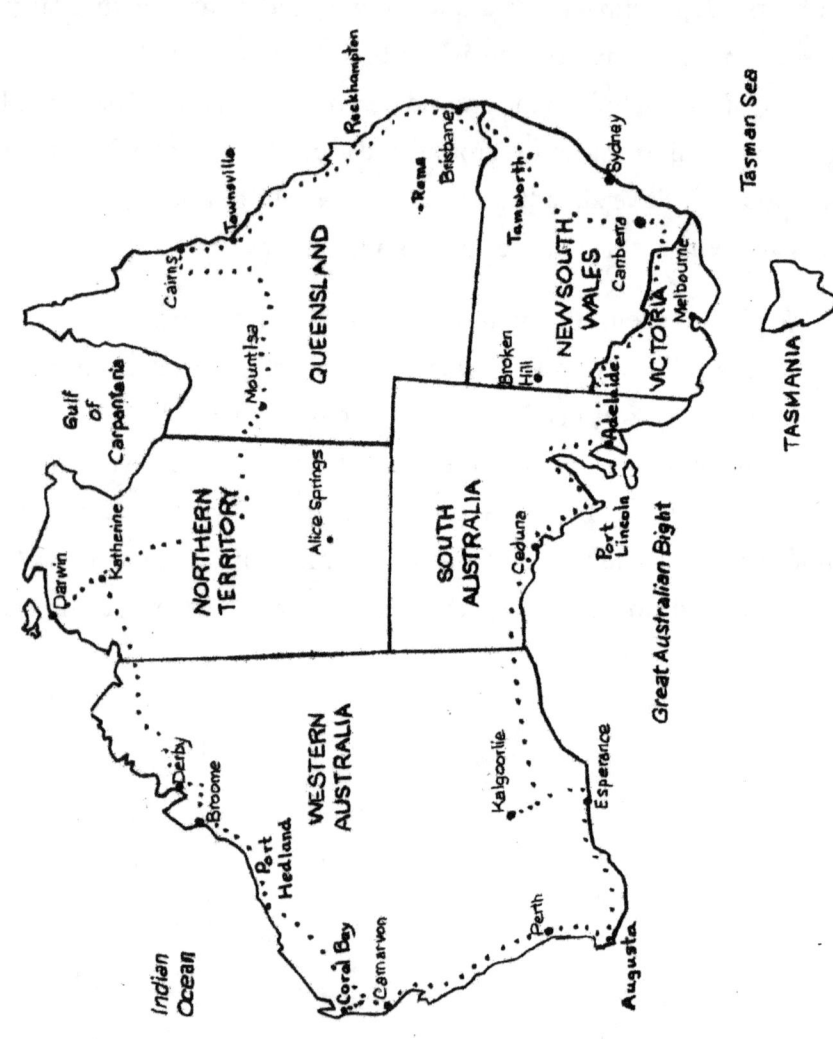

Camping Route 1

CHAPTER 3
The Wet, One-Lane Roads, and Gondwana

Having no interest in spending a wet night on the coast, we drive a short distance north of Cairns, then turn onto a road leading up to the Atherton Highlands. The road snakes back and forth as it climbs, but views of coastal plain and ocean described in my travel guide are hidden by low cloud and rain. Heavy rain falls for another hour, and the late afternoon sky is still dark and sullen when we arrive in Atherton. With only one other camper, we have our pick of sites at the 'van park and set up the tent about three feet from a low-roofed camp kitchen. Although it's cold and wet outside, we're dry and comfortable inside as we prepare supper and linger over tea.

Next morning, low clouds again threaten rain, but Dave manages a stroll about the yard during a lull in the storm. He talks to a man laying pipe in a trench, who explains, "I'm just helping out my mom; she owns the place." He then continues, "I'm actually a sales rep for a feed company. I spend most of my time on the road, as my area is huge and I visit each station twice a year." After chatting briefly, he turns back to work but first points to the sky and offers a word of advice, "You might want to stay on the bitumen when you head south. This rain could make the side roads a bit risky."

Just outside of Atherton, we stop at a quarantine roadblock and unhappily give up the tomatoes, oranges, and mangoes that we bought on our way out of town. The women are very nice about it, explaining that they're trying to stop the spread of fruit flies. We then turn into a small park on the headwaters of the Baron River; it's a pretty spot, described as high-altitude rain forest. There's not much water coming over Dinner Falls, but I'm intrigued by the tall, slim trees that I see, as the lower trunks are supported by large, wide buttress roots that keep the shallow-rooted trees from blowing over. At ground level, the trees are maybe ten-feet wide.

Close by, Mt Hypipamee volcanic crater is described as an explosive pipe. It has a diameter of 200 feet and sheer granite walls that plunge down 190 feet to the surface of a stagnant, algae-covered pool. In times past, gases from molten rock built up beneath it, causing an explosion that hurled volcanic bombs across the landscape.

An hour down the road, the good two-lane highway ends at Mt Garnet, and we leave the village on a narrow, one-lane paved road. When meeting a vehicle, Dave now slows and steers the passenger side of the car off the bitumen. At least, that's the plan, but some drivers will not move over, and he is forced onto the narrow, dirt shoulder, which is soft due to recent rain. Road trains also barrel down the center of the road; normally they haul three trailers and are 150-feet long, but here they pull only two.

The shoulder is just wide enough to accommodate the car, with a steep bank down into the ditch, and I'm feeling like potential roadkill by the time we've squeezed past a second truck. In fact, the ditch is strewn with the remains of kangaroos, cows, and one enormous wild boar.

Before long, the parched grasslands of the Atherton Highlands give way to the endless miles of bush and countless dry washes of the outback. We now drive through a scrub-vine forest that my guidebook dates back to a supercontinent called Gondwana, which included Asia, Africa, Australia, and Antarctica. I know little about the earth's history and am fascinated to read that this supercontinent began to breakup 180 million years ago. My education is actually just beginning, as in the weeks ahead, the Australian landscape provides many examples of the earth's geological history.

Rain appears imminent when we come to a sideroad leading to a cattle station that I want to visit. A sign beside the dirt track reads *30 km*, but recalling the advice Dave received that morning, we stay on the bitumen. The day then heats up and we drive with open windows, as neither of us likes the side effects of air conditioning. By the time we drive 300 km to Greenvale, the car interior is an oven.

Parking downtown, we walk through deserted streets that bake in the heat, then come to a small shop that is open. There's not much on the shelves, but we find a brochure that explains the town was built to service a nickel mine that shut down in 1994. The property was repackaged as a retirement community, complete with Olympic-sized pool, tennis courts, and 9-hole, sand-scraped golf course. The current population is 270.

We duck into a pub and enjoy large, cold beers while talking to the innkeeper about a report we heard on the radio that morning. Five aborigine groups have signed onto a plan for a gas pipeline between Papua New Guinea and Gladstone, on Australia's east coast. Smiling, the man pulls out a glossy brochure, which explains that the venture will provide energy for several projects, including a new aluminum smelter. His eyes lighting up, he adds, "The pipe for the project will be trucked from Townsville right past our front door. It's going to require major road improvements, and the town should benefit significantly."

A scruffy, overgrown 'van park on the edge of town appears deserted when we pull into the site, but we track down the owner at work in a nearby machine shop. Later, as we relax in our lounge chairs after supper, the quiet is broken by the harsh cries of a small flock of galahs (ga-lahs') feeding under the trees. The birds are a type of cockatoo, with rose-colored throat and breast, soft gray back and wings, and black tail feathers. We also see a white cockatoo, two rainbow lorikeets (smaller birds with blue, green, red, and yellow feathers), and a large cottontail rabbit.

Dark clouds have been massing in the west and the sound of distant thunder now rolls across the plains. As night falls, a lightshow spreads across the sky, with sheet lightning outlining massive thunderheads and jagged streaks of fork lightning sporadically darting down to the ground. Two hours later, the storm is overhead and heavy rain chases us into the tent. With every flash, the stark outline of a tree is visible through the tent wall, but we remain snug and dry and I fall asleep as the storm rages.

Next morning is bright and clear, but we see signs of the storm as we leave town. Water has pooled in ditches and beneath bridges, and a wide, shallow stream runs down one wash. After days of seeing only dry riverbeds and creek bottoms, it's a reminder that we need to keep moving. One-meter gauges in areas marked *floodplain* now take on new meaning, as do six-meter gauges (twenty feet) in creek beds.

We meet seventeen vehicles on the 200-km drive to Charters Towers, and three of them are road trains. Roadkill is frequent along this section of one-lane road and the smell so foul that I try not to breathe as we pass. Magpies feeding at the road's edge usually provide advance warning, rising into the air when we approach, and I then hold my breath. But sometimes the feeding birds are wedge-tail eagles and I get a good whiff before they reluctantly give way.

Charters Towers (pop. 10,000) proves to be a hot, dry, dusty cattle town dating back to an 1871 gold rush. It reached its heyday about 1900, with a population of 30,000 and a stock exchange. Several large, elegant old buildings stand along the extra wide main street that once provided camel trains with the room needed to turn around, and we check out a few of the stores before looking for a 'van park.

We are now 150 km inland from Townsville, having spent the last three days making a 1,000 km loop to the north. From here, a good two-lane paved highway leads west into the sparsely populated, dry, red center of the continent. Mount Isa is 770 km away, and we're back on the route Dave followed 35 years ago.

With a sense that the real adventure is just beginning, we set off with renewed enthusiasm next morning. We're soon stopping at a viewpoint in the Great Dividing Range, where we look back across the coastal plain from an elevation of 1,800 feet. Ahead of us, the land flattens out, and long, dry grasses and scattered trees extend to the horizon. Soon, only an occasional scrub tree shimmers in the distance. In the heat of late afternoon, we spot a number of camels kneeling in sparse shade under a few trees in a corner of a paddock.

They're large animals, much bigger than the Brahmans that graze near the road, and appear to be domesticated.

When we stop at the visitors' center in the small town of Hughendon, we learn about the dinosaur fossils in the area; in fact, there's a major attraction in the back room. *Hughie* is a life-sized replica of the bird-footed dinosaur (muttaburra-saurus langdoni); its 24 feet long, 11 feet high, and the real one weighed about 27 tons.

The local 'van park bakes in the unrelenting heat as we set up our tent on bare, dusty ground, and there's no relief even when the sun goes down. A large flock of galahs and a smaller group of sulfur-crested cockatoos then raise a ruckus as they settle in for the night. We sit at a picnic table and visit with our neighbors, who come from a small town in South Australia. They drive a Ute with a snorkel, tray top, canvas cover, extra supplies of water and fuel, and a 12-volt refrigerator. While the men talk about traveling outback, the wife is very quiet.

She then hesitantly explains, "We've just spent six months in Cairns." Before long, a dam seems to break and the words pour forth. "Our son was involved with an aborigine girl and he's trying to raise their two-year-old daughter on his own. He works full time, so we tried to support him while he sorted out his life." As she talks, I sense that she's become attached to her grandchild and is now torn by divided loyalties, not wanting to leave but unable to stay. I also suspect that she hasn't talked to another woman in a long while.

The tent is an oven when I crawl in at 2200, and I can hardly breathe. It stays that way for most of the night. The temperature drops briefly toward morning, but the day heats up quickly, and my wash is dry an hour after I hang it out at 0700. The Aussie now brings over a map and spreads it on the hood of the car. Tracing tracks across the empty interior with his finger, he describes various routes to Dave and ends by advising, "The best months to travel are July and August, and we always take a four-wheel drive."

A few pools of muddy rainwater sit in the ditch as we leave town, and I see three emus, their long necks and bodies dark against the dry grass. We drive through more unfenced, sun-bleached grasslands that day, and the ripe odor of roadkill again hangs over the road. We also pass two dirt sideroads, both posted with signs that read, *No fuel or water for 1,200 km.*

I filled our insulated jug with tap water before leaving, and by midmorning it's so warm that it's not fit to drink. With hot air blasting through the car windows, I'm soon desperate for something cold. We stop in Julia Creek about 1230 and learn that the temperature is over forty degrees. After a cold beer, a sandwich, and half an hour in air-conditioning, the heat is even more debilitating when we continue on.

We're soon crossing a tabletop-flat plain that was once the bottom of an ancient, shallow inland sea that stretched across the interior from the Gulf of Carpenteria to the Great Australian Bite. At the time, Australia and Antarctica were still joined together. On the far side of this plain, the country grows rougher, with small hills, gullies, and scattered rock stretching away on either side of the road.

We spend the night in the mining town of Cloncurry, and the heat is just bearable if I don't move. I find a spot of weak shade in the 'van park, then sit and read until dark. For years, the town held the Australian high temperature record of 48.8 degrees Celsius (127.5 degrees Fahrenheit). It lost that distinction when miners moved into the northwest of the country, where a temperature over 50 degrees Celsius was recorded.

Unwittingly, we've set up our tent beside a path that goes through a nearby hedge, giving Dave the opportunity to quiz a passing neighbor. The man admits to being a permanent resident of the campground and says he works for the railroad. In response to Dave's questions, he explains, "The track crews you've seen are replacing wooden ties with cement sleepers, but the sleepers are easily damaged when a car jumps the track, so many of them have to be replaced, too." He then volunteers, "I worked out of Darwin for seven years and sure wish I'd stayed there."

As I lie awake that night, unable to sleep in the heat, I think about Dave's conversation with the railroader. I'm reminded of how easily he connects to the men we meet, no matter their backgrounds. They all strike me as being confident, capable individuals, who knew how to work with their hands. I've since heard that relationship described as a *brotherhood,* and it seems fitting.

I think back to what I know of his life growing up in small towns in southern Saskatchewan, where his dad had also worked on the railroad. He'd been a big lad and a willing worker, and while still in school had summer jobs as a farmhand, a section hand on the railroad, and a roughneck on an oilrig. He joined the air force as soon as he graduated and later worked at an oil refinery.

But I'd seen men turn to him in a way that made me think something else was going on. That maybe his stature, his height and bearing, had once played a role in an ancient male hierarchy. In musing about this, I come to understand something that had annoyed me intensely for the past three years. He would not read instructions and had no patience with me when I wanted help with something. For him, the process of accomplishing the job was a journey, and he needed to figure it out himself.

Trucks wake us at 0500 next morning, and a brisk wind keeps the air cool for two hours before the heat starts to build. We stop at a memorial park on the way out of town and learn that copper was discovered here in 1867, and a uranium mine opened in 1958 and operated for twenty years. After climbing a small knoll for a view of the town, I stop at a public toilet before we again set off. When I turn to flush it, I'm appalled to see two green, four-inch-long legs hanging below the rim.

CHAPTER 4

3,000 Feet Underground

The drive to Mount Isa takes an hour and a half, and the terrain becomes rockier and more broken as the road winds through low hills. We then turn a corner and find ourselves in a world of red earth and rock. The high stack of the smelter comes into view about eight km out, and soon the mine itself appears. Mount Isa is a company town (pop. 24,000) and the mine produces silver, lead, copper, and zinc.

After stopping at the visitors' center, we tour through the town while Dave looks for his old watering holes. We locate the boarded-up, cement-block barracks where he stayed, and immersed in the past, he now explains, "I was tired of Saskatchewan winters and came to Australia seeking sun and sand. The middle of the desert wasn't really what I had in mind though. There was no air conditioning, and it was hot in the barracks and hot underground. The food in the dining hall was also pretty basic."

His voice growing more animated, he continues, "By the end of a shift, my clothes would be dirty and dripping with sweat. I'd hang them in the locker room, where air was pumped in, and they'd dry overnight. Come morning, they'd be stiff as boards, but I'd put them on anyway, as soon enough, they'd be dripping again." He adds, "We only washed clothes once a week because really, after two hours, it didn't make any difference."

We locate a 'van park about two km up the dry bed of the Leichardt River, and as we set up camp, the sky grows darker and thunder rumbles in the distance. The storm hits half an hour later, with the wind nearly flattening the tent, rain bucketing down, and thunder crashing overhead. We place our chairs in the vestibule, then sit and watch the lightning flashes through the fly. When a corner of the fly pulls loose, wind drives in the rain and we're soaked. Dave quickly fixes it, but we spend the next three hours reading in the car.

When the rain stops about 1630, we're off to the Irish Club, which provides accommodation and meals for the single men at the mine. The air-conditioned club takes up half a city block and appears much like a casino, with restaurant, buffet, bars, poker machines, TV screens, live music, and pool tables. We have supper in the buffet where the miners eat, choosing from a wide selection of foods. Dave is speechless the whole time, unable to believe his eyes.

We spend next morning at the Frank Aston Underground Museum, where we inspect old mining and farming equipment, then study rock and crystal samples displayed in several cabinets. We climb seventy feet up a shaft and emerge near an old water tank on a hilltop, where tools and furnishings used by early settlers are on display (many are familiar to us). Two aborigine encampments are also set up; one has a shelter made from long grasses and a few wooden tools and bowls (Kalkadoon), the other has a driftwood shelter and small dugout canoe (Gulf Islands).

Our last stop is at *a tent house*, a style of building once prevalent in the desert. Long and narrow, it has a double roof constructed of corrugated iron and canvas that is supposed to keep the building cool. As we leave, we stop to chat with the woman on duty at a kiosk near the entrance. Her husband is with her and happens to work for Mount Isa Mines; two hours later, the men are still talking.

The miner happily answers Dave's questions and tells him about a labor dispute in October of 1963 that shut the mine down for eighteen months. Shaking his head, he declares, "The strike nearly broke the union, and it never really recovered. Drug tests are now mandatory for new hires, and all employees are subject to random tests." He then adds cheerfully, "On the other hand, chilled air circulates in the lower levels of the mine, and equipment is operated by remote control."

Meanwhile, the wife tells me that they've lived in Isa for 25 years and waited years to become eligible for a house. New mines in the area now fly workers in from Sydney for ten-day shifts, and while the policy has cost the town jobs, it's resulted in a more settled population. We end with a discussion about living and camping in the outback and have much on our minds as we drive away through the afternoon heat.

The aborigines I saw earlier, wandering through downtown streets, have moved into the shade under the bridge and along the riverbank. They're particularly noticeable because it's Sunday and no one else is around. The people have very black skin, deep-set eyes and wide noses, and for the first time in years, I think of the girl I bunked with when working at Orwell Station in 1968.

Next morning, as we start Week 3, we're the ones searching for shade, even before we've finished our breakfast coffee. As Dave needs a sandal repaired, we're downtown waiting in front of a saddlery when it opens. The clerk sends us to a small shop that repairs leather, where we're directed to the home of a pensioner, who we're told has a machine that will do the job. The pensioner, Brian, invites us to wait in his small three-room house, and we perch on a broken-down, blanket-covered settee in a cluttered room while he works in a corner a few feet away.

As he works, Brian talks non-stop and tells us, "I had to take a disability pension five years before I was due to retire. Figured I didn't need much, so bought this house, intending to live out my life here." I look around as he's speaking and through an open door glimpse the back wall and a narrow kitchen. The house is barely big enough to turn around in. I then listen in shocked silence to the tirade that follows. Brian is a very bitter man and obviously feels that he's lost control of his life.

He directs his vitriol at the federal government and aborigines, protesting, "I worked hard all my life and most of them don't work at all, but the government pays them $50 a month more than I get." He then goes on, "Taxpayer money is just handed out to the tribes, and they throw it away and demand more. They hold mineral rights to their land too, but my freehold title doesn't give me any."

With his sense of injustice rising, he spits out, "Land claims will probably take my house, and even now they squat in my backyard and police do nothing. When a drunk passed out on my porch and vomited everywhere, the police came and took him away, but laid no charges."

Beside himself with rage, we now hear about *the Brisbane Line*, a WW II policy established by the federal government. Brian asserts that the Labor Government did not intend to defend the land or the people north of that line, which included over half of Australia. He rants on and on during the half-hour we're there, and not believing a word, we can't get away fast enough. It's a shame, as he does a bang-up job on the sandals, fixing one shoe and reinforcing the other for two dollars.

Subdued by our encounter, we quietly drive to the visitors' center for our scheduled tour of Mount Isa Mines. Of the ten people who climb onto the bus, three are women, and Dave and I are the only ones over the age of 25. At the mine site, we watch a nine-minute-long safety video, and then our tour guide, Henry, shepherds us to the stores room where we're issued coveralls, belt, socks, boots, hardhat, goggles, respirator, and gloves. After changing in locker rooms, we stop at a warehouse and pick up battery packs and lights, attaching them to belt and hat.

After a ten-minute wait, we're loaded into *the cage*, an elevator that takes us down 3,150 feet below the surface. It holds 100 people, so we have lots of room to spread out. Henry asks a couple of the men to pull plates off several holes in the floor and then turns off the lights so we can peer down. The lights in the shaft flash by too quickly to count, and two minutes later, we're at the bottom.

We follow him across the rough dirt floor of a large, dimly-lit shaft to the *cribroom* (lunchroom), a huge cavern in the rock that is well lit and air-conditioned. Sitting on wooden benches at a long table, we listen to his spiel about the good life that mining can offer, especially the money. He then tells us to switch on our lamps and shepherds us down the shaft and across rail tracks to a Toyota truck.

The truck runs on batteries and has a video camera mounted on the front fender. A monitor in the cab provides the driver with advance warning of any obstacles around the many blind corners. Stepping up into the back of the vehicle, we crowd onto two narrow benches running down either side of the box, and as Henry climbs into the cab, he warns, *"Don't look forward when I'm backing up because your lights will blind me."* In fact, I quickly learn to direct my light elsewhere, whenever I speak to anyone.

With our individual lights playing over the walls, we travel through shafts drilled through solid rock. The tunnels are unsupported, and cables and pipes dangle from the ceilings. There is just enough clearance for the equipment working in them to pass, and at one point, only about three inches separates the light on top of the cab and the equipment hanging down. Sometimes the road surface is rutted, with mounds of dirt on either side, and sometimes it's hidden by a pool of water.

Heat released from the rocks tends to build up in the passageways, and as we come close to a rock wall on a tight corner, a drop of surprisingly warm water falls onto my hand. Where men are working, however, the shafts are chilled and well ventilated. I only notice the dust when we watch a 40-ton ore truck dump a load down to the primary crusher, and then pull my respirator over my face.

Henry explains that the ore goes on to a secondary crusher before going up to the surface, and adds, "All the equipment used in the mine is disassembled on the surface, brought down in the cage, and reassembled." We soon pass by a huge cavern containing a machine shop that looks just like one above ground.

At the end of an unused drive, we examine a rock face that shows the ore body currently being mined (silver, lead and zinc), and I pick up a souvenir, a small piece of copper-bearing rock. At another face, a worker drills two deep holes into the ore body, where explosives will be placed. Our final stop is at the cab of a mucker operator, whose machine is located one level up and a kilometer away. He has two video screens to help him do his job, one looking forward and the other back. However, his machine has been down for an hour (a fire extinguisher went off), and he waits while a maintenance worker checks it out.

There's just enough room in his air-conditioned cab for the women, so we're invited in to chat with him. After answering our questions, he asks each of us where we come from, and when I tell him that we sailed from Canada, the most extraordinary exchange follows. "Why would you do that?" he queries incredulously, then adds, "I've seen TV news reports of yachts in trouble at sea and the waves are *huge*! It's got to be dangerous!"

I'm dumbstruck, immediately recalling every mining disaster I ever heard about. Feeling sure that it would be bad luck to mention such things underground, I can only roll my eyes and vaguely murmur, "Well, I would have said that your job isn't all that safe!"

He continues to stare at me for a moment, then grins sheepishly and says, "Yeah, I guess it does depend on how you look at it." He then reassures us that this mine is absolutely safe and talks about their training and safety procedures. Nodding my head in agreement, I reply, "Well, we do the same thing; sure, there's risk, but we do our best to manage it!"

Henry now decides it's time to move on and herds us back to the Toyota. By the time we return to where we started, we've driven twenty km through the dimly lit shafts, climbing up to 2,440 feet and descending to 3,250. He escorts us to a very small elevator, cramming nine of us into it, and it drops down to 3,900 feet before starting up; it's a long, ten-minute ride to the surface. At the top, we learn that the two missing members of our group rode in relative comfort in the bottom level of the cage. After turning in our gear, we shower and dress, and when I fill in the visitors' book, I write, *experience of a lifetime.*

That night, the wind disappears at sunset and the heat is stifling. I toss and turn on my air mattress until 0400, then fall asleep. Next morning is warmer than usual, so my tee shirt is damp when we leave to tour the Royal Flying Doctor Base. After a half-hour in air-conditioning, I have to go outside to thaw out.

The base serves 40,000 people spread over 500,000 square miles and is funded by donations matched by the federal government. The staff of three doctors and three nurses is supported by two airplanes and four pilots, with landing strips available on many stations. In the adjoining museum, we study old photographs and numerous exhibits, including a pedal-driven shortwave radio, and learn that in an emergency, a pilot has landed on a highway.

It's then on to the Riversleigh Fossil Museum, where we study life-sized models of extinct animals, including snakes, bats, carnivorous kangaroos, and rhinoceros-sized marsupials. Afterwards, we climb a small hill in the middle of town and admire a view of green trees and lawns that creates the illusion of an oasis set in spinifex hills. That is, until I look to the west, where the brooding presence of the mine with its large buildings and tall stacks dominates the skyline.

Upon returning to the 'van park, we visit with two Austrian men, who have heavy Yamaha motorcycles sitting in front of their tent. Dave has learned that they bought the bikes in Sydney and are touring the country. The men are in their early twenties, bronzed and fit looking, except that one hobbles around with his leg taped from foot to thigh. He wears a tee shirt that reads: *There are no kangaroos in Austria!*

The men followed the Plenty Highway from Alice Springs to Isa, and much of the 600-km-long backcountry route was rough, corrugated dirt track. The one chap fell and his bike landed on his leg, breaking it; he fell three more times during the three days it took to complete the journey. They've waited days for the swelling to go down.

Early next morning, they're off to the hospital and the chap returns with a fluorescent lime-green cast from knee to ankle. Within an hour, their gear is packed and tied on the bikes, and they are sedately riding through the 'van park. They've told us that they promised to be home for Christmas and have many miles to travel before catching their airplane.

Later that day, a full-sized bus towing a trailer pulls in across the road, and we watch in astonishment as thirty passengers step off. They find their way to the pool, while the driver, tour guide, and cook set up tents and tables and prepare supper. Dave chats up the cook next morning and learns that the tourists are from Germany. They left from Sydney and are *doing* Australia in twenty-nine days; some days, they travel almost 1,000 km.

He happens to mention the Austrian biker who broke his leg and is taken aback when she responds bitterly, "Good thing he didn't need the Flying Doctor Service." Seeing his look of surprise, she explains, "Last year, I guided a group up through Alice Springs. One of the members, a German woman, broke her leg, so we called on the service for help. They wouldn't come," she recalls grimly, "wrong color!"

While we're in Mount Isa, we discover the pleasure of Australian pools. Swimming in the evening, after dark, we do a few lengths, then relax and study the night sky. After the heat of the day, the water feels cool and silky against my skin and is most enjoyable.

CHAPTER 5

Daly Waters, Hot Springs, and Homesteaders

Next morning, December 4, we're on the road early and heading west. At the edge of town, we pass a large sign that reads: *Camooweal 185 km, Alice Springs 1155 km, Darwin 1606 km.* We initially drive through open, dry grasslands, then the ground cover changes to low bush, with a few, hardy trees and a scattering of termite mounds.

Red-dirt tracks occasionally branch off and disappear into the landscape. Near each one, maybe on a stand or up a tree, a forty-five-gallon drum lies on its side. I assume they are supply drops for the large cattle stations in the area. Weathered-looking windmills pump water into stock tanks for the scattered herds of Brahman that graze near the road, the water coming from a huge aquifer contained in underground limestone caves.

The termite mounds are about eighteen inches high, and we're soon passing sites where there are so many that they look like headstones in a cemetery. During the next two days, we see mounds that are twelve feet high and maybe three feet wide, while others are half that high and ten feet wide. White ants bring dirt and water up from below ground to build the mounds and live in them upward of fifty years. When they eventually erode, the mud crumbles into the surrounding dirt, providing the only means of replenishing the soil over much of the desert.

We top up the gas tank in the small Queensland town of Camooweal, and as we leave, a large sign warns: *No Fuel for 378 km.* Heat waves shimmer off the bitumen as we near the Northern Territory (NT) border, and Dave now sees something on the road ahead. Slowing the car, he brings it to a stop a few feet away from a very large lizard occupying the middle of the road. The reptile is at least five feet long, with a very long neck, and holds its head about fifteen inches off the ground.

Turning to me, he demands, "Are you going to get out and take a picture?"

"Are you crazy," I retort, "That thing's bigger than I am!"

Grabbing a camera, he hops out, leaving the car in the middle of the road, then calls out, "Why don't you go stand beside it; I need something to give a sense of its size." I don't leave the car.

The lizard is a perentie, the largest variety of goanna, and it's carnivorous. When we talk to Aussies about the sighting, most delight in repeating stories that they've heard. The reptile can be intimidating, even aggressive, with a flicking, forked tongue and loud hissing. When in danger, it instinctively wants to climb a tree, and if one isn't handy, it'll climb whatever is—including a man.

After driving for hours on the lightly traveled road, we arrive at the Barkly Homestead Roadhouse. The place is busy, as every passing vehicle seems to stop. We check out the campground, but it has no shade and the heat is oppressive. I'm not feeling nearly as debilitated as in previous days, as we've had cold water to drink, so we opt to carry on. (I put water in the camp fridge the previous night.)

An hour or so down the road, we come upon a vehicle parked on the verge with the hood up. Having grown up at a time and place when no one passed a vehicle stranded on the road, we pull over. A large aborigine man is looking at the engine, and as Dave walks over to join him, I uneasily notice the rough-looking tattoos covering his arms. After a few minutes, the men conclude that the vehicle has electrical problems and will have to be towed into Tennant Creek, about an hour away. We aren't equipped to tow anything, so I offer to contact someone in town, but the man shakes his head, saying, "Naw, I'll wait; someone will come along."

Before long, we are at Threeways, where the road we're following joins the Stuart highway, which runs south-to-north through the center of Australia. We turn south and check into a 'van park at Tennant Creek, some twenty minutes down the road; we've driven 660 km and it's been a long day. The first thing I do is check the camp kitchen for a fridge. When it doesn't have one, we find a store and buy an eight-liter cooler and a bag of ice. The ice becomes a daily purchase, as it fills the jug and cooler and gives us cold/cool water for 24 hours.

After supper, a vehicle pulls in beside us, and a man gets out and unrolls a bedroll. He tells us that he lives in Alice Springs and is making the 2,000 km return trip to Darwin to attend a sports association meeting. He's a typical Aussie and we have only to nod or grunt occasionally, and he happily talks on and on. When I study his bedroll, I see that it consists of a sleeping mat enclosed in a canvas bag, with a cage to hold the material off his face and mosquito netting covering the air holes. Next morning, he's on the road at 0400.

We follow him north three hours later, and just outside of town, a large emu wanders alongside the road; after that, there's only green bush and long, sun-bleached grasses. The highway is well maintained and busy, with a steady stream of road trains carrying live cattle north to Darwin and returning empty. Heavy clouds keep the temperature down for a couple of hours, but when they start to break up, the heat builds quickly.

After 400 km, we turn off the highway and drive into the few buildings that make up Daly Waters. It claims to have the oldest, continuously licensed pub in the territory, reportedly beginning life in the 1930's by serving passengers off the fledgling Qantas Airline. We sit on wooden stools in the open-air bar in stifling heat, with sweat pouring off, and listen to three young people arguing about who should serve us. In truth, I'm disgusted; the place looks like it hasn't been cleaned or repaired since the day it was built and is a likely home for all kinds of crawly things.

We check into a 'van park back on the highway, setting up the tent on a dusty, bare patch of ground. A cloud of flies instantly surrounds us, flying into eyes, ears and nose, and we now learn the Aussie salute, a quick, repeated movement of hand across face. I try a swallow of water from the tap but choke and spit it out; it's bore water, coming from deep underground, and tastes salty and smells of sulfur. We use the emergency water we carry to prepare supper, and don't even consider the swimming pool. Daly Waters will prove to be my least favorite spot in the entire country.

Although it's only 275 km to Katherine, we're away early next morning as we plan several stops. Within a few miles, the desert shows a slight greening around the edges, and a bit of water has pooled in the ditches; there's obviously been some rain. Just before noon, we turn off the highway and drive seven km into Mataranko Hot Springs; it's a popular spot but not busy at this time of day.

A loud, shrill screeching fills our ears as we leave the car, and the noise grows louder under the trees. Thousands of small, red fruit bats have taken over the site, as they do for three months every year during breeding season. The population is now so large that they break off tree branches with their weight, and leaves, railings, and ramps are dripping with guano. We follow a path down to the Waterhouse River, catching a glimpse of azure water through the trees, then stroll back beside a narrow, deep ditch of crystal-clear spring water.

Carefully avoiding bat droppings, we change into our swimmies in a screened-off section of the walkway leading to the pool. We then join a dozen people relaxing in the water, which is warm but refreshing. American airmen developed the pool during WW II, blending rock steps and cement retaining walls into the small pocket of rain forest. Storyboards tell us that the spring comes from rainwater caught and held in underground limestone caves. The water heats up and bubbles out of the earth at a rate of 30.5 million liters/day.

Located nearby is a replica of Elsey Homestead, built for the filming of *We of the Never Never*, an Australian classic about pioneer life in the area in 1903. We tour the farmhouse, studying storyboards, and peer curiously at two humpies in the yard outside, which are rough lean-tos used by black fellows for shelter. I buy a copy of the book by Jeannie Gunn, which proves delightful, as she joyously recreates her characters and, in the process, relates much of the attitudes and habits of the age.

I am particularly fascinated by her description of hauling freight with bullocks, thinking it speaks volumes about the land and the people. To cover a distance of 50 miles (80 km) without water was a complicated business. Late on the first day, the bullocks would haul the wagons ten miles down the trail, then they would be returned to water. By sundown on the second day, the animals were back at the wagons and they hauled all that night, or as long as it took to reach the 40-mile mark. The wagons were then left and the bullocks taken forward to the next water. After resting for a day or two, they returned and hauled the wagons in during the night.

Feeling a strong connection to the land and the people, we follow the route of the pioneers north to Mataranko. I can only imagine the heat, the dust, and the sheer physical effort required to settle in this area. Day after day, both here and at home in Canada, those early settlers gave their lives to a harsh land, leaving a legacy for their children that benefited us all. A fact that I appreciate as we cover that same 80 km in an hour, in relative comfort even without air conditioning.

After admiring the bougainvillea and a huge termite mound in the town of Mataranko, we continue on to Cutta Cutta Caves. While waiting for a tour guide, we walk about the grounds, feeling sweaty and sticky in the unfamiliar heat and humidity. When our guide appears, we ask about well-worn paths through the high grass and he tells us that they were made by a nearby wallaby colony.

Leading us across the rock-strewn meadow, he explains, "These caves were formed by erosion that began two hundred million years ago." Gesturing with his arm, he adds, "The piles of rock you see around us are all that is left of what was once an upper level of solid rock." Stopping to look around, I find myself struggling with the enormity of such a concept, the time involved.

Shaking my head in wonder, I follow the men down into a shallow ravine and through a black opening in the hillside. After we've climbed down several steps at the mouth of the cave, our guide flicks a switch and a few well-placed lights reveal a fairyland. White and gold sculptured rock surrounds us, and here and there, the walls sparkle. We're told that the entire cave sparkles when the walls are wet, thus the aborigine name, Cutta Cutta, which translates as many stars. (Only white light is used inside, in an effort to preserve the natural appearance.)

Walking on a metal screen ramp, we follow a narrow, twisting passage through several chambers, where *stalactites* hang onto ceilings, and *stalagmites* grow up from floors. Water running down the sides of the cave has left layers of deposits called *shoals*, as well as *curtains* of stalactites. Recent rain has continued the process of dissolving calcium from the limestone, and these areas sparkle in the light.

The air remains surprisingly fresh and reasonably cool as we go deeper but is noticeably more humid. We see three baby brown tree snakes curled up on the wire mesh, looking for all the world like they've already been stepped on. Another one is stretched out on the rock, pencil thin, and about fifteen inches long.

We descend only halfway to the water table, which is 100 feet below the surface. Our guide points out the roots of a banyan (fig) tree, stretching downward for water, and then to a crooked crack that he says is a termite track. The ants follow it when coming down for a mouthful of water, which they take back to the surface to make mud for their mounds. Bats also live down at the water table.

Ending the day in Katherine (pop. 10,000), we check into a grassy, shady 'van park named for the red gum trees that grow on the site. We spend the early evening in the pool, which we have to ourselves, and I linger in the water, thinking about the events of the day. We've been reminded of our roots, as both Dave and I are descendants of folks who homesteaded in the Canadian prairies in the early 1900's.

Dave's family settled in southern Saskatchewan, and his Grandfather Ball started out by living in a cave in the side of a knoll. Granny Ball lived with the family for half of each year while he was growing up and he remembers her stories well. She talked about working as an upstairs maid at Belvoir Castle in Leicestershire, England, and about the family's move to Canada. After breaking her hip at age 93, she refused to go to hospital and died four days later. Dave was given the task of digging the grave and laughs sheepishly as he confesses, "I dug the hole six inches too short and had to lengthen it while everybody waited, which really annoyed my dad!"

Members of my family settled in the Red Deer area of southern Alberta, but at the end of the depression (1938), my parents moved to Giscome, BC, where there were supposed to be jobs. My dad then reported to the lumber mill every morning for weeks before getting one. By the time I was born in October of 1946, he was working in the bush, falling trees. As he was no longer eligible for a company house, my mom brought me home to a small cabin outside of town.

I grew up in bush camps at a time when life was still governed by the land and the seasons; we had no electricity, no telephone, and not much radio. I became addicted to books as soon as I could read and was fascinated, as a pre-teen, to hear the story of my paternal grandmother, a small woman I saw only once.

She left her home in central Europe and crossed an ocean, as well as most of North America, to marry a man she'd never met. Seven years later, he was seriously ill. He died four years after that, leaving her dependent on the goodwill of neighbors as she struggled to raise two sons on a poor homestead near Condor.

I wondered how she'd coped with the isolation that was then the reality of Canada, the long winter nights, the black forests. I think she came from a populated area, as she spoke four languages and understood seven. And even before my grandfather died, he'd spent the winters working at a coalmine in Nordegg, and she'd been left on her own.

When Dave and I were growing up in the 1940s and 50s, we witnessed the struggles of our parents, friends, and neighbors. We knew that our grandparents' lives had been even harder. I think we inherited their work ethic, their fierce independence, and their commitment to community. I suspect that other members of the cruising community shared those traits, or none of us would have set out to sail across an ocean.

CHAPTER 6

Discovering Katherine Gorge and the Brisbane Line

Katherine is an important waypoint on the route north, as it has the first permanent water supply north of Alice Springs. We want to spend a day on the river and make plans to canoe the Katherine Gorge, which consists of thirteen canyons, separated by rapids, with walls up to 200 feet high. Expecting temperatures above forty degrees and high humidity, we wear long-sleeved cotton shirts, put on big, shady hats, and take along a jug of ice water.

After driving upstream for an hour, we're able to rent a canoe at a kiosk on the river bank below the last canyon. The young man on duty informs us, "The river is low and the water muddy, but it's perfectly safe to swim." He adds reassuringly, "Don't worry about crocodiles; the ones in the river are *freshies* and only grow to six feet. They don't bother people."

Being back on a river is a treat, although we're surprised by the number of tourists paddling the lower canyon, given that it's off season. Heading upstream, we paddle through the first three canyons, having no difficulty with the rapids but portaging around a rocky ledge. Signs on the riverbank identify crocodile nesting sites, bat caves, hanging gardens, and aborigine paintings. I blister the soles of my feet while climbing over hot rocks to view the paintings, then find the overlapping stick figures unremarkable, even though very old.

The only wildlife we see is a darter, a large water bird with a long, eel-like neck, although I could almost swear that I see bubbles and the top of a croc's head near the river's edge. The heat finally overcomes my concern about *freshies*, and we swim for a half-hour below the first rapid.

After a most enjoyable day, we stop at a mall in downtown Katherine to buy a few groceries. As we walk across the parking lot, I see a group of aborigine men standing around the entrance. Several more sit on the floor on either side, backs against the walls, and I stick close to Dave as he winds his way through their outstretched legs. Inside, more men and women loiter outside the liquor store. They are loud, foul-mouthed, and dirty looking, with stick legs and swollen bellies.

The wind dies at sundown, leaving the air oppressively hot. When I go to bed, heat from the ground transfers through my air mattress, and I stew in my own sweat until 0200, when a thunderstorm brings rain that cools the air. I'm then able to sleep.

(Six weeks later, a tropical cyclone brings torrential rain to the area. The river peaks at 68 feet, and the gorge outside of town is only 65 feet deep, so huge areas to the south are flooded. Three highways are closed for days and it takes weeks for the water to drain away because the land is so flat. Elsey Homestead suffers flood damage and supplies have to be flown into Mataranko. A news story reports that a fourteen-foot crocodile is seen swimming down Katherine's main street. If so, the reptile is a *saltie*, not a *freshie*, and came out of the river system, which is disturbing.)

We start Week 4 by driving 320 km to Darwin in *the Top End*, as the upper half of the Northern Territory is called. The countryside grows noticeably greener along the way, and an astonishing number of WW II airstrips line the highway. We puzzle over a large diameter pipe that parallels the road for miles, and eventually learn that it carries the city's water supply from a reservoir on the Darwin River.

Darwin (pop. 80,000) sits on the edge of the Timor Sea and spreads out over a very large area. We drive into the visitors' center, which is downtown, and learn that the closest 'van park is an hour away, while the cheapest hotel room is $50/night. A staff member then advises, "We have a special arrangement with MGM Grand and can get you a $250 room for $75."

So, after spending three weeks sleeping on the ground, we check into a luxury hotel, where our main concern is living up to the dress code. Putting on our least wrinkled clothes, we visit the casino, which is very quiet by any standard. We really enjoy the beautiful 25-meter pool, and one afternoon watch with interest as a three-foot goanna slowly and deliberately picks its way across the wide back entrance.

Although we spend three nights at the hotel, we otherwise continue our camping lifestyle. In the mornings, we eat breakfast at a picnic table overlooking the bay at East Point, where it's cool and quiet. In the late afternoons, we visit a deli and eat supper at one of the shady tables set up on the grassy verge that separates the esplanade from the harbor. Two or three times a day, a storm rolls through, bringing heavy rain for twenty minutes, but then it clears, never interfering with our plans.

Dave has the car serviced, and I have my camera repaired, then we visit the many small shops in the Smith Street Mall and nearby arcades. We check out a flag shop, as we're always looking for flags for *Windy Lady*, and the proprietor insists on taking us for coffee, wanting to know all about our travels.

In turn, he tells us that trade with Southeast Asia is booming. Exports of live cattle have exploded in the past ten years, and more opportunities are available to trade north than with the rest of Australia. He also assures us, "Statehood is coming. People were upset when the federal government overturned the Euthanasia Bill, which was NT legislation. Besides, Western Australia became a state with the same population!"

Dave is keen to buy a didgeridoo, and when he hears a low moan drifting down the street, we follow the sound to a small store. The German shopkeeper tells us that the didgeridoo was originally made from a tree branch hollowed out by termites, and the longer the tube, the deeper the sound. He happily explains the breathing cycle, and the two men stand in the store entrance, blowing and vibrating their lips, until Dave finally produces a sound. Deciding that he wants one with a deeper tone, he then realizes that we don't have room to safely store one amongst all our camping gear.

While touring through the downtown, we visit a rock-faced colonial building and study a series of pictures displayed on the veranda. We now learn about the devastation caused by Cyclone Tracey on Christmas Eve in 1974, and by Japanese bombing in February and March of 1942. Unaware that Australia had been bombed during the war, we curiously make our way to the Oil Storage Tunnels.

Tunnel Five is a huge, underground tank that is hot, humid, dimly lit, and occasionally muddy under foot. We study more wartime photographs here and learn that Japanese planes attacked northern Australia 64 times, and 46 of those raids hit Darwin. Eleven above-ground oil storage tanks had served as beacons for the enemy and all were bombed. Five steel-lined, concrete tunnels were then built but never used.

On our way out, we talk to the ticket agent, who isn't at all busy. The man was once a city tour guide, loves to talk, and we stay for two hours. He explains that as early as 1926, naval bases were being reinforced in Darwin and Singapore in order to defend the interests of the British Empire. He then continues, "After spending many years in opposition, the Labor Party won the federal election in Australia just before the start of WW II. They believed the Poms (the English) would take care of us, so military funding was not high on their list of priorities."

Tersely, he goes on, "After the onset of the war, the new government decided to defend only the southeast corner of the country, an area defined by a curving line between Brisbane and Adelaide, *the Brisbane Line*. Then, when Darwin was bombed, fleeing residents were held in camps for up to three weeks, as the government didn't want word of the air raids to get out."

Seeing the looks of shocked disbelief on our faces, he nods his head, saying, "Darwinians felt betrayed. Even today, resentment is strong against the national government, and the Labor Party, in particular." (At that point, I silently send an apology to Brian in Mount Isa; we simply hadn't believed him.)

But there is more to the story. If the Aussies didn't protect their northern coast, the enemy would control shipping into SE Asia. That situation was not acceptable to General Douglas MacArthur, Commander of Allied Forces in the Pacific. He apparently told them that if they didn't defend their territory, the Americans would. Ultimately, the policy was cancelled.

We are incredulous at first, then appalled. Australia and Canada had a similar history of British democratic institutions and values. How could duly elected representatives abandon their fellow citizens, along with much of the territory they were duty bound to protect? Looking at each other, we ask the same question, "What's to stop something like this from happening in Canada?"

In fact, our confidence in our federal system had been shaken the previous year when we were in Fiji. We'd learned that the Prime Minister and his entire cabinet had been kidnapped in a coup d'etat shortly after a general election. We couldn't believe that such a thing could happen in a Commonwealth country. What made it worse was that neither of us had even heard news reports about it.

We now recall that during the national referendum in Canada in 1992, we were harangued by politicians, professors, business leaders, and the media, who repeatedly told us that the world as we knew it would end if we didn't vote *YES* to constitutional change. Canadians overwhelming voted *NO*. Thinking about it now, it seems obvious that the elites of country had been on a different page than ordinary Canadians, which didn't bode well for the future.

CHAPTER 7

Across the Top to Derby

From Darwin, we take a roundabout route back to Katherine, driving 550 km on secondary roads through two national parks (NP). The land around Mary River NP is extremely flat and subject to frequent flooding. Millions of dollars were once spent trying to establish a rice plantation here, but it failed. Water buffalo were then introduced and destroyed thousands of acres of wetland, many of them important crocodile nesting grounds. A park ranger tells us that 10,000 head were removed from an area to the south in just two years.

A few miles farther on, we cross the Alligator River and enter Kakadu NP. The riverbed is maybe 100 yards wide and lined with mud bars; the water is muddy and shallow. Several hundred magpie geese feed in a flat meadow on the far side, then all we see is high bush growing at the edge of the road. As the day grows hotter and more humid, the sky darkens and a ten-minute deluge floods the windshield. Showers continue for an hour afterward, leaving the air deliciously cool.

Above the line of bush, I now see the Escarpment of Arnhem Land, an ancient sea cliff that runs for 500 km. It's part of a huge aborigine homeland covering the entire eastern half of the Top End. In order to visit it, we need a permit from the Aborigine Land Council, which we don't have, so we continue on to a campsite at Jabiru, where we set up the tent in a lush, grassy site.

After supper, we relax in our chairs, enjoying the evening quiet and the freshness of the air. We study the sky as the stars appear and then a big full moon rises up over the horizon, casting long shadows across the grass. It would be idyllic but for the cloud of flies that attacks our eyes, nose, and ears; I endure them only by continually fanning my face with a fly swatter. Mosquitoes then rise up out of the grass, so I pull on long pants; Dave doesn't and scratches for days. Overnight, the humidity climbs and I wake up several times, bathed in sweat.

Next morning, we check out the pool, which is large and round, with a waterfall tumbling over rocks on one side; it's a beautiful spot and we swim for a half-hour. We then visit the interpretive center, but only video and slide rooms have air conditioning. We attempt to study the outside exhibits, but with sweat pouring off and flies tormenting us, we don't stay long. We do learn that much of Kakadu is aboriginal land, leased to the national government for use as a park.

The drive that day is again monotonous, with high bush lining the road, but I catch sight of a few brolgas (cranes) and a jabiru (a black and white stork). About mid-afternoon, we arrive at Yellow Waters Billabong, where hundreds of egrets, ibis, and jabiru feed in a grassy meadow. But heat and humidity have taken their toll, and we're really only interested in sitting in the shade in the pool in Katherine.

At the park boundary, we stop at an isolated roadhouse for fuel, and a scrawny, middle-aged woman behind the counter sells Dave a meat pie. She insists that he eat it the Aussie way, with tomato sauce, instructing, "Just punch a hole in the center with your thumb and pour in the sauce." She talks on and on and then laughs, confessing, "I'm a true Aussie, all you have to do is say hello and I'll talk for a week."

Katherine is again hot and humid, without a breath of wind, and there's no relief when the sun goes down. I toss and turn on my air mattress when I go to bed, once more feeling like I'm being stewed. An hour later, I crawl out of the tent and sit in a chair for three hours, until the temperature begins to drop.

Next morning, we start west across *the Top*, following an inland route for 1,400 km to Derby on the North Coast. The vegetation, which is green around Katherine, quickly becomes sparse and bleached. As we near the Victoria River, red rocky bluffs and mesas stand out against the sky. We are now in the land of the Boab tree, and the blocky lower trunk and branched top remind me of a chunky vase filled with flowers.

A long band of rimrock trims the hills on either side of the narrow valley at Victoria River Crossing, where the roadhouse is closed for the season. We continue on to Timber Creek, the only other community on this 500-km stretch of road to Kununurra in Western Australia. When Dave goes inside to pay for gas, I notice a group of black fellows sprawled in the shade nearby. One man goes into the store and returns with something in his hand; a second man then does likewise.

On the far edge of the parking lot, a faded sign promotes a river tour looking for *salties*. As a result, a camping spot beside the river a few miles down the road is of no interest. Since leaving Brisbane, we've heard that a crocodile attacked a man swimming at night near Cairns, and another one killed a man on the Daly River, downstream of Katherine. The Wildlife Service also trapped one in Darwin's harbor, where about 100 are caught every year.

Two fast-moving thunderstorms pass overhead as we're driving across the wide flood plain of the Baines River, and with rain flooding the windshield, Dave slows to half our normal speed. The roadbed is only a foot or two above the surrounding terrain, and the heavy rain pools almost instantly on both sides. On one corner, a four-foot-wide sheet of water runs across the highway, and with water pooling and rain reflecting off bitumen, we seem to be driving into a lake. Fortunately, the storms don't last long and the water disperses quickly when the rain stops.

The birds now come out and we see several white egrets and two dancing brolgas. The cranes are bobbing up and down to some unheard rhythm when I notice their red head patches flashing against the green bush. When their large, grey bodies come into view, I recognize them as the graceful birds depicted flying into the sun in the NT's tourist emblem.

We gain one-and-a-half hours when we cross the border into Western Australia, which doesn't really affect us, as we get up and go to bed with the sun. After clearing through another quarantine roadblock, we stop at a 'van park in Kununurra, the small, lush, green town at the center of the Ord River Irrigation Project. The reservoir here is the second largest in Australia and supports agriculture on a massive scale, with farms producing melons, bananas, mangos and dairy products.

For the next three hours, thunder rumbles over nearby hills and lightning flashes in the dark sky. Although we see no rain, the air cools pleasantly. Nearby, some twenty black cockatoos are etched against the lush, green grass as they feed under the trees. I creep closer to take a picture, but a sentry croaks a warning and the birds take flight, their red tail-patches flashing. After dark, we do forty lengths in the campsite's beautiful pool, watching the lightning flashes as we swim. I'm then so tired that I sleep despite the humidity, simply rolling over and exposing the other side when it gets too damp.

Our campsite backs onto Hidden Valley NP, a pocket-sized park containing a range of 300-million-year-old sandstone hills. Next morning at daybreak, we scramble up one of two nature trails and emerge on the other side thirty minutes later, drenched in sweat. When we return, we do another forty laps in the pool.

I'm intrigued by the small lizards we see here, especially a little one that scampers around on its hind legs. It remains standing when it pauses and waves a front foot back and forth, as if motioning others forward. Another is small and husky, with a broad white stripe on its throat; it freezes for a few seconds with its nose high, displaying the stripe, then is off again.

As we push into the Kimberley on the second day, the highway leaves the broad, flat valley bottom behind and climbs into hills that grow progressively higher. The country becomes rockier, with piles of accumulated rubble that look as if a giant hand had gathered them up and dropped them haphazardly across the landscape. Communities are few and small, and only infrequently does a road turn off.

Toward midday, I notice a scattering of sand on the bitumen and uneasily realize that water covered the road not long before. Looking around, I notice that the bottom of every shallow gully in the rolling terrain appears to channel water. A few minutes later, there is water on the road in front of us, and we cross four streams in quick succession, each about twenty feet wide and a few inches deep.

I'm suddenly worried about being stranded by flooding rivers, so am struck dumb when the Ord River comes into view. Rushing, muddy water fills it from bank to bank and it's at least a hundred feet wide. It's hard to tell how deep it is, but the water is moving fast. I then see the narrow, single-lane causeway spanning the river; it's still safe, with water gushing through a few feet below the road surface.

We spend that night at Hall's Creek, a small, dusty community on the edge of the Great Sandy Desert. The park operator is an English woman, who tells us that it has rained daily for the past two weeks, which is why roads are flooded. We notice a larger aborigine presence here, with some people sitting in scattered shade on the roadside, and others driving vehicles into the general store when we stop for gas.

The next morning brings gusty winds and high overcast, and for the first time in days, I'm not covered in perspiration when I wake. We're on the road at 0630, now starting Week 4, and have a pleasant three-hour drive before the cloud cover breaks up. As the day progresses, we pass through flat grassland with rocky mesas, tree-covered plains and then the bush returns. I see several galahs and flocks of tiny birds, one of which attacks a wedge-tail eagle, causing bits of feather to float down.

We fuel up at Fitzroy Crossing, then have a bite to eat and stretch our legs. It's very hot and the scene at the roadhouse is familiar, with a group of black men sitting in the shade, and one or another occasionally going inside to make a purchase. I find myself studying them more closely because of a radio report that morning. As a result of continual harassment, a group of five nurses left their post at an isolated aborigine village southwest of Darwin.

Roadside gauges now mark the flood plain of the Fitzroy River, and they go on and on for miles. The river is flowing from bank to bank when we cross, but it's not yet at flood level. Large tracts of land have been burnt, and I soon grow tired of looking at the blackened skeletons of trees and bush. As traffic is light, we break the monotony by trying to be the first to spot the next communication tower or oncoming vehicle.

After driving 600 km, we're hot and tired when we pull into the 'van park in Derby (pop. 4,000). The town sits on King Sound at the edge of the Indian Ocean, and we're cheered by the sight of water shimmering in the bay across the mud flats. We'd really like a swim, but the park doesn't have a pool and the town pool is closed that day.

Instead, we visit the port, enjoying the freshness of the breeze as we walk out onto a deep-water dock, where a new conveyor system loads lead and zinc concentrates directly onto ships. The tide is high, with the sea flooding back into the mangroves, and I'm appalled at how grey and muddy the water is. I then remember that tides here are the highest in Australia, up to thirty-eight feet, and currents are strong.

The town is very spread out and we have trouble finding the supermarket. When we do, it looks like it's in a war zone, with bars protecting windows already covered by heavy mesh screens. We then stop at a bottle shop, where Dave cannot find a four-liter box of wine. An employee explains, "The large boxes are illegal in Derby and Broome, as they're supposed to encourage binge drinking. We carry only the smaller ones."

Back at the 'van park, a neighbor provides more detail, "The large boxes were banned because aborigines bought them, disappeared into the bush, and returned as *box monsters*.

We've bought a bag of ice, and I now dig out the large, plastic wine glasses we purchased in Darwin, fill them with ice, and top them up with white wine. We then relax in our lounge chairs and watch the setting sun. It's much like at sea, with the sun sliding down to the edge of the world and disappearing. The breeze then drops and we put in another drippy night.

Next day, we visit *the Prison Tree*, a thousand-year-old Boab tree that was used as a lockup when transporting aborigines in custody. The tree is forty-five feet around, hollow inside, and has an outside wall that's maybe eighteen inches thick. We climb in through the one entrance and gaze around in amazement; it's clean, cool, and dry.

Two days after leaving Derby, we hear a news report about a ruckus in the supermarket parking lot involving twenty aborigine men. Two police officers arrested two of the men and were then attacked by the others, who roughed them up and took their vehicle and prisoners. The police have issued an APB for the missing vehicle.

CHAPTER 8

A Glimpse of Life on the North Coast

From Derby, we follow the coast of the Indian Ocean for 1,500 km. We cross the Dampier Peninsula the first day, driving on a highway that mostly sits on top of a series of dikes, twenty feet above a bush-covered flood plain that's recently been burnt. The final crossing of the Fitzroy River is anticlimactic, as the riverbed is dry except for a string of small pools near the mouth. After driving 220 km, our spirits soar when we glimpse the golden sands and turquoise waters near Broome (pop. 10,500).

We now drive around impatiently, trying to find our way into a van park on Roebuck Bay. The site is beautiful when we find it, but after a few minutes, we're less impressed. The sun is scorching, there's no real shade, and tents are crowded together beneath a few palm trees. Two warning signs are also posted nearby, one for box jellyfish and one for crocodiles. (Box jellyfish are plentiful across *the Top*, and stings can occur while paddling about on the beach, or launching a boat in shallow water.)

We locate another 'van park inland and select an attractive, shady site for the tent. But as we set it up, tiny black ants swarm across the ground and crawl up our legs. Occasionally, one bites and I brush off maybe fifty at a time. We're also camped beside the main route to the port, and heavy trucks haul for most of the night.

When I wake in the morning, a column of ants marches about a foot from my head. They carry a dead fly toward a corner of the tent, where I later discover several pin-sized holes; I have no idea how they plan to get it out. We now discover holes in the floor near the door, so cover them with duct tape. (We'd been warned in Timber Creek that ants would eat through the tent floor.)

We start the day with a visit to the public pool, which is separated from the older part of Broome by two or three miles of bush; the 25-meter pool is beautiful and we swim sixty lengths before it gets too hot. We then stroll along the Town Beach and wander through a small cemetery set under a few trees on a grassy knoll. Although called the Pioneer Cemetery, headstones both old and new are scattered about haphazardly. One is only a few years old, a young man, a diver, who lies for all eternity looking out to sea.

Nearby, a larger plaque memorializes Broome's One-Day War in March of 1942. Dutch nationals and injured/sick American servicemen were being evacuated from the Dutch East Indies (Indonesia) ahead of the Japanese advance. The planes overnighted in Broome, with the flying boats moored a kilometer offshore because of the tides. Everyone stayed on board, as there was no way of getting ashore and no facilities there anyway. The next morning, nine Japanese Zeros flew out of the sunrise. Their bombs destroyed eight land aircraft and fifteen flying boats, killing seventy-two Dutchmen and thirty Americans.

This glimpse of the past is haunting, kindling our interest in the area, so we search out a small local museum where we spend three fascinating hours. The building houses a treasure trove of old photographs, newspaper clippings, and scrapbooks on every subject that ever affected the town, and also has a few artifacts.

Focusing first on Broome's history as a pearling center, we read about the equipment used, the difficulties faced by divers, and the sometimes-violent rivalry that existed between divers from different Asian countries (most were Japanese). After examining an early diving suit, we move on to current pearling operations.

We then learn about the Overseas Telegraph Cable, an early aviation company started by a local pilot, aborigine history in the area, and the paths of cyclones along the coast. As we're about to leave, I'm sidetracked by an incredible shell collection, including a crown of thorns starfish, which was assembled by a local woman decades before, then by an Indonesian fishing boat sitting in the backyard that was confiscated in local waters.

Later, we stroll through the downtown, looking in the windows of pearl shops and glancing curiously at chairs set up in a fenced garden, which my guidebook describes as an open-air cinema dating back to 1916. I also read that bars on windows are not meant to prevent theft but rather to minimize cyclone damage.

We save Cable Beach for last, as this twenty-km stretch of golden sand is the town's main attraction. A few people are in the water, but the quickly receding tide catches my eyes, and I think of that early March morning so many years before. Apparently, the wrecks of the flying boats are still visible, and it's possible to walk out to them at low tide.

We spend two nights in Broome, and the evenings are pleasant with bright, starry skies, but the tent is a humid oven overnight, and neither of us sleep well. We're up early on the last morning, eager to be underway, then wait two hours because the staff had a Christmas party the night before and no one's around to check us out.

We drive 600 km that day, passing through an area where the Great Sandy Desert meets the sea. Traffic is light, and for half the distance, the roadway is bordered by four-to-five-foot-high bush. There are no dry creek bottoms, termite mounds, or roadkill, so it's just hot and boring. By the time we see the large sand dunes at Eighty Mile Beach, we're more interested in shade than sand. We stop and fuel up at Sandfire, another expensive oasis situated so far from anywhere that almost everyone stops.

The bush isn't nearly as high or as thick from there on, and about 100 km from Port Hedland, we cross a creek bottom, then see power lines, a railway, and smog. The barren-looking landscape gradually fills with roads, railway tracks, power lines, and the occasional industrial plant. Heavy trains almost three-km long bring iron ore from mines in the Pilbara to this Indian Ocean port for shipment overseas. The Pilbara, in the northwest corner of the state, is immensely rich; its iron ore and natural gas reserves account for much of the state's prosperity. It is also isolated and harsh, containing some of the hottest country on earth.

The town of Port Hedland (pop. 12,500) slowly emerges from the grey smog as we draw closer. We check into a 'van park fifteen km out, where shabby caravans provide homes for permanent residents, workers who came for the money and found nowhere else to stay.

The buildings need maintenance, the pool is closed, and a few taps leak in the amenities block, a phenomenon that has become more frequent as water has grown scarcer. The block is also home to countless small frogs, reminding me to scan walls and floor to see what else might be hiding in a cubicle when I enter.

We buy our groceries at the shopping mall downtown, and with only a week to Christmas, the place is bustling. All manner of community life appears to take place in the forecourt, with people sitting and talking, and children playing underfoot. I get the impression that many are there to escape the heat.

Returning to camp, we put supper on, fill our glasses with ice and wine, then relax in lounge chairs in the shade. A workman now walks past, his face streaked with dust and sweat, his dirty coveralls stained with red dirt. Upon seeing us, he calls out, "You only have to close your eyes to imagine you're in Bermuda!"

Curious, I respond, "We've just traveled thousands of kilometers to get here, so why would we do that?"

His emphatic reply, "*Because this is the worst, gawd-damn place in Australia!*"

In fact, the flies are miserable, and the night brings no relief from the oppressive heat and humidity. Unwittingly, we've also placed the tent on a patch of grass beside a path to the local watering hole. Small groups walk around us on the way to the pub, and stragglers trip over the tent pegs when they return after midnight.

The next day, we drive 200 km to Karratha (pop. 11,500), and as we walk from the car to the visitors' center, I feel the sun burning my arms. We're told that it's five degrees cooler in Dampier (pop. 2,500) on the coast, so half an hour later we're standing in a small, sun-drenched 'van park on the rocky shoreline of King Bay. But we're not too impressed, as there's a wharf on either side of us, with iron ore being loaded at one, and commercial fishing boats tied up at the other. Natural gas from the Northwest Shelf also comes ashore nearby. Some of it is liquefied and exported to Japan and South Korea, the rest is pumped on to Perth and the Pilbara.

As there's very little shade, we return to Karratha and check into a 'van park that has a few gum trees. The temperature is 43 degrees Celsius (109.4F). Setting up the tent in an open, grassy area, we spend the next two hours shifting our chairs around, trying to stay out of the sun. Unfortunately for us, what shade there is mostly falls on a large double tent that has an air conditioner.

We watch as two men wrestle a large refrigerator out of the tent and onto the back of a truck, then see two other men armed with sticks warily trying to re-direct a four-foot long perentie that wants to come through the fence. They persist until it eventually waddles across the parking lot and disappears out the other side. Meanwhile, a flock of galahs occasionally raise a ruckus in the gum trees.

One of the birds then lands on the grass nearby and walks back and forth, cheekily cocking its head from side to side while looking us over. When Dave throws out bits of cracker, it balances on one leg and picks up the tidbit with a claw and nibbles on it daintily. It even takes a piece from his fingers but runs a short distance away before stopping to eat.

As the sun nears the horizon, we find our way to the public pool downtown. It's only open for another hour, but we've waited because it doesn't have a sunroof. The fifty-meter pool is gorgeous, with a large attached wading pool, and in the area in between, five women lean against a round table in about three feet of water. We each do thirty lengths and come away feeling refreshed.

When we return to the 'van park, two more tents have been set up and one is practically on top of ours. We then trip over our new neighbors as we bring supplies from our vehicle. The young couple, Robert and Rebecca are from Townsville; he's in the army and she teaches school. She tells us, "We're driving to Perth to spend Christmas with my parents. We'll spend a few days with Robert's parents in Brisbane on the way back. We'll be gone five weeks and drive 15,000 km."

Robert then describes a shortcut that he attempted to take through the backcountry and tells Dave, "The Victoria River was running deeper and faster than I expected. When we started across, the current pushed the frontend of the vehicle downstream, and I had to turn back. Instead of saving 200 km, we added 100."

The following morning, the battery is dead in their Nissan Patrol, and Rebecca announces triumphantly, "Robert left a light on." As he has jumper cables, the men try to jumpstart it using our car but aren't successful. The local rep of the Royal Auto Club arrives within minutes of a phone call, and after starting the vehicle, the men decide that Robert's cables were too light to carry the required current.

The day is already hot when we depart at 0900, and a sign at the edge of town reads, *Limited Water for 643 km.* We see only red earth, green bush, and blazing sun as we drive southwest; it's hotter and drier than anything we've yet experienced. During the afternoon, dust devils out on the plain whirl red dirt hundreds of feet into the air.

We buy expensive gas at Nanutarra Roadhouse, a desolate spot some 300 km from Karratha. Sacking is draped around the lower half of the fuel pumps, and we're told that on very hot days, it is soaked with water in order to cool them. Apparently, they develop vapor locks, causing customers to wait hours for fuel. A handwritten sign beside the sunbaked-dirt parking lot proclaims: *No Filling of Vehicles from Jerry Cans.* Another, at the entrance to a shaded patio, warns *Do Not Bring food onto the Patio.*

CHAPTER 9

Christmas on the Northwest Coast

About mid-afternoon, we turn off the highway and head north to the small resort community of Coral Bay. To our surprise, some of the facilities are full when we arrive. We check into a pleasant 'van park tucked beneath scattered trees amongst the sand dunes, and the manager explains that holiday visitors from Perth fill up west coast resorts during school break, which runs from Christmas to mid-January. They prove to be a different type of camper, bringing propane lights, fridges, negligees, and Christmas decorations. They also go to bed at midnight and sleep until 0900, although it's light at 0530.

The temperature is a bit cooler beside the ocean, and a strong sea breeze blows clouds of fine white sand about as we erect the tent on a small patch of grass. The slender trees prove a mixed blessing, providing a bit of shade but dripping a sticky sap during the night. Potable water is available in the amenities block, and each campsite also has a tap that provides artesian bore water for washing and watering the grass.

The water comes from 2,600 feet down, tastes salty, smells of sulfur, and is so hot by late afternoon that I can't hold my hand in it. A fine spray head on the sprinklers cools the water, but it says a lot for the hardiness of the saltine couch grass that it survives, as do the birds and lizards that are frequent visitors.

During the four days we're here, my neck and shoulder are bothering me, which makes the extreme heat and humidity harder to bear. But I go through the motions, joining Dave and walking for hours along white sand beaches and swimming and snorkeling in turquoise waters. But after six weeks on the road, our 24-hour/day companionship is starting to chafe, and we don't have much patience with each other.

When we return from the beach late on the first day, Dave discovers that his wallet is missing. Although we frantically search car and tent, it's nowhere to be found. Thinking that he might have left it in Nanutarra, we set off in search of a telephone, so he can put a hold on his credit cards. After driving up and down hot, dusty roads, we come across four phone booths baking in the sun; he tries all four before one works. After a very frustrating hour, American Express has put a hold on one card, but MasterCard has insisted on cancelling the other.

Robert and Rebecca pull into the site next to us on the second night, which is a surprise as we thought they'd be miles ahead. Two young Americans occupy the site on the third night, computer types who live and work in Sydney. Dave tells them about the two Austrians we met in Mount Isa and that one had broken his leg. They respond in unison, *"We know them! We camped beside them in Alice Springs!"* One then runs back to their campsite, calling back over his shoulder, "I've got to show you what they gave me." He returns with a tee shirt adorned with a picture of a kangaroo and the words: *There are no kangaroos in Austria.*

The wallet surfaces in the middle of our last night, falling onto Dave's chest when he pulls up the sleeping bag. As much annoyed as relieved, he doesn't get any more sleep. Next morning, he's back on the phone. American Express is not a problem but MasterCard is, as it will take at least four days for a replacement card to reach us. As we don't know where we'll be, he decides to leave it until we return to Brisbane. He then nearly explodes when the agent scolds, "If you weren't sure what had happened to your card, you should have had a hold put on it; we didn't have to cancel it."

In need of supplies, we leave Coral Bay the day before Christmas, now starting the 1,500 km drive south down the west coast. Under a searing sun, the car is again an oven, and the landscape grows harsher, with patches of gravelly soil visible amongst small, twisted trees and scattered clumps of grass.

Dave continues to be irritated that his MasterCard was cancelled, as many businesses don't accept AmEx. I'm not particularly sympathetic as I have a Visa card we can use, but that's not something he wants to hear. I spend the morning studying the landscape and see ten emus, including a nursery group with a single adult and four chicks. Interestingly, the adult would have been a male, as once the eggs are laid, females have nothing to do with raising the young.

After driving 240 km, we arrive in Carnarvon (pop. 9,000), a pretty town situated at the mouth of the Gascoyne River. The town is subject to cyclones and floods, so is encircled by a levee, and the long, narrow, one-lane bridge over the river has been underwater several times. When we cross it, we see only the dry, sandy riverbed and a few scattered pumps. I now read that a permanent stream of water flows beneath it. The pumps bring up water for the town and nearby farms, many of which grow bananas.

We're puzzled to find seven 'van parks and numerous motels here, then discover that the town caters to its own version of the Canadian Snowbird. Some folks in Perth pack up their caravans and head north for six months every winter. As it's now offseason, we have our choice of sites and pick a campground with good-sized leafy trees and respectable shade. It also has a full-sized bowling green, mini-golf, and a recreation hall. The hall, a large shed, has just been built and is to be christened with a sausage sizzle that night and a potluck dinner on Christmas Day.

We make a quick trip downtown, and although the stores are going flat out, manage to buy the groceries we need, as well as some Christmas goodies and a strip of red tinsel for the outside of the tent. Taking chairs and drinks, we then join other guests at the sausage sizzle. Our hosts provide a karaoke music video, with which they've been practicing, but first-timers like us keep everyone entertained as we have trouble following the melody, reading the words, and keeping time.

The guests sitting around the shed that night are a varied group. A German couple are on a three-week holiday, and a flat tire brought them to the campground. A slim, quiet, fortyish-bloke named Doug is riding around the country on a bicycle. Two other couples, traveling separately, have come from Coffs Harbor, south of Brisbane. They are the first of another breed of camper that we meet, retirees who are taking two-three years to drive around Australia. One of the men explains to Dave, "I'd been retired seven years by the time we left—had to wait for the cat to die!"

Snowy, a rough-looking character in his sixties, has just returned from spending ten months up the coast. He takes a break from playing the spoons to watch his wife Wendy, who can't stop dancing. Then there's the taxi driver and his wife, who want the melon scraps to take home to their worm farm.

A beat-up pool table with sloping surface has been set up in a corner and keeps a group of local young people entertained. One of them, with hair and beard hanging halfway to his waist, looks like a refugee from a previous century. Two other good-looking lads get a bit rowdy as the evening progresses, and the young woman who joins them is quite free with her hands. Dave makes up a fourth for a game and is astounded to find she considers him fair game.

Christmas Day is by far the hottest we've ever spent, but our generous hosts at the Wintersun Caravan Park make sure no one feels homesick. There is more food, more drinks, and more hijinks, including a swim in the pool. The German couple tell us that they flew into Perth, rented a four-wheel-drive vehicle, and are heading to Mt Augustus, some 450 km east of Carnarvon. They then explain, "We have three weeks to make the journey, but today it's supposed to be 50 degrees Celsius (122 F) inland and that's just too hot." They then confess, "This is our second attempt; we tried last year, too, but were stranded by flooding rivers and had to turn back."

Curious, I now research Mt Augustus and learn that it's Australia's largest rock; it's twice the size of Uluru (Ayres Rock), inclines in only one direction, and low scrub grows on the surface. The rock dates back 1,000 million years, to sand and boulders that formed an ancient sea floor. Those deposits became sandstone and conglomerate strata, and eventually uplifted and folded. The granite rock beneath is between 1,650 and 1,750 million years old. When I try to wrap my head around the massive forces and the time involved, my brain is simply overwhelmed.

We intend to leave on Boxing Day, but stay over when the forecast calls for a temperature of 47 degrees Celsius (116.6 F) farther south. Although Dave isn't very enthusiastic, we drive out to the blowholes instead, passing the dry bed of Lake Macleod on the way.

With low rainfall and high evaporation rate, the lake is reputed to be the ideal spot for solar salt production. The salt is then hauled twenty km by truck, dumped on the edge of a cliff, pushed onto a conveyor system, and loaded directly onto ships. Nearby is the wreck of the *Korean Star*, a bulk carrier hit by Cyclone Herbie in May 1988. The ship had discharged its ballast and was waiting to take on salt when it went aground and broke in two.

We park the car amongst the rocks near the blowholes, then walk down to the shore, where a large sign warns, *King Waves Kill!* The view is spectacular. Huge waves from the Indian Ocean pound the coastline, and jets of water shoot sixty feet into the air as water is forced through the rocks under pressure. Every twenty minutes or so, a series of bigger waves sweeps in across the rocks, and water that was ankle deep then swirls above the knees. These waves, breaking high on rocky points, are the ones that sweep fishermen to their deaths.

South of the blowholes, a small lagoon nestles in the shelter of an island and adjacent reefs. A sliver of white sand curves along the beach, and a few sun worshippers are propping up umbrellas and laying out towels. On the outer edge of the reef, swells break in a long, white curl, sending crystal-clear water surging across a wide, rocky shelf into the lagoon. With the thunder of the surf in my ears, I stand on a low cliff and look down into deep holes in the shelf, watching numerous fish, large and small, drift back and forth with the current. It's magic! Dave then breaks the spell, as he's had enough sun and wants to return to town.

When we leave Carnarvon the next day, a sign at the edge of town warns, *Limited Water for 432 km.* The land is now some of the most desolate we've seen, with large patches of barren ground broken infrequently by twisted clumps of bush. Eventually, scrub bush gains a foothold and spreads across the landscape, growing higher with every mile. Soon, a few trees appear, followed by flowering bushes and some scruffy-looking conifers. We bypass the tourist resorts of Shark Bay, including the dolphins of Monkey Mia, sure that they will be hot and busy, and finally come to the northern fields of the wheat belt.

The town of Geraldton (pop. 34,000) is impressively clean and well cared for, and we stop to watch two tugs maneuver a freighter into the small deep-water harbor. A line of tall Norfolk pines shelter the street beside the harbor, big, beautiful, shady trees that I'd have paid money to sit under just a few days earlier. Huge, tarp-covered hills of wheat are piled nearby, as a bumper crop was harvested in early December. I can't help but compare the number and frequency of harbors on the Australian coast with the distances that Canadian farmers and miners have to haul their products to tidewater, then wonder how they compete in a world market.

A few miles to the south, we pass a small bay where the activity reminds me of a ski hill back home. A few windsurfers carry equipment up from the beach, others secure boards on top of vehicles, load gear into the back, or change their clothes. Farther down the shore, long, high piles of seagrass are piled above the tide line, explaining the ripe odor of seaweed that hangs heavily over the town.

After checking into a nearby 'van park, we set up the tent under a sun shelter, then walk down the beach. The strong, cool breeze pushing up whitecaps in the bay now blows fine sand into our eyes. When we return and are setting out our chairs, the woman in the next campsite comes over. Talking a mile a minute, she looks at our license plate and asks, "What part of Queensland are you from?"

When Dave responds, "Canada," she roars with laughter. It strikes her as so funny that she repeats it to everybody who walks by.

Telling us that she and her husband are from Tasmania, she explains that they bought a retirement home in Townsville and have just installed their daughter and her family there. They've been touring the country for several months now and she loves it.

Dave then innocently asks, "So, you didn't have to wait for the cat to die?" Upon seeing the blank look on her face, he describes his conversation in Carnarvon.

She laughs again and exclaims, "Wait for the cat to die? I'd have killed it!"

When we leave next morning, huge white sand dunes, the size of low hills, glint brightly along the coastline. We then drive through wheat fields where the after-harvest stubble shines like burnished gold. We take a short detour into the old fishing village of Dongara, then drive up to Fishermen's Outlook in Port Denison for a wonderful view of the bay and a very active small boat harbor.

This section of coast is dotted with the wrecks of 17th Century sailing ships that were bound for Batavia in the Dutch East Indies (Jakarta in Indonesia). Leaving from Europe, the vessels followed sailing directions that are mindboggling in their simplicity. They sailed down the west coast of Africa, rounded the Cape of Good Hope, then steered east for 8,500 km. Upon sighting the western shore of Australia, they turned north. But sometimes wind and sea didn't cooperate, and some of the boats ended their voyage here, on what is now called *the Batavia Coast.*

CHAPTER 10

New Year's on the Southwest Coast

From Geraldton, it's 400 km to the city of Perth (pop. 1.4 million). We expect the northern suburbs to extend out for miles, but they don't. We simply pass through a few vineyards where the bitumen is patched and rough, and then are on a busy four-lane highway entering the city. With traffic moving quickly, I have difficulty spotting the street signs, and when I do see one, I can't find the street on our pocket-sized map. We end up missing turns, getting lost, and shouting at each other.

We're in the adjacent port city of Fremantle (pop. 25,000) before I figure out where we are. We then take in a few sights, again get lost, and end up at a 'van park in Rockingham (pop. 50,000).

As we set up the tent on a quiet, shady site, I notice a big flock of crows watching from the nearby trees, which pretty much finishes my day. But to my surprise, there is no chorus of raucous *caws*, just individual birds calling *awh, awh, awwwh*. The last note drops away, as if the bird was expressing sympathy for the entire world.

Returning to the beach, we buy fish and chips at a take-away and eat at a picnic table on a grassy verge. Vacationers saunter up and down the sidewalk in front of us, or struggle through a strip of sand along the water's edge. Very few are in the water, as the wind is strong, blowing up whitecaps on the bay.

A thick cloud of smoke lies over the coast to the north and we figure it comes from an industrial area that we drove through earlier. We'd seen an aluminum smelter, a nickel refinery, a huge oil refinery, salt works, and I believe, a coal-burning power generator. Through the haze, we can also make out the long causeway leading to an island naval base.

The following morning, now going into Week 7, we return to the port of Fremantle, which sits at the mouth of the Swan River. As we stroll through the downtown, peering into markets and museums, we very much enjoy the cool sea breeze that tempers the heat of the sun. As I admire the well-maintained, stone-faced colonial buildings, Dave reminds me that both the port city and Perth were built with the help of convict labor.

We now drive north along a straight, sandy coastline, occasionally glimpsing some of the thousands of sun seekers enjoying the beaches. Watching the surf break, covering the sand with white lace, I recall a news report from last year. A big white attacked a surfer on one of these beaches, crunching his board, and the young man had survived. The world swimming championships are to be held here next week, and a team of navy divers will accompany the long-distance swimmers to protect them.

As we drive into Perth, I can't help but notice how fresh and clean the city looks, with spacious public grounds and smart, new commercial edifices. With a state population of 1.8 million, it's not hard to figure out that both state and city governments have benefited from a booming mining industry. Shoppers crowd the sidewalks in the city center, and a vacant parking spot can't be found anywhere, so we continue driving and end up at the entrance to Kings Park.

The park is one of the city's main attractions, but with the current drought, grasses are dry and bleached, and leaves hang limply on trees and bushes. One area has recently burnt, and black skeletons of trees stand starkly on the hillside. We end up following a memorial drive that is lined with gum trees, their branches stretching out over the road. A small plaque beneath each tree bears the name of a fallen soldier and the date and cause of death. The avenue goes on and on, as do the trees, and the sheer number is mind numbing.

After parking the car, we wander through a botanical garden, where I recognize a few plants that are currently blooming in the desert. Banksia is easy to spot, as many varieties are in flower along the highway. A large tree covered with orange flowers also stands out; it's sometimes referred to as Western Australia's Christmas tree, but is known locally as moodjar (Nuytsia floribunda).

Unknowingly, we save the best for last, and as we round the brow of the hill, spectacular views of the city lie before us. Walking in the shade of beautiful, tall gum trees, we drink in views of the Swan River and the downtown. At the base of the hill, black swans (the state bird) swim in a pool. Wandering on, we stop to inspect a huge karri tree lying on its side; the tree is 200 feet long and twice my height in diameter, but has been cut into sections and is supported by a cradle.

We now walk back to the State War Memorial, which also overlooks the city. It's very impressive and a lump forms in my throat as we approach. I step down two or three steps and read the names of battles engraved on the low wall encircling the entrance, then follow a path around to the lower level, where we read the names of the state's war dead, a very long list.

Next day, we continue our journey south and soon are driving over the shiny black surface of a new highway, passing the entrances to shiny new subdivisions where *For Sale* signs litter the roadside. It's a beautiful, sunny day, and after 220 km, we stop near a two-km-long jetty in the resort town of Busselton (pop. 9,000).

As we walk along the beach in the shade of tall, leafy trees, small family groups sit on white sands and young children play in shallow waters. After buying hamburgers at a kiosk, we lay claim to a shaded picnic table, and soon another couple approach and settle on the far side. The man has a well-established middle-age paunch, and the woman is slender and well dressed, with fine gold jewelry. He spreads out a newspaper and reads aloud a letter to the editor, and we listen unashamedly because the topic is one that we've been following in Canada.

The letter writer complains that he doesn't understand the uproar about the Commonwealth Government's refusal to apologize to aborigines for past wrongs. He continues, "I've lived all my life in Australia and have done nothing that would require me to apologize! What is the point of asking this generation of Australians to apologize to the current generation of aborigines for wrongs committed by and to past generations?" In obvious agreement, the reader is now incensed.

At this point, Dave interjects, "We've just heard that the Canadian government has apologized to native Indians for their mistreatment at the hands of religious groups operating state-funded schools. They've set up a compensation fund of $600 million!"

This gets a fiery response from the man, and he complains bitterly about the black fellows, and the uncertainty created by land claims. We now learn that he is a real estate developer in Perth, and his wife, who is South African, murmurs softly, "And we're the ones who are supposed to be racist."

As I listen to the conversation, I think of the aborigines we've seen and the comments we've heard about them. Australian government policies are definitely not bringing people together. Nor do I believe that the Canadian initiative will provide real change in the lives of indigenous people. The policy forces them to identify as victims and simply continues their plight as wards of the state. As long as they look to government for answers, I don't see how they will ever be free to live their lives.

That afternoon, we drive another 100 km down the rugged west coast, watching mighty ocean swells break on reefs and sweep into bays, while sea haze obscures the far horizon. Small parking lots are crowded with vehicles, people, and surfboards. We briefly stop at the surfing destinations of Yallingup and Margaret River, and from a bluff at the latter see half-a-dozen surfers far from shore, waiting for the right wave. Closer in, two snorkelers swim in a large pool worn in the rock, while a couple of nude sunbathers lie on the sand beneath the cliff.

As the day wears on, we round a corner and find ourselves in a Karri plantation. The slanting rays of the afternoon sun soften the green of the undergrowth and cast a ghostly glow on the pale, smooth trunks, giving the trees a mystical quality. I want to stop but it's late, and only have time to recognize that the trees are probably a mature stand of second growth. They're uniform in size, evenly spaced, and the branches form a canopy high above the ground.

By 1700, we are in Augusta (pop. 1,000), and are as far south and west as we can go. We now locate an extraordinary 'van park tucked behind heavy scrub alongside the Great Southern Ocean. Although it's nearly full, the pounding surf drowns out most of the noise made by campers. After we've set up the tent, Dave starts supper while I finish pumping up air mattresses and unpacking sleeping bags. A man from the campsite next to us strolls over, sees what Dave is doing, and demands, "What's wrong with her, she got a broken hand?"

Peter, for that's his name, doesn't wait for a reply and soon has volunteered that he's 67 years old, a fourth-generation Aussie, bushman, and land surveyor. His tall, spare frame carries his years well, although white hair pokes out from under his fishing hat and he wears glasses. In response to Dave's questions, he reveals that he's familiar with most areas of the state. But he's also domineering and opinionated, and only by being quick or forceful can we get a word in edgewise.

His companion is a tall, big-boned woman about the same age, and they seem the most unlikely couple. Joy comes from Perth, a townie according to Peter, and is a well-established ceramics painter and teacher. She seems the independent sort and I find their relationship puzzling, so am not surprised when she admits that Peter can be overbearing, even arrogant on occasion.

When the sun goes down, the temperature drops abruptly, and Dave disappears into the tent, as he refused to pack warm clothing. I dig out sweater, socks, and boots, and enjoy the evening for a few more hours.

Next morning, we drive down to Cape Leeuwin on the extreme southwest point of the continent. Under a grey, overcast sky, we scramble over rocks to the water's edge, then watch waves from the Indian and Southern Oceans mix together before breaking on offshore rocks. The sun soon burns through the overcast, warming the air and brightening the sea, and a light breeze ruffles the surface of the water.

We now turn toward the lighthouse, and as we approach, I feel as though on a pilgrimage, thinking of the many similar structures we'd seen and the network of safety they provided for sailors. This lighthouse was dedicated to the world's mariners in December of 1896, so is over 100 years old. Built with local stone, it towers 182 feet above the sea, with four-foot-thick walls at the base and deeply inset windows.

We each pay $7 for the pleasure of climbing the 200 steps that wind tightly up the inside walls. While catching our breath at the top, we study the old clockwork that rotates the lens. Originally driven by a counter weight, it now depends on a small electric motor. The light sits directly overhead and, at one million candlepower, is visible for 46 km.

The ramp around the tower provides spectacular views in all directions, including dense windblown bush covering the rising ground to the northeast. When trying to determine what marks the boundary between the two oceans, we discover that only Australia recognizes the Southern Ocean; to the rest of the world, it's part of the Indian Ocean. Later, as we explore the surrounding grounds, we find a freshwater spring and an old, salt-encrusted waterwheel that once directed water to residences near the base of the lighthouse.

On the way back through town, Dave has the car serviced and is told that a rear tire has developed a bulge. They have no tires, so we cross our fingers, knowing we'll have to drive 400 km to Albany to obtain a replacement. We're back in camp by 1500, setting out our chairs in the sun, welcoming the warmth for a change.

Our neighbors drive in an hour later, and Peter immediately comes over and announces, "Guess what you're doing for tea tonight. You're coming over for fish and chips!" He explains that they've had a successful day fishing and Joy is making "real Aussie fish and chips".

Thus, we spend New Year's Eve, 1997, with Peter and Joy and enjoy it immensely. The evening stays reasonably warm and we sit under the trees for four hours, drinking wine, eating, and talking. The fish are small but Peter caught at least twenty, and Joy divulges that her batter recipe includes half a can of beer.

Peter now reveals himself as a staunch supporter of Western Australia, complaining that the state provides 80% of federal government funding but has no say in policy because of its small population. With her teaching and painting, Joy has led a completely different life. She travels across the country frequently and is also involved in looking after her mother, who has become very dependent. According to her, "Peter takes me away from all that, and I really enjoy the time we spend fishing."

She has vivid memories of the war years, as her dad was away fighting, leaving her and her mother alone in Perth. When I ask about the Brisbane Line, she tells me about the terror her mom felt when she learned that the town would not be defended. Turning to her daughter, she'd desperately asked, "What do we do if the Japanese land?"

Although barely a teenager, she'd responded, "We'll go into the hills."

Her mother then pleaded, "But what about the abos?"

Joy had assured her, "We'll be okay as long as we never turn our backs on them," and then tells me, "I knew that from school."

Peter then explains, "Young teenagers living in the country, like me, were prepared to defend themselves. We banded together, stocked up on weapons and supplies, and stashed them in the hills." With a sly grin he adds, "I don't know what would have happened if the townies had shown up, as the bushies and townies didn't get along."

Both reinforce sentiments that we'd heard before; they felt betrayed by their government and still didn't trust Canberra. I suspect that that distrust plays a role in their attitude toward aborigines. Joy is actually the more disparaging of the two, telling us that they had their own method of birth control, and then whispers in horror, "When food was scarce, the men ate the piccaninnies!"

We'd read about that claim but never heard anyone mention it, and Dave now asks, "Was that really true?"

Joy assures us, "Oh yes, it happened. It wasn't uncommon."

CHAPTER 11

The Great Southern Ocean and Nullarbor Plain

Next morning, under a grey, gloomy sky, we start our journey eastward along the south coast. I'm looking forward to seeing the karri forests that day, but we mostly pass through farmland and see only a few, small pockets of the tall, graceful trees. Disappointed, I persuade Dave to make a side trip into the Valley of the Giants, where the big trees can be viewed from a ramp extending out over the valley floor. But when we get there, the parking lot is overflowing with holiday visitors, and a clamor of excited voices and clanging footsteps carries from the direction of a metal ramp. Looking at each other, we don't even get out of the car, just shake our heads and drive on.

After driving 400 km, we arrive in Albany (pop. 19,000), the oldest European settlement in the state. Established in 1826, it's a quiet, pretty town with many old, well-maintained buildings. When we drive past the harbor, the tide is out and a large flock of black swans are resting on the mud flats.

The first 'van park we come to is full, but the second squeezes in everyone who shows up. It's not too bad when we first set up the tent, but late arrivals then squeeze in around us. One camper parks his van very close to our tent, turns up his stereo, and plays loud Irish music while preparing supper. We're not too happy, but suffer through it. After supper, the cold again drives Dave into the tent, and when he can't hear his radio, he turns the volume up as loud as it will go. The competing sounds drown out each other, and no one can hear anything. After ten minutes, peace is restored when the camper shuts off his music and Dave turns down the radio.

Next morning, we have both rear tires replaced, and while we wait, I read up on the town's history. The port is located in Princess Royal Harbor, off King George Sound, and at one time provided coal to steamships bound for the east coast. It was also a staging point for Australian forces during WW I. Of even more interest to us, an old whaling station that operated from 1952 to 1978 is now open to tourists.

We spend the afternoon at the station in Frenchman Bay, studying pictures and examining equipment, while reading about methods used to hunt the whales. We watch a video of a whale being harpooned, towed into the station, and winched ashore. A forty-ton sperm whale was reduced to eleven tons of product, with nothing wasted.

Humpbacks were the initial targets, but after a few years, the whalers concentrated on sperm whales, which roamed the continental shelf thirty miles out of the harbor. The whale hunts have long since ended, and now Southern Right whales visit the sound to mate and give birth, bringing in tourists from July to October.

We end the day by driving to the outer coast, where the constant pounding of huge waves over millions of years has created formations like the Natural Bridge and The Gap. The afternoon is sunny and pleasant, and we spend half an hour climbing over the smooth granite rock, enjoying spectacular ocean views. We then tear ourselves away in order to find a supermarket before it closes. Dave and our neighbor have an unspoken truce that night, and the cold again drives him into the tent at sunset.

I put in a restless night and am awake early, so quietly get up, leaving him snoring softly. In the quiet of a grey dawn, I follow a winding path through brush and sand dunes down to the beach. The morning is exquisite. The sky is clear, the air cool and calm, and the bay a mirror, perfectly reflecting the images of three small fishing boats. I stop and gaze about as the sun bursts over the horizon, then walk down the firm, white sand at the water's edge.

I turn back half an hour later, and soon feel the sun warming my shoulders. At about the same time, a light breeze stirs the air and a gentle surf begins to roil the sand. When I come across a smooth, flat spot, I decide to do some tai chi, although I haven't done it in years. My muscles are stiff after weeks of sitting in the car, and I have difficulty remembering the form, but go through it twice.

I then notice a figure walking down the beach toward me and turn to leave. Hearing a voice call out., I stop, look back and see a young woman approaching. She's attractive, fit looking, and it turns out, a kindred spirit. She asks, "You were doing tai chi, weren't you?"

Nodding my head, I confess, "Yes, but I'm afraid I'm rather rusty!"

"I watched you and it was beautiful," she responds, then waves her hand toward the backdrop of sea and sky, and exclaims,

"Inspirational!" Bubbling with enthusiasm, she tells me that she's made a New Year's resolution to take up tai chi with her son.

After chatting for a few minutes, we go our separate ways, and I'm almost purring with satisfaction at the thought that I could have added something to such a perfect morning. Dave is still asleep when I get back, so I keep busy with laundry until he gets up, then eagerly start to tell him of my encounter.

Not really interested, he rains all over my parade, and as the magic of the morning disintegrates, I angrily turn and stalk away. We spend the rest of the day avoiding each other. Next day, we exchange two short sentences while driving 500 km. I fixate on the small trees with bright orange flowers that dot the fields and line the highway, and on flocks of sheep grazing in the stubble of wheat fields. At one point, a bandicoot crosses the road in front of us, at least it's a small animal with a hopping run, long snout, and a short tail that sticks straight out behind.

We're in Esperance by 1300, and again have to go on to a second 'van park. After organizing our gear, we return to the esplanade downtown and stroll beneath huge Norfolk pines that line the beach. With a cold southerly breeze pushing up whitecaps out on the bay, I'm happy for the protection of a low berm that runs beside the sidewalk.

Something then flashes out on the water, so we climb up on the berm and gaze out to sea. Under a brilliant, sunny sky, a 25-knot breeze is blowing the tops off waves, and clear, cold water crashes onto the beach in front of us. Another flash then focuses our attention on a dozen windsurfers racing across the water.

The gossamer wings of their sails follow a course parallel to the beach, and fascinated, we watch as they continue down the course to the last buoy, where the onshore breeze tests their mettle as they round it and start back. When they're finished, another race starts on a second course half a mile to our left; this one is angled more offshore. We've stumbled upon the Ninth Annual Esperance Races, which have brought world-class surfers to the Southern Ocean.

The heats are staggered, and there's always something to watch, but the wind has a cold bite and sand occasionally stings our faces. After a half hour, we leave the berm and watch as we walk. Soon, we arrive at a stretch of sand littered with racers and their belongings; all wear neoprene wetsuits, most appear short and muscular, and only three are women. I stop and talk to a woman with a baby carriage who is also watching, and she tells me that her husband is one of the organizers. When I ask about the conditions, she replies, "Oh, they're excellent! They always are at this time of year."

As we marvel at the skills of the competitors, Dave and I are again pals, all traces of ill humor forgotten. Our relationship at this time is still based on a shared enthusiasm for adventure, for new experiences. We're probably best described as two travelers keeping each other company while going in the same direction.

When the races finish, we tour the port, then find our way to the coast road, where views of the Southern Ocean grow grander around every corner. From atop high cliffs, we look down on blue, crystal-clear water breaking on reefs and granite outcroppings, and see strips of sandy beach nestled in protected coves. We watch a few windsurfers, their sails mingling with breaking waves, and conclude they are dedicated enthusiasts when we see the difficult climb from beach to parking lot.

Next morning, as we start Week 8, Dave hears on the radio that a large piece of mining equipment is to be moved 1,000 km from the port to the town of Lenora. It will be hauled over the route we're taking, so we quickly pack up, not wanting to be stuck behind it. Police and highway vehicles are waiting in a marshalling area as we drive out of town, but there is no sign of the equipment. Spectators stand on street corners for the next two blocks, however, their cameras ready.

The ground is flat when we turn inland, with well-spaced, hardy trees growing amongst dry patches of low bush. As the terrain becomes more rolling, the bush grows higher, then gives way to grasslands near the goldfields. While driving through the hamlet of Norseman, Dave notices a small-diameter pipe paralleling the road and figures it carries water north. At Coolgardie, the site of a major gold strike in 1892, the pipe grows bigger and he realizes water is actually flowing south.

In fact, the pipeline comes from Perth, some 600 km to the west, and was built in 1903 in order to sustain the mining industry. This part of the state is so dry that many early miners reportedly died of thirst or succumbed to diseases in unhygienic shantytowns.

After driving 400 km, we arrive in Kalgoorlie (pop. 30,000), the only large town remaining in the goldfields. Deep pits and flat-topped mountains of earth surround the town, with head rigs and ventilator shafts visible in all directions. Gold was discovered here in 1893, and an open pit mine and the Mt Charlotte underground complex are still operating. It's known as a frontier town with legal brothels, two-up gambling camp, and a reputation for heavy drinking.

The sun burns my arms as we set up the tent on a patch of gravel beneath a small square of sunshade, but the 'van park turns out to be quite pleasant, with a few trees providing shade and a bit of breeze. Next morning, we're off to the visitors' center, which overlooks the largest open-pit mine in Australia. Only one loader and half a dozen ore trucks are working, and we watch the huge trucks, loaded with rock and earth, inch their way up the steep road to the top. The trip seems to take forever, but requires only seven minutes.

Afterwards, we tour through the downtown, where several striking turn-of-the-century buildings line the wide main street. It's too early to see any activity outside the brothels, and we assume it'll be the same at the 2-up camp, which is seven km out. (The game involves tossing two coins in the air and betting on the outcome.) After poking about in the shops, we stop at a nearby pub for a couple of expensive beers.

We pass an aborigine encampment while driving back to the 'van park. The occupants look dirty and unkempt, and I'm dismayed at the amount of trash littering the site. We've seen so much garbage in so many places that I have to believe it's a huge problem for the planet. I wonder whatever happened to the slogan of *reduce, reuse, and recycle,* which was used to promote individual responsibility a few years earlier.

Living on Windy Lady has made me very conscious of our own consumption habits, as we had to be self-sufficient when at sea or at anchor. We caught rain water for washing in order to preserve the limited drinking water that we carried, and eliminated most of our garbage by not buying canned drinks or frozen food. We stored what garbage we had until able to dispose of it in port.

Our electricity came from batteries that had to be charged, which meant running the diesel engine every fourth day for at least four hours. That provided power for a few lights, computer fans in the berths, and navigation and communication equipment. We used the large fans and refrigerator only when hooked up to shore power, and had no air conditioning.

Next day, we're away early and take an alternate route back to the crossroads at Norseman. As we round a corner of the two-lane paved road, we meet a pilot truck with a wide load sign. Behind it is a police vehicle, which swerves to a stop with its front end in our lane. Dave pulls over onto the shoulder and also stops, but the officer orders him off the roadbed, pointing to trees at the edge of the right-of-way. Realizing that we're meeting *the Road Train*, Dave acknowledges the instruction then asks, "What happened to you? We thought you'd be through here yesterday."

"Yeah, so did we," the officer responds, "but you know that long hill coming out of Norseman? It was so hot yesterday that the pavement started to melt under the tires, so we had to wait until early this morning."

Dave then asks, "How far is the train behind you?"

"About a minute!"

We quickly drive off the road, crossing through the ditch and stopping in the shade of the trees. Within seconds, a second police vehicle sweeps around the corner followed by a Dept. of Transport vehicle and then the convoy. At first, I see only a cloud of dust swirling up around the load, but it clears as four big Mack trucks roar by. They're pulling a trailer on which sits something that looks like a huge oil-tanker car. Two Mack trucks are behind, pushing, followed by maybe a dozen vehicles that are unable to pass.

The convoy is 300 feet long and moves quickly. I have time to take only three pictures before it's gone. The outside tires on both sides of the trailer are off the pavement, stirring up dust on the shoulder, and the pictures reveal eight sets of dual tires across the width of the trailer, and at least nineteen sets along the length. The load is reported to be 23 feet wide, almost that high, and weighs 770 tons. The engines in the six Mack trucks are each rated at 610 horsepower.

We've heard that four such units will be taken to Lenora, and actually saw two of them in an enclosure at the port. This huge piece of equipment is an autoclave, used by the mining industry to separate gold, although other industries use it for sterilizing. Incredulous at what we've just seen, we talk about the convoy all the way down to Norseman, where we stop to fill up the gas tank and water jug.

We now turn east across the Nullarbor Plain, a huge expanse of flat, semi-arid/arid land bordered to the north by the Great Victoria Desert and to the south by the Great Southern Ocean. The next community offering any variety of services is 1,200 km away, although roadhouses are located about every 200 km. The gently rolling terrain soon flattens out, trees become more scattered, and then there's only bush. Before long, we're crossing a 90-mile (146.5 km) straight stretch, the longest in the country.

Although it's mid-summer, the wind has a freshness due to the proximity of the ocean and the day is very pleasant. I read that a telegraph line was built across the plain in 1877, and miners followed it on their way to the goldfields. The first bicycle crossing was made in 1896, and the first car was driven across in 1912. (Bicycles were reportedly used by sheep shearers to travel between stations.)

At Caiguna, we pay the highest price yet for gas, and at Madura, the road drops down over the escarpment and we drive along a narrow coastal plain, with 200-foot-high cliffs paralleling the road on the north side. At Eucla, the long line of limestone cliffs edges back out toward the ocean and the road climbs back up on top. It's now 1700 and we've driven 930 km, so we stop at a roadhouse.

The sky has been overcast for the last fifty km, and the manager tells us they've seen the sun for only a few hours in the past week. The wind has a definite bite as we set up the tent, and as soon as the sun goes down, the cold drives us inside. Before leaving next day, we walk over to the edge of the escarpment and admire a magnificent view over the coastal plain, where huge, white sand dunes border the blue waters of the Southern Ocean.

Not far down the road, we cross the border into South Australia, and several times that morning, we drive out to the edge of the escarpment and admire the views of deep, blue waters frothing white at the foot of towering limestone cliffs. The sky then clears, providing a beautiful, sunny afternoon. Eventually the dry-looking, grey-green bush gives way to a field that looks cultivated, and I see two bulls, a flock of sheep, and a house. After refueling at Penong, we donate a few tomatoes, onions, and oranges to a quarantine station located just outside of Ceduna, where our journey across the Nullarbor ends.

CHAPTER 12
Ayres Peninsula and the Murray River

Ceduna (pop. 3,600) is a quiet community nestled beside the sea at the top, west corner of Ayres Peninsula. We check into a 'van park and set up the tent in a shady, fenced enclosure, where a cool, refreshing sea breeze offsets the afternoon heat. It's really very pleasant, but before we have time to enjoy it, we're rushing off to a store, as we've lost almost two hours due to time zone changes.

Our neighbors that night are from Melbourne and explain that they took the train to Perth and paid $1,600 for the one-way passage for themselves and their car. They also tell us that we shared the same campsites for the last three nights, but I remember seeing them only in the crowded camp kitchen in Kalgoorlie. Enjoying their company, we stay up late, then pay for our sins come morning, when motor homes start rumbling out at 0430.

With the day bright and sunny, we spend the morning doing chores, then walk about the community for a few hours. We end up at an abandoned wharf that local kids have claimed as their own. Some are fishing, using large hooks on the end of strong cord, and one young boy excitedly tells us, "I just saw a hammerhead shark!"

Next day, we take an inland route 400 km down the Ayres Peninsula. The heat starts to build as soon as we leave the coast, and fields are drab and brown, with crops long since harvested. We're surprised to learn that there's little fresh water on the peninsula; most of it has to be piped in. We then stop beside a field and study wind-worn granite rocks known as Murphy's Haystacks that are over 1,500 million years old.

Turning off onto a rough dirt road that loops over to the coast, we are again treated to spectacular ocean views. We stop and walk along the edge of rugged cliffs, looking down on clear, blue waters, with swells breaking white on rocks below and long curling waves rolling into sheltered bays. A few surfers are out at Blackfellows, enjoying one of Australia's premier surfing spots. Scattered across the ground underfoot are small, clay-like objects, known locally as clogs; they are believed to be up to 100,000 years old and are the fossilized cocoons of weevils. But when we return to the highway, the engine has an unfamiliar growl, as we've put a hole in the tailpipe.

We camp that night in Port Lincoln (pop. 13,000), at the tip of the peninsula. The 'van park is very pleasant, with dried yellow grasses spreading across a hillside dotted with gum trees. Setting up in a shady spot at the far end, we pretty much have the place to ourselves, and soon are relaxing in our lounge chairs, enjoying a beautiful, warm afternoon. I must admit, however, to being envious of the many small boats out on the sheltered waters of Boston Bay.

The temperature cools pleasantly overnight, and next morning, we're on the road early, driving through grain fields up the east side of the peninsula. An isolated hill looms high on the horizon as we near the north end, and signs identify it as *Iron Knob*, the site where iron ore was discovered in 1894. The BHP Company (Broken Hill

Proprietary) developed several mines nearby, and in 1964, a fully integrated steelworks was built at the nearby port of Whyalla.

Port Augusta is hot and windy, but for once, we have a luxuriously grassy campsite. After dinner, we sit and enjoy the sunset, then watch a big, full moon rise over the eastern horizon. We only notice the ants come morning and then we are swarmed as we approach the car. My legs are black to the knees when I swipe them off, and they're back a minute later. We pack up and leave as quickly as we can, but the humidity has us dripping with sweat before the tent is stowed.

We start Week 9 by stopping at the Wadlata Outback Center on the way out of town, where we learn about the first Europeans to explore the country. Dutch sailors visited the west coast between 1600 and 1650, and Captain Cook mapped the east coast in 1770. Exploration inland began on the southeast coast in 1824.

Eyre crossed the Nullarbor in 1840-41, traveling from Port Lincoln to Albany. He found virtually no water or food, and his companion was killed by their two aborigine guides. Leichhardt led an expedition from Morton Bay to Darwin in 1844. The journey up the east coast was expected to take seven months, but took twice that long, by which time he was given up for dead. He then attempted an inland route in 1848 and was never seen again. His name is familiar to us, as we saw it reflected in place names while driving through the area.

The expeditions through the harsh, dry center were even more extraordinary. Eyre left Adelaide in 1840, heading north to Darwin, but turned back when he ran into a large lake (it fills about once every hundred years). When Sturt headed north four years later, he looked for an inland sea and dragged a rowing dory amongst his supplies. Burke and Wills succeeded in making the trip from south to north in 1860-61, but they disappeared on the return journey. Forrest crossed from east to west in 1874.

It's almost noon when we set out on the 300-km drive to Adelaide. Heat and humidity have been building, and soon angry black clouds are hanging low in the sky. The ensuing storm brings heavy rain and cools the air considerably. We check into a downtown 'van park in a gloomy dusk and find the campsites squeezed between a paved lane and the riverbank. There's barely room for the tent beside our car, and as the trees are dripping from the rain, we rent a caravan for the night. We then walk through the quiet neighborhood and find a pub to have supper.

Next morning, we drop off the car to have the tailpipe repaired, then spend the day exploring the downtown. Adelaide, (pop. 1,070,000), is a beautiful city with interesting brick and stone buildings and tree-lined streets. We inspect the statues in Victoria Square and stroll down King William Street to the Rundle Street Mall, where pedestrians rush about, dodging trees and sculptures. As it's the noon hour, many of them are smartly-dressed young businesswomen, looking most attractive in brightly tailored tops and skirts.

That night, the mosquitoes are dreadful. I wrap myself in a sheet, trying to hide, but it's so hot and humid that I wake up at 0200 with nightshirt and sheet soaked through. Locating a bottle of *deet* in the car, I splash it freely on face and arms, but only drift off to sleep when a breeze finally stirs the air. Humidity is still high next morning, and we're dripping by the time we've finished breakfast.

Our route now takes us inland for 1,300 km, first across the 3,000-foot Mount Lofty Ranges, then out into the desert. We pick up the 2,500-km-long Murray River near its mouth, and looking down at the muddy, slow-moving stream that slides through a canal-like channel, I find it hard to believe that the river was once a bustling thoroughfare, carrying goods between ocean and interior. Only 20% of natural flows now make it to the sea, and they are heavily polluted with agricultural runoff and community waste.

After driving through more wheat fields, we cross into the state of Victoria, where the river forms a 1,000-km-long boundary with New South Wales (NSW). We seldom see the river, but pass over numerous canals running bank-to-bank with irrigation water for market gardens, citrus fruit orchards, and vineyards. We also listen to a radio report about the long-term effects of using flood irrigation; apparently, it raises the water table, bringing salts to the surface, and reduces the productivity of the land.

After driving 500 km, we stop for the night at Swan Hill (pop. 9,800). The 'van park seems idyllic, with large, shady gum trees scattered about a grassy meadow on the bank of the river. But the manager points to lowering clouds while showing us to a site and suggests we face the tent southeast. Heat and humidity grow more oppressive as we sweat through our chores, but the storm holds off until after supper. With the first scattered drops of rain, I take refuge in the tent, but notice that the lower part of the sky seems more brown than blue-black.

Minutes later, a fierce gust of wind flattens a wall of the tent, then rain buckets down. The heavy rain doesn't last long but showers continue for an hour. The storm passes directly overhead, bringing brilliant flashes of lightning and ferocious crashing and banging of thunder, and when it moves on, the air is ten degrees cooler. We then have a wonderful night's sleep.

The cool temperatures bring clear, bright skies next morning, and just after daybreak, a flock of corellas (cockatoos) start a ruckus that carries on for three hours. It somehow seems appropriate given that the explorer who named Swan Hill did so after spending a night listening to noisy black swans. Later, two flocks of corellas dispute the use of a large weeping willow overhanging the water, while several eastern swamp hens, the size of small chickens, forage in the grass.

We now learn that last night's storm spawned several mini-tornadoes, and one blew over trees and ripped off roofs just south of town. A group of campers had waded out into the river for safety, but lost their vehicle, tent and equipment.

We drive only 160 km that day and stop on route to visit a bird sanctuary in the Kerang Lake wetlands. Using binoculars, I study white ibis, straw-necked ibis, royal spoonbills, black swans, pelicans, cormorants, and one brilliant blue wren; many more ibis feed in the wheat fields when we drive on.

We spend the night in the town of Echuca (pop. 10,200), checking into a 'van park located behind the high walls of a levee on a flood plain dotted with gum trees. After setting up our camp, we stroll beneath the trees as we head downtown. In the 1880s, 300 steamers had operated from this port, which was then second only to Melbourne in the volume of cargo handled in the state.

A few paddle wheelers now wait for their next load of tourists at a massive wharf on the riverbank. Built with long, straight pilings made from red river gums, it has three levels to accommodate changing river levels. The street next to the riverfront has been restored and boasts a steam-driven woodturning shop, sawmill, and blacksmith's shop.

When we return to camp, we find a couple in the process of erecting a tent beside us. Bill is tall and well-built, looks to be in his mid-forties, and tells us that he spent fifteen years in the navy. Margaret is a bit younger, dark-haired, slim and confident, and explains that she's from Melbourne.

Before long, Bill is confessing that he recently bought a house on the Murray and laments, "It seemed pretty cheap until I found out about the white ants! I've had to rip out and replace one whole wall!" He's also not bashful about giving his opinion when he learns that we sailed across the Pacific Ocean. "Anyone who would go to sea is crazy," he states bluntly, then observes, "And you look so normal." They introduce us to another form of camping, as they've brought along several bottles of wine and later depart for a club.

Next day, the heat is scorching, and despite muddy water filling irrigation ditches, the countryside looks parched. We drive past the town of Yarrawonga, which sits on a reservoir behind a dam on the Murray. It's supposed to be a tourist destination, but I'm put off by the dead trees in the water. We then pass the twin towns of Wodonga-Albury, which sizzle in the midday heat. Lake Hume is another reservoir with more dead trees, and open bare ridges that bake in the sun.

The road starts to climb as the hills grow higher, and open grasslands now give way to forest. Plantations of pine soon intermingle with native forest, and we meet several trucks loaded with logs; in fact, clear-cuts are visible as we cross through a saddle. Even more surprising, a small herd of bison graze in a high valley.

We arrive in Corryong (pop. 1,300) about mid-afternoon and check into a 'van park that reminds me of camping at home. Big, leafy trees shade the spacious, park-like meadow, and a creek runs through the back of the property. A low weir spans the creek, making a shallow pool 100 yards long, and kids of all ages swim, float on air mattresses, or just sit in the cool water. We set up the tent on the creek bank and don't move out of the shade.

We leave early next morning, but the day is already hot and the road winds tortuously as it climbs into the Snowy Mountains. As it cuts through gaps and follows high valleys, we cross from Victoria into New South Wales. At Khancoban, we buy a permit to drive through Kosciusko National Park, which includes most of the area that records snowfall in Australia, as well as the highest mountain, Kosciusko, at 7,352 feet.

At the visitors' center, we watch a video describing the jobs and wealth creation that resulted from the Snowy Mountain Hydro Electric Scheme. The Snowy and Murrumidgee Rivers were both dammed, their waters diverted from the eastern slopes of the mountains into the Murray River drainage on the western side. The project was massive, involving 126 major dams, 134 km of main tunnels, 7 hydroelectric generators, and 1 pumping station.

The Murray system now provides irrigation water to three states, and the power generated goes to communities in the southeast. A water management commission regulates the waters of the Murray and four other rivers, effectively controlling the water drainage for one-seventh of the Australian land mass.

Beyond Khancoban, the road is steep, narrow, and winding for 100 km; six sections (8.5 km) are unpaved. We stop at a viewpoint to admire a panoramic view of the western face of the range, and then again at the Swampy Plains River campground, where several trails lead along the river. Much of the forest here consists of wattle trees and peppermint gums, but a crowded stand of slender snow gums catches my eye.

After cresting the summit at 5,140 feet, we drop down to Thredbo, Australia's premier ski resort. The town is located in a narrow, steep-walled valley that is really just a deep ravine. The chairlift is busy taking people up and down the hillside, and several strings of ponies stand with saddles on, awaiting riders. The bypass road is closed for repairs, as it was damaged by a landslide that killed nineteen people the previous year.

Entering a saddle of low, rolling hills, we come to Lake Jindabyne, the reservoir behind the last dam on the Snowy River. The two gates of the spillway are huge, and the sight of a small stream of water cascading down and disappearing into the cracks of the dry riverbed is a sobering reminder of the river that once was.

We stop for groceries in Cooma (pop. 7,385), and in the downtown come across a WW I memorial depicting the actions of a stretcher-bearer, a local lad awarded a Military Medal for *acts of gallantry and devotion to duty under fire*. Stopping to pay our respects, I find myself strangely moved to learn the veteran had only recently died. It touches Dave too, and he reminds me, "I remember waving at the troop trains when the soldiers came home from WW II; I would have been six years old."

We find a shady campground on the edge of town and that night share stories with a camo-wearing Pom. He lives in Adelaide, has been in country twenty years, and is on a walking tour. He tells us that wild pigs are seriously damaging vegetation in the backcountry of the park, then complains about the water wasted by farmers using flood and aerial irrigation along the Murray, noting that too much water brings salts to the surface and kills plants.

I don't say much, but he's speaking to the converted. I'd recently spent four years researching water management issues and had concluded that we all waste water and electricity. I suspected consumers were encouraged to do so in order to justify big hydroelectric projects.

CHAPTER 13

Canberra, Cowra, and Coonamble

Next day, it's a short drive to Canberra (pop. 300,000) in the Australian Capital Territory. This inland site, midway between Sydney and Melbourne, was selected for the capital in 1908, seven years after the Commonwealth of Australia was formed. Fifty years later, a dam was built on the Molonglo River, creating an 11-km-long lake in the city center. In 1988, a new parliament building costing $1.1 billion was opened. It was an exorbitant amount of money at the time and caused a huge uproar.

The heat is stifling as we approach the city and the countryside looks parched. Several small, green, tree-clad hills then appear on the horizon, along with a jet of water shooting high in the air. Minutes later, we turn onto a wide boulevard and cross a bridge over the lake. The National War Memorial is behind us on one side of a shallow valley and Capitol Hill before us. A three-column bell tower stands on a small island nearby, and the Captain Cook Memorial Water Jet can be seen to the east.

The imposing home of the federal government merges into the profile of a hill, and a thick mat of green grass covers much of the roof. On top, a huge flagstaff supports an Australian flag the size of a double-decker bus. Leaving the car in a parking lot out front, we follow a walkway that has water flowing in low riffles down either side. It takes us to a large shallow pool in the forecourt, where a mosaic using aborigine sand painting traditions represents a gathering of tribes. Low steps then lead into the building.

Inside the main foyer are forty-eight tall, marble-clad columns that are unbelievably beautiful. Grey-green in color, they symbolize a eucalyptus forest. Two marble staircases lead to the upper floor, which is finished with all manner of Australian wood. Joining a guided tour, we peer down at a water sculpture in the Member's Hall, a silent pool with a surface like glass that overflows in a thin, constant sheet on all four sides. From the visitors' gallery, we also look down into the House of Representatives and the Senate Chamber.

As we wander through the public rooms, I squeeze in beside other visitors and study one of only four copies of the original 1297 issue of the Magna Carta; it is written in Latin on vellum, with a translation on the wall behind. Also on display are the original copy of the Commonwealth of Australia Constitution Act 1900 and the Australia Act of 1986, which severed legal ties with the British Parliament.

Taking an elevator up to the roof, we stroll across the grass while admiring the magnificent view down the avenue to the War Memorial. When we return inside, we stand for a moment at the top of a marble staircase, taking one last look around. I'm still awestruck at what imagination and an unlimited budget can create.

A nearby guide, who keeps an eye out for anyone looking lost, now speaks to us, and on hearing our accent, volunteers that she visited America by ship in 1962. Dave's ears perk up because he sailed to Australia aboard the *Oriana* that year. As they reminisce, she recalls, "I went over early in the year and returned later that same year. In fact, our liner was hit by an aircraft carrier in Los Angeles harbor." Dave's jaw drops and he exclaims, "No! I was on that boat!" They speak for only a few moments before the woman returns to work, and we're left stunned. How extraordinary!

After returning to the car, we drive across the lake to the War Memorial, where we pay our respects at the tomb of an unknown WW I soldier in the Hall of Memory. The cloisters outside record the names of over 102,000 who died as the result of wars (46,000 from WW I). The stained-glass windows, the mosaic on the dome, and even the small tiles stuccoed to the walls seem to speak of the sacrifice of the men and women who went overseas, and the caring of those who stayed home. I leave with the feeling that the Aussies succeeded in honoring their war dead without glorifying war. The message was simply that as a people, they forged a nation, defended their country, and met their responsibilities.

The wind whips up clouds of dust as we settle into a 'van park, then brings a pleasant, cool rain. Come morning, the dust has turned into mud. We pack up between showers and stop at the National Science Center on our way out of town. It's something of a madhouse, with youngsters rushing from exhibits that have puzzles to those that have computer-generated imagery. I find myself lingering in front of a display that repeatedly produces a miniature tornado and bolts of lightning.

Five strange-looking, solar-powered vehicles are parked in front of the building when we leave. They're participating in a cross-country race. One has a molded solar panel for a top and the driver peers out through a peephole; it's said to have cost $1,000,000. A second vehicle resembles a tabletop, with a bicycle supporting one front corner, and the opposite rear corner resting on a wheel. We're told that the team have disputed the right-of-way with a wedge-tail eagle and a big red 'roo, and so far have won.

As we go into Week 10, we're only 1,600 km from Brisbane, but take six days to get there. We drive 200 km that afternoon, and when we arrive in Cowra (pop. 8,600), dark clouds fill the sky and lightning flares on the western horizon. A strong wind hits as we're setting up the tent, blowing up clouds of dust that sting hands and faces. We escape into the car, where we wait an hour for the rain to end before preparing a late supper in the cool aftermath.

Cowra is located in a peaceful farming district, but has its own story of WW II. The town was the site of a prisoner-of-war camp housing Italian, Korean, Formosan, and Japanese POWs. On August 5, 1944, over 1,000 Japanese prisoners attempted to break out, and when the incident ended, 234 prisoners and four Australian soldiers were dead. An avenue lined with cherry trees now leads through quiet fields to two cemeteries, where local residents maintain a Japanese War Cemetery in addition to their own.

We visit the site of the POW camp next morning, where only a few foundation stones are visible in a grassy field. We continue on to the Japanese Garden and Cultural Center that was established in 1973. The garden is a delight, with naturally occurring rocks and tall gum trees blending into a formal design of waterfalls, shrubs, and colorful flowers. After wandering along winding paths, we rest in the shade of a teahouse, peer through latticework at miniature plants in the

Bonsai house, and study beautiful displays of pottery in the pottery shed.

The cultural center features many exquisite objects, including ceremonial masks, kimonos, miniature dolls, and a 300-year-old painted scroll. Outside, in a dry garden, large rocks are transformed into islands by a sea of pebbles raked into varying designs. The theme continues even in the parking lot, where a row of twelve large rocks runs due north. Shaped by nature and carved by man, they're said to symbolize the oneness of the world and represent peace. Deeply impressed by what I see, it occurs to me that ordinary, caring people of these two nations have created something extraordinary from tragedy.

The images stay with me next day as we drive 200 km through lightly treed, rolling pasture and farmland to Dubbo (pop. 40,000). I'm hot and sticky when we arrive, and we're soon waiting out another storm in the car.

We prepare supper in the camp kitchen that night and are entertained by three kookaburras that perch companionably on the branch of a nearby tree. (We've heard the birds at dawn and dusk for several days now.) They occasionally leave to catch flies in the grass, and I'm struck by how ungainly they look. They're the largest kingfisher and have heads and beaks that seem much too large for their bodies.

Next morning, we're off to Coonamble (pop. 3,500), where I worked on a station thirty years before. It's pretty country and the 160-km drive stirs vague memories, but nothing about the village seems familiar. We stop at the local visitors' center, hoping to find someone who can job my memory, as I can't recall the names of either the owner or the station. The volunteers who staff them have been very helpful in other communities, but the woman here is a newcomer and sends us to the Shire office.

The staff at the Shire office are unable to help, as stations have been sold and subdivided in the intervening years. One of the staff suggests we talk to John O'Brien, the local stock and property agent, saying, "He's been around forever."

Mr. O'Brien is not in when we locate his office and I'm beginning to think we're just wasting time. However, I repeat my story to the woman there and she unexpectedly responds, "I'm Mrs. O'Brien. My husband and I were married in 1967, so maybe I can help."

Having now thought about it, I'm able to recall a few more details and explain, "I was hired through an agency in Sydney and traveled out to Coonamble on the night train. I was met at a rural siding by an old man in a wagon; he had a bad leg and limped, and his grandson lived with him." Suddenly, I also recall, "He hired only girls and four of us worked there at the time."

After thinking for a few minutes, Mrs. O'Brien replies that only one person comes to mind and his name was Skinner. As the name pierces the hazy veil of my memory, she takes us into an office, where an old wall map shows Orwell Station. I'm now sure that this is the place and ask for directions, but she hesitates, asking us to wait for her husband to return.

When John O'Brien appears, he remembers Clary Skinner as a strange duck who hired only girls, but says another station farther from town also hired jillaroos. After thinking about it, he concludes, "You probably got off the train at Combara siding, where there were two or three houses. Skinner would have picked you up there and driven back to Orwell via Morning Star Station."

He continues to reminisce, telling us that Skinner had been on the outs with his daughter, and that his grandson, Rodney, occasionally stayed with him. The daughter inherited the property when the old man died in 1970, and she had passed on two years before. "Her husband still lives there," he continues, "His name is Ralph Parsons and he's a friendly, likeable man. He's now 84 years old and I'm sure would be happy to talk to you."

He draws us a mud map, and after thanking them for their help, we retrace our route eighteen km south. Turning off onto a side road, we soon come to the railway siding at Combara, which now has facilities for loading grain. A cloud of red dust rises behind the car as we continue down a dirt road, and ten minutes later, we turn off and follow a long drive into a farmyard. The place seems deserted, and then a large aborigine man carrying a rifle emerges from a shed. When Dave asks him for directions to Orwell Station, he shakes his head and mumbles, "I'm just visitin'."

When I ask, "Is this Morning Star Station?", he nods in response.

Returning down the drive, we continue on for a few more kilometers, and the road then splits, and splits again. This time, a weathered sign, *Orwell Station*, hangs from a tree. As we turn onto the road, a small troop of kangaroos appears beside the car and bounds away. When the road turns ninety degrees, intersecting their path, they cross in front of us and I count ten animals. Turning again at a nearby fence line, they race us down the road and Dave clocks them at 40 km/hr.

I see nothing familiar as Dave drives into a deserted-looking yard and parks in front of a modern two-story house. A jacked-up pickup truck sits in the driveway, and a pocket-sized front lawn is roped off. Ralph Parsons turns out to be a small, slight man, with alert, bright blue eyes in a tanned face. Upon hearing my story, he invites us in, asking us to sit down and visit awhile.

He confirms that he and his wife Chum moved to Orwell Station in 1970. They built the new house in 1987, and he shows us through the main floor, which has bright, airy rooms and hardwood floors. A bore was drilled at the same time, so he now has water to weather the droughts. When I ask about the quality, he runs a glassful from the tap; it's cool and sweet.

He tells us that he's lived alone since his wife died and explains, "My son visits occasionally, and I have wonderful neighbors down the road, who help out and keep an eye on me. For nothing," he asserts, then admits, "They do have the use of a 300-acre paddock." He also confides, "I got rid of the sheep after my wife died; they were just too much work." Although his neighbors have switched to grain, he now has 500 head of cattle on his 5,000 acres.

We then wander about outside for a few minutes, and I recognize the farmyard that once was. The small, old farmhouse still stands, looking like a breath of wind could knock it over, but the orange tree out front is long gone. Grass grows under the trees where the rickety two-room bunkhouse once stood, the corrals are gone, and the barn has been rebuilt.

As I look around, I remember riding out to a paddock, where we'd spent the day digging up and piling brush. Margaret, an aborigine girl, had chased several kangaroos on the way and they'd escaped by jumping over the fence. I then recall old man Skinner standing in the yard that morning, watching as we saddled the horses. When I prepared to mount, he had mockingly said, "You're going to have to do it yourself; nobody's going to help you here." I just stared at him, wondering why he would assume that I needed help.

I quickly discovered that Orwell Station was not a happy place. Two of my workmates were from Sydney and did nothing but complain; they were also leaving within a week. I shared a room with Margaret, and she was leaving in ten days. The idea of staying on alone didn't appeal to me, and when we ran out of eggs, bread, and potatoes that first week, I had to face some hard truths.

I didn't have much money and had a month to find a job, as that was when my return plane ticket expired. A week in Sydney had convinced me that it would take every penny I made to live there. Working as a jillaroo paid less but room and board were included and I'd figured on saving most of it. Now Orwell Station wasn't looking that good and time was passing quickly, so I made the decision to return to Canada.

I take one last look around before climbing in the car, and then the memories start to fade. The time here has been unreal, not like a dream, but more like a past that belonged to somebody else.

CHAPTER 14
Country Music and King Parrots

After driving south for an hour, we turn onto a second highway that takes us northeast, around the end of the Warrumbungle Ranges. The scenery is incredibly beautiful, with grassy valleys dotted with trees, timbered hills, and tall, strangely shaped rock domes and spires. According to my guidebook, active volcanoes covered the area with several hundred meters of lava thirteen million years before, and natural erosion had since created this work of art.

A couple of hours later, we arrive in Coonabarabran (pop. 4,000). My first question at the visitors' center is, "How do you pronounce the name?" With a laugh, the woman responds, "Just like it's spelled, *Coo-na-bar'-a-bran*." She then tells us, "We haven't seen many tourists because of news reports of bush fires in New South Wales and South Australia." We're surprised, as we saw no evidence of fires along the way, and with some frustration she explains, "The closest fire was 100 km to the north."

In fact, we passed through heavy rain a few hours earlier, and the rain starts again while we're setting up camp. The storm dumps an inch of rain in an hour, during which we take refuge in the car. I'm just thankful that the tent floor stays dry. Next morning, the air is clear and fresh, and we drink our coffee and eat bacon and eggs with relish.

We chat for a few minutes with a neighbor, who rides a big Harley-Davidson and reveals a lot more face when he removes his helmet. He tells us that he's just spent four days at the country music festival in Tamworth. "It's really very good," he enthuses, "You should stop and take it in." He then warns, "But you won't find a camping spot anywhere nearby."

The world looks freshly scrubbed when we drive on, with forested hills rising up on either side of the road. Within fifty km, however, the green trees have been replaced by bare, dry-looking fields. We now notice a new road sign, a large black circle painted on a yellow background, with the words *Fatigue Black Spot Ahead*. We've seen similar signs throughout the country, encouraging drivers to stop and take a break.

Tamworth (pop. 35,000) lies in the heart of NSW's agriculture plains, and its population reportedly doubles during the ten-day country music festival. A green strip alongside the Peel River is filled with tents when we arrive, and pedestrian and vehicle traffic are heavy near the town center. Several streets are closed off, providing space for kiosks and entertainers, and it takes a while to find a parking spot.

When we walk through, performers are stationed close together, their heavy-duty sound systems doing battle with each other. I then hear someone playing a polka on an accordion and am instantly transported forty years into the past. When I was thirteen, my folks started taking me to the monthly winter dances at the hall in Hixon. The whole community had turned out, and dancers had laughed and twirled in front of three local men, who'd spent hours playing polkas, waltzes, two-steps, and even the Mexican Hat Dance. A good family friend, Frank McKelvie, had played the accordion.

Coming to an outdoor stage, we find a spot to stand under a big, shady tree, then listen to performances that vary from polished professionals to green beginners. The music is mostly 60s to 70s country, with a few Aussie tunes thrown in. On our way back to the car two hours later, we stop and watch the line dancers, then see a large woman in western garb cracking a bullwhip, and a young girl with a huge voice belting out songs. She's maybe eleven or twelve and rakes in the money.

Amongst all the visitors, we see only three police officers, and I subconsciously contrast that to Noumea in New Caledonia, where a police presence had been noticeable. But it's a different story on the highway north, where we see more police vehicles than we've seen in total over the past ten weeks. After driving 100 km, we stop at a 'van park in Armidale (pop. 22,000), the home of the University of New England.

Next day, we drive 300 km through the Great Dividing Range, passing through hilly, timbered country where the road climbs above 4,000 feet in elevation. The area is extremely fertile, producing peas, potatoes, and wool at higher elevations, apples, pears, and apricots at mid-level, and maize, tobacco, dairy, and timber at lower levels. After crossing the border into Queensland, we arrive at Warwick on the Darling Downs, an area famous for its cattle and horse studs.

Not yet ready to return to Brisbane, we take a side trip to Queen Mary Falls on the western slope of the Great Dividing Range. On the way, we pass a field of bearded grain that looks ready to harvest (sorghum), then cross a steep-walled ravine and climb a ridge into a eucalyptus forest. After setting up the tent on a grassy slope in the 'van park, we give in to temptation and order Devonshire teas at a small café near the office; the scones, with cream and jam, are sinfully rich and delicious.

At 1600, everyone is off to watch the feeding of the King Parrots, brightly plumaged birds a bit smaller than a robin. Some of the birds have red heads and chests, with either blue or green tail feathers, while others are entirely green. The birds fly in amongst the visitors, brushing against heads and shoulders, so it's quite entertaining.

One little boy (about age eight) has a handful of feed, but the birds make him nervous. His mother tells him to stand still, then jumps a foot when a parrot flies by her head, which amuses everyone. But eventually, the boy is beaming, with one bird standing on his hand and another on the back of his shoulder.

We then walk down a well-groomed trail that takes us into the forest and down into a 130-foot-deep gorge, where we admire the view of Queen Mary Falls. After crossing the creek, we climb up a sloping path on the other side. It's an enjoyable hike, well worth the effort, and on the way back, we spot a wallaby.

The tenting area fills up while we're away, and at least three other campers now overhear every conversation. One couple, John and Debbie, have two young children and tell us they dream of one day going offshore, so we have lots to talk about. She also comments, "I can't believe how quickly you set up your camp! I saw you arrive, and when I looked again, you were sitting in your chairs, sipping wine, and waving flyswatters!"

Laughing, I confess, "That's because we've done it 43 times in the last 70 days."

The sky is clear that night, the moon in its last quarter, and the stars are brilliant. The temperature drops, bringing a heavy dew, and by 0600, birds are calling and kids are moving around. We warm up by hiking the trail, then have breakfast and pack up the car for the last time. Soon, we're back on the highway and approaching Cunningham's Gap, the deep saddle that leads through the Great Dividing Range to Brisbane.

As we descend on the eastern side, the coastal plains are hidden by rolling masses of dark, moist cloud, and the day quickly grows hotter and more humid. Traffic is light in the city and we're soon approaching Scarborough. In the marina parking lot, we run into Jeanie off the cruising boat *Max*, and when she asks about our trip, we respond in unison, "It was absolutely incredible!"

CHAPTER 15
A Different Side of Australia

With *Windy Lady* waiting down on the dock, we feel like we've come home. We quickly settle into marina life, walking along the beautiful beaches of Moreton Bay in the early morning, working out at a gym three times a week, and freezing in the air-conditioned iciness of the malls. Within days, however, we're listening in horror to reports that two American scuba divers were left at a dive site on the Great Barrier Reef. The charter boat doesn't report them missing for a day and a half, and the site is 40 km from shore. They are never found.

The hot, humid air mass sitting over Brisbane remains for most of February, and frequent, fast-moving thunderstorms bring intense thunder, lightning, and heavy rain. The rain leaves black streaks down *Windy Lady's* sides that I try to scrub off, but they never actually disappear. Despite the heat, we work on the never-ending list of jobs on our *to-do list*. Dave also buys a 220-volt battery charger, so that he can charge the house bank without running the engine. Power failures then cause rotating blackouts across southeast Queensland near the end of February.

We hire a rigger to replace the furling gear on the headstay, and after looking over the boat, he warns, "Your standing rigging is too light; you really should have heavier cable. The spreader is unstable too and needs to be redesigned." Shaking his head, he adds, "I see this all the time on yachts from North America." Having seen how the boat twists and heaves in heavy seas, we take his advice.

During a fierce thunderstorm one afternoon, lightning strikes the tall mast of a boat at the end of the dock. We're sitting in the cockpit at the time, and Dave sees a cloud of smoke at the top of the mast, while I see sparks fly. The resulting magnetic field affects our electronic equipment, turning on depth and wind speed gauges in the cockpit, and knocking out the inverter and EMON (energy monitor) in the cabin. Alarms sound up and down the dock, as other boats experience similar problems.

Except for a VHF antenna lying on the dock, there is no sign of damage to the boat, but the owner's away and no one checks inside. Months later, a live-aboard notices that the boat is sitting low in the water. Efforts are made to contact the owner, but it's much too late as the boat contains three feet of water. The lightning strike fried all the wiring, causing the electric bilge pump to fail, and damage is extensive.

As the weeks roll by, we start planning for the upcoming cruising season, and I work on a budget. But when push comes to shove, we really want to make a winter camping trip outback. So, on a beautiful, spring-like day in mid-August, we pack our camping gear into the station wagon and head inland. In the next seven weeks, we will drive 9,000 km and see a completely different side of Australia.

Upon leaving the city, we drive through rolling, green countryside, where a fringe of trees grows along the verge of the road, and every pond and basin is filled with water. With clear skies, sunshine, and a temperature of 23 degrees C, the air has a freshness that causes Dave to roll up the car window. We then cross over the Blackbutt Range, named for a eucalyptus tree that looks like it's been through a bushfire, with black patches on the trunk and exceedingly rough bark. We next see tree-clad hills and a beautiful valley near the forestry towns of Blackbutt and Yarraman.

By noon, we're in Kingaroy, the self-proclaimed peanut capital of Australia. We now turn south and follow a narrow, paved road along the ridgelines to Bunya Mountains National Park. The road frequently deteriorates into a single lane, and at one point, a thick wall of bush closes in on both sides and meets overhead, making it cool and dark, like a tunnel.

We plan to camp in the park, but the air is surprisingly chilly and we stay only long enough to examine the Bunya trees. These remarkable-looking conifers have giant puffballs of needles growing at the very tip of branches that are otherwise mostly bare. The cones take eighteen months to develop and are the size of footballs; each contains about 120 almond-sized nuts.

When we drive on, a few wallabies graze near the road, and three ponies in a paddock are looking rather shaggy in winter coats. Views from a lookout at the top of the range (3,250 feet) are hazy, then the road abruptly drops 1,000 feet. Before we've reached the bottom, the acrid smell of hot brake pads seeps into the car.

Having driven 330 km, we spend the night in a 'van park in Dalby, a livestock and grain center in the eastern downs. We're swarmed by mosquitoes while setting up the tent, so flee to the camp kitchen and discover that it has a roof and potable water, but no walls. The mossies aren't a problem for long, as the sun goes down at 1700 and the temperature drops to 5 degrees C overnight. Come morning, the tent is covered with moisture, and we stay in our sleeping bags until the sun brightens the walls.

Next morning, we drive across tabletop-flat fields that we believe grow cotton, at least, we see a cotton mill at the edge of town, and bits of white fluff are caught in weeds in the ditches for miles. Cultivated fields then give way to bushland, and now the brilliant yellow blooms of wattle trees dot the roadside. Bottle trees also appear for the first time; they're a native deciduous species that store water in bulbous trunks and provide a bit of shade. Cattle purportedly will eat the leaves and soft interior of newly fallen trees during a drought. There are also many prickly pear cactus, a non-native species brought in by early colonists that spreads easily and is difficult to control.

By noon, we've driven 270 km and are in Roma (pop. 7,000), where we stop at the visitors' center. A 1920's-era drilling rig set up next door is a reminder that this area was the first in Australia to develop oil and gas fields. We eat lunch at a round cement table near a duck pond, where we enjoy the sunshine and watch the birds. I'm particularly taken by several Apostle birds, medium-sized grey birds that wander across the grass, heads bobbling as they search for seeds. They bring to mind the image of a little, old woman shaking her head and muttering to herself.

The many Bottle trees lining the streets create an image of a pretty, well-cared-for town, but that's only part of the story. The first tree was planted in 1918, in memory of a district man killed in WW I. Over ninety memorial trees have now been planted. Descendants of those fallen heroes gather every year on Anzac Day and place wreathes. If a relative isn't available, someone adopts the tree and does so.

That night, we share a picnic table at the 'van park with our neighbors, two teachers from Melbourne. Jim and Christine are about our age, and soon mention that they'd recently spent fifteen months teaching at an isolated aboriginal settlement in the outback. The two of them filled one position, and they taught basic English and math to thirty children. Interested, we ask a few questions, then sit back and listen quietly as they talk about events that they are obviously still trying to process.

Jim first tells us, "After signing on, we learned that the school had been closed for four and one-half months, as the previous teacher left without giving notice. We were then warned that if there was any sign of trouble, any problem at all, we must leave immediately." He emphasizes, "I was told not to pack anything; just get in the car, pick up Chris, and leave. The situation would be reviewed and the aborigine response ascertained from afar; if safe, we could return."

He then continues, "While we were there, we made it a rule to be home by 1700 every day, with our vehicle parked safely in a compound. There was only one incident that threatened to get out of hand, and it involved a kid with a rock."

The settlement had an aborigine population of 175, with a resident nurse, and a doctor who visited for half a day every three weeks. The buildings all had water and sewer, and the school was set up in two air-conditioned trailers. Only a few of the children spoke

English, and their own language was limited to a brief vocabulary, accompanied by lots of grunts and body movements.

According to Chris, the children attended class willingly, probably because it allowed them to escape the heat and the flies. The first ones straggled up the steps about 0700 and were immediately whisked into a shower for a scrub and shampoo. She quietly explains, "Because we had such close contact with the children, the showers were mandatory, especially on Mondays. They not only smelled bad, but had body lice, sores on arms and legs, and two candles below the nose."

Trying not to be judgmental, she goes on, "Children often came to school hungry, not having just missed breakfast, but maybe not having eaten in two or three days. Parents didn't raise their kids," she clarifies, "at best an auntie kept an eye on them."

With obvious frustration, she continues, "After the showers, towels had to be washed, then hung on a fence to dry. We showed two of the older girls how to peg the towels, and everything went well the first day. The next day, the girls stood back and threw the towels at the fence, turning it into a game. Some landed on the fence, but none were pegged, and the wind soon scattered them across the ground. We were never able to get the girls to do the task properly on a regular basis."

Jim now chimes in about the community's water supply, something he obviously found exasperating. "Everyone in the community learned to turn on a tap, but most didn't see the need to turn it off."

Fuming, he continues, "They'd just walk away and leave the water running!"

Funds came into the community through unemployment benefits and child welfare programs, and the local council administered a work-for-the-dole program. With money in their pockets, adults sat down and gambled until most of them were broke. The winners would go into Alice Springs to spend their stakes, leaving the losers to struggle through another week. Four families received about $4,000 annually in royalties, and the money was spent on cars that lasted anywhere from three days to six weeks. The community was supposed to be dry, but with a roadhouse seventeen km away, booze was brought in frequently.

It's my impression that teaching the kids wasn't very successful, although they lined up to play on the school's three computers. The two teachers were also very disappointed when a promising young student followed in the footsteps of the elders. Then there are stories about the Red Ochre Man, a local enforcer who acted on instructions from the elders, and about the rape of a twelve-month-old baby.

Jim now reveals, "We loved living there and were able to get by as long as we kept a sense of humor. But toward the end, every Sunday morning would see us decide to stay, and by 1000 on Monday, we knew we had to leave."

I believe the couple are sincere; they had hoped to make a difference in people's lives. Shocked by the hopelessness inherent in their story and needing reassurance, I ask, "How do these people move forward? What is the future for this community?" They both slowly shake their heads and remain silent.

Next day, I realize that the couple hadn't asked us a single question. I then recall that we'd had that same kind of tunnel vision after the difficult crossing from Hawaii to Palmyra. We'd spent hours talking to the folks on *Byjingo* about our doubts and frustrations, and just by listening, they'd helped us process that experience. My hope is that we may have done the same for Jim and Chris.

The temperature drops to 7 degrees before morning, and while we wait for the sun to brighten the tent wall, we hear the other couple pack up and leave. We're underway by 0900, driving north under a bright sunny sky, with herds of beef cattle grazing in rolling pastureland alongside the road. Scattered trees and open grassland soon replace the fields, and in the next hour, we see a wedgetail eagle, an emu, and eight brolgas.

After driving 400 km, we turn off the highway onto a dirt road that takes us 25 km into Carnarvon National Park. We cross several dry creek beds as we bump and squeak our way in, so assume that heavy rains would close the road. With towering sandstone cliffs, a permanent water supply, and remnants of rain forest, the park is a major tourist attraction and August a peak month for visitors.

Happily, we have no difficulty finding a vacant campsite, and while eating a late lunch, we watch grey kangaroos grazing on nearby patches of green grass, the females with little ones in their pouches. We then hike a 3.2-km trail through open forest up the side of the canyon. The last section is very steep, with many steps and ladders, and we meet a fellow coming down who tells us that he counted 700 steps. It's a tough climb for a couple of out-of-shape cruisers, but we manage to huff and puff our way to the top. The effort is well worth it, as the view across the mouth of the gorge is magnificent.

The temperature drops to 10 degrees overnight, and we are up in the chill of the morning, preparing for a 23-km hike. Wild grasses five feet high border the wide dirt path leading into the canyon, and soon we're walking through a forest of majestic grey gums, spotted gums, graceful cabbage tree palms, cycads, and grasstrees. White sandstone cliffs now rise up against a deep, blue sky, and as the rays of the sun penetrate deeper into the gorge, they chase away cool air lurking in dark shadows under the canyon walls. Within an hour, we've stuffed sweaters into backpacks.

We cross Carnarvon Creek on large, flat stones, the first of twenty such crossings, and halfway down the canyon stop at Cathedral Cave. A huge bulge of overhanging rock shelters aboriginal artwork on the lower part of the cliff wall, and a boardwalk protects the ground in front. Signs explain the images, which include stencil art, engravings, and freehand drawings. Many of the images are outlines of hands or boomerangs, created by spraying red ochre paint by mouth; the engravings are female vulvas and animal tracks.

At the end of the canyon, we bushwhack into a smaller gorge that looks like it could have been carved out by floodwaters. The floor is roughly thirty feet wide and walking is not easy, as loose rocks litter the bottom. The walls slope inward as they climb up sixty to a hundred feet, so they're not very far apart at the top. We turn back after half a kilometer, when the passage opens up and sunlight begins to filter down.

We follow several paths up the sides of the canyon on the return hike. The first leads to stairs that climb up and around an overhanging rock, then through a huge split rock to more aboriginal artwork. We eat lunch here under the watchful eye of a large, black raven perching on a nearby railing. The view is extraordinary, with lush, green vegetation and flowing water framed against a backdrop of high, white canyon walls draped in dark shadows.

The next trail takes us to *Ward's Canyon*, where we climb steep stairs beside a waterfall, then follow a narrow passageway into a small fenced area where giant King Ferns grow. The air feels cool and humid as we pause to read a sign asking the public to respect the site, as the Angiopteris fern is the largest in the world and dates back 300 million years. The trail ends at an inner cavern, where a low waterfall flows like a pipe into the far end of a pool that covers the entire floor.

Our last stop is the most impressive, as the *Amphitheatre* is magnificent. The narrow path up the side of the canyon ends at the base of a solid rock wall that soars upward some two hundred feet. A long climb up a ladder takes us to a narrow crack in the wall that's maybe ten feet wide at the base. From there, a 100-foot-long passageway leads back through the rock into the bottom of a deep pit.

I feel dwarfed as I look up at the soaring, vertical walls and wonder whether we might be standing at the bottom of another explosive pipe. The walls are so high that a small colony of ferns grows only in the very center of the pit. The air is actually cool, a fact I only appreciate when I feel a brisk, chilly wind following us back down the passageway.

We spend the next day in the lower part of the canyon, first climbing up to the Moss Garden, an idyllic spot that is shady, cool, and secluded. Water seeping from the bottom twenty feet of a sandstone cliff supports a mass of ferns and mosses growing on the rock, and a small stream tumbling across a large overhanging rock drops into an icy pool. Apparently, rain in the highlands soaks into the sandstone, seeps down through faults in the rocks, and permanently supplies these creeks and secret gardens.

We then bushwhack up Hellhole Gorge, climbing around large boulders and over rocky shelves as we follow a creek bed at the base of high sandstone cliffs. We come across several deep pools joined by a gurgling stream of clear, cold water, but the stream then dries up and we see no obvious sign of its source.

Upon returning to camp, I study the crow-sized, black and white currawongs that perch on cars and chairs. Watching with bright yellow eyes, they keep the grounds clean but are a bit of a nuisance. As dusk falls, a half dozen apostlebirds wander through, heads bobbing. Next morning we awake to a symphony of cheeps and chirps, and I hear the clear, bell-like peal of a currawong, then the sounds are drowned out by the raucous laughter of several kookaburras.

As we drive back to the highway that morning, I am content. I've found the Australia that I was looking for. The canyon was magnificent and park management deserved a lot of credit, preserving the unique features of the site while providing access to thousands of visitors.

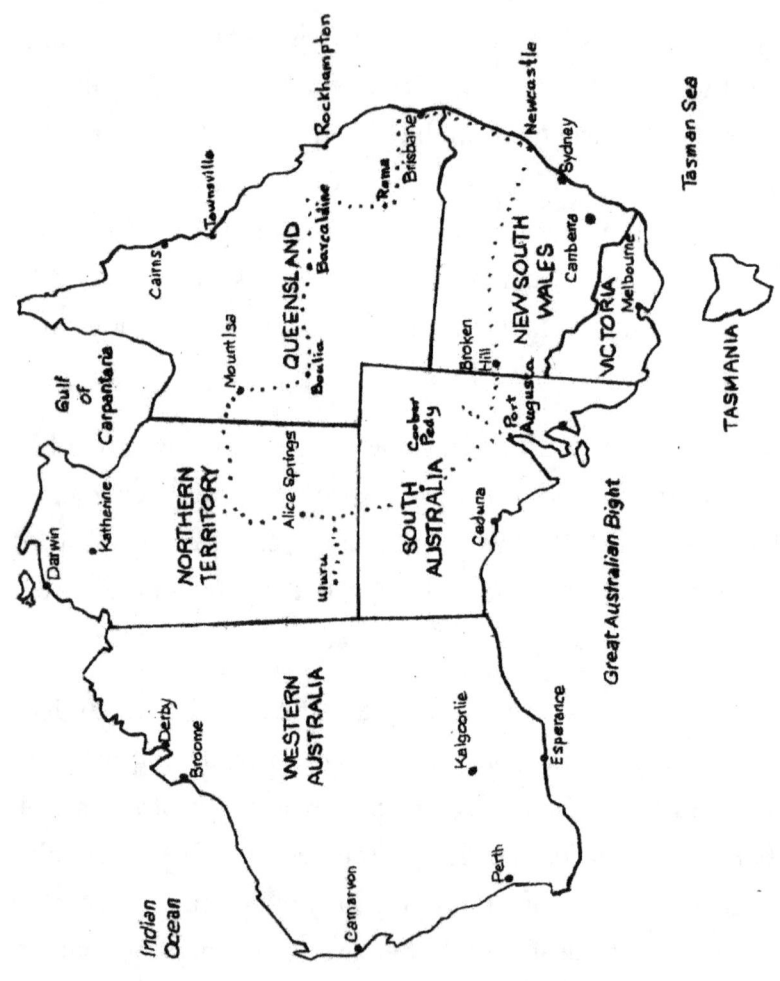

Camping Route 2

CHAPTER 16
Outback Queensland

We are now 600 km northwest of Brisbane as the crow flies and continue driving north and west for the next four days. The first day, we drive through grain fields and then a range of bluffs and buttes where the roadkill toll is high. Irrigation water turns the fields a deep green near the small community of Emerald, and orange trees loaded with fruit line the highway for the last twenty km.

We check into a 'van park on a ridge overlooking Lake Maraboon, then bake in the sun, with neither shade nor breeze. A bloke from a nearby cabin puts out bird feed and attracts six rainbow lorikeets, colorful birds with blue heads, green backs, and yellow and red chests. But he also brings in some forty noisy and aggressive gulls that hang around our camp long after the lorikeets disappear.

The sky is grey and overcast next morning, and as we leave town, we pass through acres and acres of sunflowers. A few hours later, we turn onto a road leading to the gem towns of Sapphire and Rubyvale. The area is popular with fossickers, who look for emeralds, sapphires, and rubies in abandoned mine workings. We toy with the idea of buying a fossicking license, but after seeing the junky shacks, flea markets, and facilities selling gems, or the promise of finding them in a $5 bucket of dirt, we don't even stop.

Dave spots three brolgas walking near a fence as we're driving back to the highway. He parks the car and we cautiously walk closer, then spend fifteen minutes studying the large birds. The cranes are about five feet tall and peck at the gravel, their bobbing red head patches emphasizing the movement of long legs.

As we continue westward, low, shrub-covered hills are replaced by stands of tough-looking, scrawny-stemmed small trees, then the terrain opens up and groves of large trees appear in open fields. Eighteen-inch-high termite mounds make an appearance near Jericho, where we're back at the edge of the desert.

Pools of water now lie in the ditches, sometimes half-hidden by fallen leaves or tall grasses, and the desert blooms. Bushes of all sizes are covered with small purple or white flowers, the wattle trees have their brilliant yellow blossoms, and the occasional tall, slender, cedar-looking tree has sausage-shaped orange blooms.

We camp that night in Barcaldine (pop. 2,000) and spend the next day at the Workers' Heritage Center, where we study a remarkable collection of photographs, videos, and artifacts. Sitting on burnished benches in a one-room schoolhouse, we study period maps and charts pinned to the walls. The building has a very high ceiling, and the walls have hinged panels about eight inches off the floor, allowing air to circulate when they're open.

We stand in front of a well-aged ticket counter from a railway station, then make our way through an adjacent passenger car. We view a holding cell in a tiny watch house and examine the leg irons bolted to a tree out front, which were used to secure a prisoner when no other means were available.

We learn that Queensland became an independent colony in 1859, and that a bitter strike occurred in 1891, when wool prices dropped and shearers refused to accept a pay cut. But of most interest are the artesian bore and billabong at the center of the complex, where we learn about the Great Artesian Basin that underlies one-fifth of the Australian land mass, including central and eastern portions of the outback.

Around 18,000 bores have been drilled, with the deepest going down 6,500 feet, and water temperature can be as high as 100 degrees Celsius. Some wells now have to be pumped, as more water is being taken from the system than is going in. One study estimates that 95% of the water accessed is wasted, and efforts are underway to find and shutdown abandoned wells. The local well, which was drilled down to 1,400 feet in the 1890s, was deepened to 2,760 feet in 1910 and water quality was then much poorer.

We end the day downtown, walking across the railroad tracks and inspecting a windmill slowly pumping water into a small tank. We continue on to an old ghost gum known as *the Tree of Knowledge*. Local lore has it that drovers and aborigines used to sit under this tree, waiting to unload their wagons, and that both shearers and the military met here during the strike.

That night, guests at the 'van park are invited to spend the evening around the campfire. Joining some fifty to sixty people, we sit at a long table, drinking tea made in a billycan and eating damper. The bread, made with baking powder, is cooked in camp ovens (big cast-iron pots), smeared with butter, and drips with cocky's joy (golden syrup).

As the night deepens, a local tour operator regales us with stories and poetry while promoting his business. He talks about an early stockman, and a cattle duffer (rustler), who was something of a local legend. He ends with a poem about a long-suffering pastoralist, who spends so much time getting the certificates required by bureaucrats that he no longer has time to run his station.

The following day, we drive 107 km across a tabletop-flat plain to Longreach (pop. 4,300) on the Thompson River. With the exception of one waterhole, the river is currently dry. A few sheep graze near the road, where new green growth pokes out from beneath the remains of last year's dried grasses. Farther out, I see a mob of twenty to thirty emus.

After settling into the local 'van park, we spend the afternoon at the Stockman's Hall of Fame, which chronicles the history of the land from the arrival of aborigines 40,000 years before to the development of present-day rural industries and their infrastructures.

The stories we heard the night before take on more meaning when we read that the stockman, Nat Buchanan, was one of two men to explore the country along the Thompson River in 1860. He and his partners settled in an area known as Bowen Downs, and it was from there that Harry Readford, the cattle duffer, set out ten years later with 1,000 head of stolen cattle. The herd was pushed overland to South Australia, and along the way, Harry sold a white bull. This event led to his arrest and a trial, but the jury found him not guilty.

Droughts were a frequent reality, and at the end of the 19th Century, half the sheep and cattle in Australia died in a drought lasting eight years; another drought occurred in the 1930's. We watch a video of the *talking drover*, which I find exceptionally moving. The drover sits on a log by a campfire and firelight flickers over his face as he reminisces. He speaks of long, hot, dusty days spent on the downs, of lonely evenings, and of the hopelessness he'd felt when moving cattle from one dry waterhole to another.

We stay over another day and spend the morning at the cattle stockyards on the edge of town, watching as the auctioneer walks swiftly from pen to pen, selling lots of up to ten animals. After each sale, an assistant marks the animals with blue paint, and we assume that each buyer has his own mark. We then visit a small opal shop downtown, where a young woman cleans and polishes a small rock opal that comes from the family mine to the southwest (or so we're told). When she finishes, the gem flashes deep red and green fire that's stunning. Amongst the jewelry and gems set out for sale, however, we find nothing comparable.

A cold wind blows through the campground that evening, the temperature drops to 6 degrees overnight, and we linger in our sleeping bags come morning. We then set off on a two-hour drive to Winton (pop. 1,750), a small settlement on the edge of the desert.

As we cross the flat landscape, I notice a low line of hills rising on the horizon to the south. According to my travel guide, the hills are 100 feet high and a cap of ancient rock has protected them from the forces that have eroded the surrounding plain. Studying the empty space around these hills brings my fascination with this ancient landscape into focus. I finally glimpse what a million years actually means, as I figure it must have taken at least that long for wind and water to have wrought such change.

The current drought has cost this area a million sheep and a hundred thousand cattle. Ten shearing crews were once based in Winton, but crews now come in to shear the sheep that remain. As jobs disappeared and families moved, the town struggled to survive. But the area was rich in folklore, in bush poetry and storytelling, and the locals built on that and created the newly opened *Matilda Center*.

After checking into a 'van park and setting up camp, we visit this facility, which is dedicated to a song written by the poet Banjo Paterson at a nearby station in the 1890s. *Matilda* was another word for swag or bedroll, and *Waltzing Matilda* meant carrying a swag. Video clips show the attachment of Australians to the song over the years, calling it the workingman's national anthem.

The center combines storytelling and visual aids in a way that captures my imagination. Storyboards describe the lives of swagmen and tales about the outback can be heard by lifting the lid off any one of ten billycans. Longer stories can be heard by pulling up on one of five taps.

In a small room near the exit, two dozen framed photographs by local artists are on display. Two of them, by the same person, are remarkable black and white photos. The first shows a man's hand; covered with thick calluses, with cracks etched deep into the palm, it looks more like a horn or hoof. Only the fingernails, broken and black with dirt, give it a human quality. The second features a horse and rider, with the animal spinning around in the dust. Individual hairs on the tail float out behind, and ghostlike, in the murky shadows, cattle attempt to move away.

As we leave, a small quilt displayed in a place of honor by the door catches my eye. It identifies Redcliffe, where we left *Windy Lady,* as a sister city. People there had raised money for drought relief for people here. This act of caring and sharing strikes a chord. I know my parents came from that same tradition, neighbors and families helping each other in times of need. More recent generations have passed that responsibility on to an impersonal government, and I wonder whether, as a people, we risk losing part of our souls by doing so.

The sun is close to the horizon when we return to the 'van park, and we make our way to a campfire burning at the back of the property. We've signed up for dinner and see that four large camp ovens sit on the coals. "You'll be eating mutton, not lamb," the cook tells us, "Because all the sheep around here are raised for their wool."

Some thirty people, bringing their own chairs and utensils, are soon sitting around the fire. We line up to have our plates filled with mutton stew, curried mutton, chops, and meatballs. The food is excellent, and we finish off with two big billycans of tea and plenty of homemade damper. With aromatic wood smoke lingering in the air and stars growing brighter, we are now entertained with stories and poetry.

Tonight's weaver of words is the cook. Gloria Hitson is an ordinary-looking woman of fifty-five and wears a broad-brimmed hat covered with emblems and pins. In the glow of the campfire, she is a storyteller extraordinaire.

Telling us that she's a buyer of 'roo skins, Glory points to several hanging off the side of her van and explains, "Thirty-four years ago, my husband and I were on our way to *the Territory*, when bad weather forced us to stop in Mount Isa. We ended up staying there and opened a pet food store, which we supplied with 'roo meat that we shot ourselves. We then ran two 'van parks before buying the Hamilton Hotel, which lies 280 km west of Winton on the road to Boulia." This lonely, seldom-traveled track brought few customers but provides the basis for many of her stories. She ends by explaining that she's now a widow and lives alone on the outskirts of town.

A cold wind blows around the fire while she speaks, chilling me to the bone, but I'm too fascinated to leave. When we do return to the tent, I lie sleepless for a long time trying to warm up. Reliving the evening, I marvel at her talent, of how she could set a stage and fill in the details with witty, colorful descriptions. Thinking about our own adventures, I wonder for the first time whether I could tell such stories.

After another 7-degree night, we have the car packed by 0800 next day. We don't rush off, however, but join other guests and listen to a lecture by Jeannette Elliot, one of the owners of the campground. Jeannette is remarkably informed about the area and happy to share her knowledge.

Pointing to the large acacia tree under which we've gathered, she starts by announcing, "This tree has been declared a noxious weed!"

She then explains, "The first such trees were brought from Africa in the 1920's and expected to provide shade and food. But in Africa, giraffes fed on the tops, forcing growth lower down, and elephants pushed them over in drought years. In Australia, the trees just grow tall, destroying the surrounding grass, and provide little shade or food. They've proven impossible to eradicate as seeds can lie dormant for ten years."

Pointing to the ground below, she then informs us, "Bedrock is three miles down and geologists have identified eight different layers in between. Four of the layers were once silt deposits on the bottom of an inland sea. The deepest dates back to a time when the sea had split the continent into four islands."

"Over eons, the silt deposits turned into three types of rock. A very fine mudstone formed in areas of little water movement, trapping all kinds of fossils. The swirls and curls of sandstone came from rough, turbulent water and contains no fossils. Ironstone formed in areas where the water deposited minute quantities of that mineral."

She now passes round several pieces of fossilized rock bearing the imprints of two very different leaves, one broad and one narrow, like a gum leaf. We also study a large piece of petrified wood that some fifty million years ago was a living tree.

Jeannette next reveals that trees can't survive in the harsh, hard ground of the grasslands. "The ground cover here is Mitchell grass," she explains, "it needs 50 mm (two inches) of rain to germinate, and that much again to grow any amount, due to the high evaporation rate. If left in the fields, the grass is a nutritious feed for up to two years, but it will rot in heavy winter rains and blow away."

On the other hand, "The Thompson River can be up to ten miles wide when in flood. With depths over three feet and strong currents, it's impossible for vehicles or horses to cross for weeks on end."

She then divulges, "The waters slowly percolating through the saucer-shaped routes of the Great Artesian Basin are replenished by rainfall in the highlands of New Guinea and on the eastern side of the Great Dividing Range in Australia. The water is estimated to take two million years to go from one end to the other."

"At Winton, the town bore is 4,000 feet deep, the water a million years old, and the temperature 82 degrees Celsius. In summer, you have to run a bath first thing in the morning to have it cool enough to climb into before going to bed at night! The town runs the water through a heat exchanger, which doesn't help much in summer, then sprays it on a pond to eliminate the smell of sulfur. Local residents pump water into high tanks beside their houses and let it cool for 24 hours; it then gravity feeds into their homes. While the water is good to drink, it's heavily mineralized and of no use for irrigation, as it turns the ground to concrete."

Jeanette answers so many of my unasked questions that I can't thank her enough. Our visit here is one of the highlights of our trip. Amazingly, we almost miss her, as the last dinner of the season is that night. She has asthma and will spend the summer elsewhere, leaving Glory to look after the 'van park.

CHAPTER 17
The Red Center

Alice Springs lies 1,000 km west of Winton, but we make a big loop to the north and drive 1,800 km to get there. We first head west on the lightly-traveled, one-lane paved road to Boulia, and I find myself gazing across the plains with new eyes, noting that few animals graze on the new green grasses.

As dark clouds build to the south, the temperature drops and I switch on the car's heater when my feet turn into blocks of ice. We then emerge from a low range of hills, with the vast spread of the plains before us. Low cloud and rain partially obscure the horizon, and soon a heavy downpour buffets the car, followed by occasional showers for half an hour.

The countryside gradually changes, with grassland giving way to scattered bush and open patches of gravelly soil, which in turn is replaced by low red-rock hills dotted with isolated buttes and mesas. Soon, we're crossing a 3.5 km-long earthen causeway over the narrow, shallow watercourses of the Hamilton Channels. The area gets little rain, but summer monsoons farther north send floodwaters rushing down several rivers toward the great depression that is Lake Eyre in South Australia. The water diverts into numerous channels, usually drying up in water holes and saltpans, but reached and filled the lake in 1970 and 1989. (I'm beginning to understand why early explorers were convinced of the existence of an inland sea.)

A lonely, stone fireplace standing near the edge of the road is all that remains of the Hamilton Hotel, and an hour later, the small settlement of Boulia (pop. 500) emerges from a bleak landscape. Surrounded by bush and dirt, with low clouds threatening rain, it's a pretty depressing sight. We stop to check out the campground, but the grounds are rough and hummocky, and a raw wind cuts me to the bone. A huge flock of white cockatoos perch precariously on the branches of trees alongside the dry riverbed, their weight causing the boughs to bend almost straight down.

We drive on to the roadhouse and order hamburgers, and while we wait, I scan the signs on the walls but see nothing promoting the rodeo scheduled for the weekend. As we eat, a few aborigines walk in and out, and the young waitress visits quietly with a friend but no one else speaks. When we're finished, we look at each other, shrug, and return to the car; it's 300 km to Mount Isa.

The barren landscape of Boulia is soon behind us, and now cattle and sheep graze in low hills, and wildflowers bloom near the road. But the sky remains overcast and road kill litters the ditches, including cows, kangaroos, a few sheep, and one emu. We meet a vehicle towing a horse trailer, then several more, all traveling fast, and presume that the cowboys are on their way to the rodeo.

As we approach Mt Isa, heavy, dark smoke billows up in the sky. Fanned by a strong easterly wind, the fire is in the spinifex and the smoke so black that tires might have been burning. We check into the same campsite as before, but instead of four or five tents, the small, grassy meadow now holds two tents and fourteen caravans.

We stay two days, and with clear skies overnight, the mornings bring a heavy dew and cool, comfortable temperatures. We buy a new battery and two new tires for the car, do chores, and discuss the road ahead. We intend to spend the next two weeks hiking in the Red Center, as the lower half of the Northern Territory is called.

As we drive west to the border, now going into Week 3, the highway is much busier than last December. At one point, I see sand dunes in the rolling grasslands ahead, but as we draw closer, they turn into waves of bleached white grass. When clumps of spinifex appear near the road, we stop for a closer look at this plant, which an early explorer described as "that abominable vegetable production".

The plant is also called porcupine grass and grows in arid regions across one quarter of the continent. Initially, the leaves grow quite normally, but in the first dry spell, they roll into hard cylinders with needle-like points that are miserable to walk through. Bending over a dome-shaped hummock, I cautiously reach down with my hand and end up with a painful stab in my finger, although I swear that I don't touch it.

Two hours later, red dust boils up behind the car when we turn onto a broad dirt road scraped into the desert floor. We then turn onto a rough track and bump and grind our way into the campground at Camooweal Caves NP. The site seems idyllic, with a few gum trees lining the edge of a billabong on the edge of a hot, dry plain. A vehicle with three young people is parked at one end, but they leave soon after we arrive, and we're alone with a few cockatoos and a million flies. As we set up the tent, the flies walk on our arms and faces, buzz in our ears, and dart at our eyes. Only now do I realize that I didn't pack fly swatters.

We then set off for the caves, walking back along the dusty track and following a path across a hot, dry field to an outcropping of limestone rock. I expect to see something similar to Cutta Cutta, but here the cavern roof has collapsed, leaving deep sinkholes. We poke about in the rocks for a while and scare up a two-foot-long goanna, but access underground seems precarious.

When returning across the field, I notice a number of trees that I'd ignored earlier, mostly because their narrow, lance-shaped leaves provide little shade. The rays of the late afternoon sun now bathe the slender, powdery-white trunks with an eerie glow that justifies the name, *ghost gums*.

A peaceful quiet settles over the billabong as the sun drops behind the trees, and the occasional puff of wind now keeps the flies away. When the breeze dies, Dave builds a small fire, and we sit and watch the sky fill with stars. Occasionally, he pokes at the fire, causing the flames to flare, and I contentedly track the Southern Cross across the sky. For me, the constellation has become a symbol of our new reality; the freedom we've found, the adventures we've had, the promise of more to come.

As we gaze into the embers, our conversation turns serious, and we speak of the small towns we've just visited and muse about their futures. It's apparent that change is coming, that rural residents are being marginalized by the growth of large urban centers; those populations are the ones now electing governments and forming policies. We wonder how it will end, as growing feelings of alienation cause rural folk here and at home to feel ever more isolated.

Next morning, I'm awake at 0600, and as it's still dark, I nestle back down, wanting more sleep. Then, out of the darkness, a mysterious warbler starts to sing, and I am enchanted. I listen to the glorious tones and range of its voice for fifteen minutes, then the sky begins to lighten and the bird falls silent. I now hear a variety of whistles, chirps, and cheeps, followed by the raucous chatter of cockatoos. (Research later reveals that I likely heard the "wonderful melodic song" of a Clamorous Reed Warbler.)

The temperature drops just before dawn, and I wait until the sun's rays strike the tent before quietly getting up. It's now 0700 and the air is cool as I cautiously investigate a ripple on the billabong's surface. Seconds later, a flock of nervous ducks flies up and lands in trees farther down. A few minutes later, the birds circle back over the pond before flying away.

As the sun climbs higher in a cloudless sky, a quietness settles over the campground, and even the flies leave us alone during breakfast. For our first outback camp, the site was perfect, and I say a little prayer of gratitude as we drive away.

We now cross into the Northern Territory and drive along the southern edge of the Barkly Tableland, a vast Mitchell-grass plain that supports a large beef cattle industry. Dozens of army trucks, loaded with gear, are also heading west. We see three kangaroos hopping away from the road, but the remains of many more lie in the ditches, where numerous hawks and wedgetail eagles forage.

By midday, the sun beats down mercilessly, and after driving 260 km, we stop at the Barkly Homestead Roadhouse. We check into the 'van park after finding a campsite with a spot of grass and a small, lone tree that gives a bit of shade. We then relax, reading and watching newcomers arrive, while swatting flies and moving our chairs to stay out of the sun.

Dave talks to a Canadian professor and his wife from Ottawa, who are camped across from us. They tell him they leased a car in Melbourne and are touring the country for ten weeks. We then watch their preparations for dinner curiously, as they bring out table, chairs, plates, cutlery, wine glasses, and a bottle of red wine. When the sound of cutlery clinking on plates disturbs the evening quiet, we look at each other, shaking our heads. Dave waves his hand toward them and quips, "Definitely not our type."

We sit in our lounge chairs, spooning food out of plastic dog bowls that are balanced on our knees. A four-liter box of Koolabah wine sits on the grass beside Dave's chair, from which we top-up our ice-filled twelve-ounce plastic wine glasses.

The temperature stays warm overnight, and next day we see more bush, spinifex, and anthills. Shortly after turning south on the Stuart highway at Three Ways, we stop at a restored telegraph station. The site includes several buildings that have two-foot-thick stone walls and green-painted metal roofs. The telegraph building and a house are joined by a flagstone patio. While admiring the stonework, we peer through windows at empty interiors, as the doors are locked.

The station is isolated and sits in a landscape that would have looked familiar to a swagman walking the line a hundred years earlier. Stopping to listen to the silence, I feel a warm, dry wind on my face and notice a ripple in the grass. I think of the days we spent backpacking in 35 degree C temperatures in the BC interior and know how welcome the sight of the station would have been after long, hot days on a dusty trail. Before leaving, we silently pay our respects to the occupants of two lonely graves that lie side by side and date back to 1910.

A short distance down the road, we stop in Tennant Creek and buy gas, groceries, and fly swatters. Dave also buys a liter of ice cream and then hunts for a cool spot to eat it. We end up parked in a narrow strip of shade in the lee of a semi.

The highway south now leads to a low range of hills, and a spectacular spot known as *the Devil's Marbles*. Huge granite boulders, some almost twenty feet high, are strewn about in a field, with some balanced precariously on top of one another. We spend an hour walking through the formations, and in the process, come across a semi-collapsed termite mound, with chambers and tunnels still intact in the honeycombed interior.

The marbles were formed in a process that extended over millions of years. Initially, an upheaval pushed a bulge of granite close to the earth's surface. Freed from previous downward pressure, the upper layer of rock slowly expanded and cracked, forming large square blocks in a small, shallow hill. As the surface cover eroded, rain seeped in through faults, causing more erosion, ultimately forming these huge, rounded boulders. Hot and cold temperatures created more cracks, sometimes splitting a boulder in half.

We camp here overnight, choosing a site on the eastern side of a huge rock pile where the shade comes early, as do the flies. Happily, our new fly swatters work amazingly well. We then watch, bemused, as vehicles pull in from the nearby highway and stop just long enough for the occupants to race up the rock pile and take a few pictures. Two blue-jeaned, tee-shirted men on motorcycles are the last to arrive, but at least they stay for half an hour. When the younger man steps off his machine, he stands gaping at the rocks as he removes his helmet, then turns to his friend and asks, "How did they get up there?"

As we're preparing supper, a small flock of zebra finches scurries past, pecking at the dirt. They're plump little birds, with red masks and white and gray stripes on heads and necks. When the wind dies at sunset, the air is so still and clear that I hear parts of three conversations, although no one camps nearby. As night creeps over the land, we search out familiar stars, and when a halfmoon climbs over the horizon, dimming the stars and casting shadows on the ground, we find our way to bed.

Stars are shining through the thin nylon roof of the tent when I wake at 0545, and suddenly I'm aware of humming in my ears. Listening to the silence, I hear the distant voice of a didgeridoo, *ah-hummmm; ah-hummmm*; a few minutes later, a dingo howls far away. An early-rising camper then starts moving around and the connection is broken. The didgeridoo is silenced, leaving me with a sense of loss.

We now set out for Alice Springs, 400 km to the south. The countryside grows more rugged as the day grows hotter, with low hills lining both sides of the highway. We visit the tiny Barrow Creek Hotel and take a lunch break at Ryan Wells, where the broken remains of an old windmill stand beside a large water tank. As we sit at a picnic table on the edge of the parking lot, I study the countryside and hear the sound of an approaching vehicle rising out of the south. Soon, a car towing a caravan comes into sight, turns off, and pulls in beside us.

An older, white-haired couple climb out and join us at the picnic table. We learn they've followed much the same route as we took in December, and the woman tells us, "It's been cold, and we only took off our tracksuits a week ago." Her husband then warns, "Alice Springs is very expensive and Ayres Rock even more so. A non-serviced campsite costs $22/night, and park permits are $15 apiece and good for five days."

CHAPTER 18

Alice Springs and MacDonnell Ranges

It's midday when we arrive in Alice Springs (pop. 22,000), and it's hot. We check into a 'van park with a five-star rating, but the campsites are small, crowded together, and have no shade. By the time we have the tent set up, the sweat is running off. We then tour the downtown and see block after block of tour offices, while shops in the Todd Street Mall mostly sell expensive souvenirs and aborigine artifacts.

On our return, a young man greets us as we climb from the car. He's tall and grubby looking, with hair tied up on the back of his head in thick, fuzzy dreadlocks. A small gold ring hangs from one eyebrow, and two swords are tattooed across his back. His companion then appears, looking more respectable; she's small and slim, with long, straight hair, and wears a long skirt.

They are camped next to us, and despite our first impressions, the four of us are soon animatedly discussing our respective adventures. The couple are in their early twenties, British, and traveling on one-year work permits. They'd spent time in Perth, Albany, and Melbourne, and now have only three months left. Before saying goodnight, we tell them what we can about points east.

I'm up early next morning, enjoying the cool freshness of the air as I do a few chores. Dave waits for the sun, then works to keep his chair in the shade. He's actually feeling last night's wine, and I have to shame him into taking me to the botanical gardens, where I poke about for an hour, while he sits on a shaded bench.

The Olive Pink Botanical Gardens feature native plants growing within 200 km of Alice Springs, and I'm delighted to recognize corkwood, ironwood, widgety bush, mulga and a few others. As well, there are flowering plants such as Sturt's Desert Rose, rosy dock, the yellow-flowered cassia bushes, and plants with white, yellow, violet, and red blooms. I also see one with a soft, grey flower tipped with purple.

Following a path up the side of a small hill, I come out at a viewpoint overlooking the town; the dry bed of the Todd River sits in the foreground, with the mountain range and Heavitree Gap behind. Clouds of dust roll along the horizon, chased by a strong wind, and next thing I know, I'm chasing my own shady straw hat across the rough terrain. Suddenly aware that Dave is waiting, I guiltily rush down the hill to the billabong, and back along the wattle path to the car.

By the time we return to the 'van park, the wind has developed a cold bite and the temperature is dropping. We take refuge in the tent after supper, and about 1930, a land cruiser pulls into the campsite below us. Setting a powerful light on top of their vehicle, the family of four spend the next two hours banging and clanging about. With the light shining directly into our tent, I'm reminded of why I don't like small campsites.

I'm up with the sun, and Dave again waits for the day to warm up before he emerges. I spend the time studying my guidebook, which describes the trails and campgrounds in the 650-km-long MacDonnell Ranges that lie to the east and west of Alice Springs. We then pack up and drive west for two hours. As the road winds and dips between two ranges of hills, the landscape is extraordinary, with burnt-red earth and rocks a startling contrast to scattered clumps of green bushes bearing small yellow, white, or purple blossoms.

At Ormiston Gorge, we have our pick of sites in the campground, then pull on our boots and start up the trail to Ormiston Pound (a word used by early settlers to describe a stock enclosure). As we steadily climb up the side of a ridge, broken chunks of red rock crunch beneath our feet, and the wind blows in long, cold gusts, keeping the temperature down. I find the harsh desert landscape enticing, with outcroppings of red rock, bright-yellow, buttercup-shaped flowers on cassia bushes, and the occasional ghost gum on a ridgeline.

After crossing through a saddle, we top a final ridge and the land falls away, providing a magnificent view of the basin, from the rim rock trimming the upper slopes, down through a dry riverbed to the narrow gorge entrance at the lower end. The trail now descends steeply, then meanders through grass and spinifex to a waterhole nestled beneath a large outcropping of rock in the riverbed.

The trail continues on down to the red and purple rocks of the gorge, where nearly vertical walls soar up 1,000 feet. The walls are maybe two hundred feet apart at the narrowest point, and large, loose rocks underfoot make walking difficult. Eventually, we arrive at another billabong at the base of the wall, and after skirting deep sand around its edge, we're only a short hike back to camp.

Darkness falls as we're eating supper, and the moon then rises over the canyon wall. It's almost full and pale light floods beneath the trees, transforming the site into a fairyland. But the temperature drops quickly, and we head for the tent as soon as our chores are done. Next morning, I'm awake early and quietly get up; the moon is just setting and stars are bright. By first light (0615), I've had a quick bite to eat and am ready to retrace yesterday's route.

Walking quickly, I reach the top of the ridge overlooking the pound just seconds before sunrise. The first rays, bursting over the rim rock, flood the ridge tops with warm color and chase gray shadows down into the basin. Moments later, light splashes across the basin and dark shadows retreat under the cliff walls. The day is magnificent, with a clear, blue sky and bright sunshine, and despite a strong, cold wind, I sit awhile, soaking up the view. I see neither man nor beast and only a few birds that morning, but can't recall another trail that provided so much satisfaction for so little effort.

After packing up the car, we return down the road a few miles to the ocher pits, which are located a short walk up a dry wash. This low wall of soft white clay contains varying amounts of iron oxide, giving it red and yellow tints, and in traditional aboriginal culture, the material was used as paint.

Originally, this deposit was sediment at the bottom of an inland sea, and eons under pressure turned it into siltstone. In the upheaval that created the MacDonnell Ranges, the rock was thrust upward in almost vertical seams and swirls from deep beneath the surface. In trying to conceptualize the powerful forces and millennia involved, I only become more aware of just how insignificant mankind has been in the long history of the earth.

By noon, we are at a large, permanent waterhole known as Ellery Creek Big Hole. It sits at the base of a high cliff in a gap carved through a range of hills by sand-laden floodwaters. After setting up the tent, we wander about and stop to watch two young men taking turns jumping off a Tarzan swing. Sunlight sparkles on the water's muddy surface as their heads emerge, and the way they gasp for breath reveals just how cold the water is.

As the campground has no picnic tables, Dave sets up the camp stove on the tailgate of the station wagon. When he then starts preparing rice and curried salmon for supper, he is instantly surrounded by a moving wall of buzzing flies. I frantically swing the fly swatter while he fills our bowls, but we end up with at least a dozen in each one. I carefully pick them out of mine, but he just stirs them in, muttering something about *more protein*. The real fight then begins because it's impossible to raise a spoon from bowl to mouth without ingesting more. Covering the bowls, we flee into the tent, where I pick off the flies that accompanied us.

The air cools quickly after sunset, then the wind picks up and the flies disappear. A big, full moon now rises through a gap in the hills, its bright light throwing shadows across the desert floor. Flames flicker at nearby campsites, and when I look closer, I see a dingo sneaking through the shadows at the edge of the road. Dave disappears into the tent about 1900, and I follow after finishing my chores.

The air is still chilly next morning when we pull low gaiters over the tops of our shoes and set off down the 8-km Dolomite trail. The trail gives access to rocks exposed by the up thrusting of the MacDonnell ranges, some of which date back 500 million years. We take a wrong fork at one point, and it peters out high on the side of a ravine. We then have to work out way down a steep slope to pick up the original trail. I slip and throw my arm back for balance—and encounter a clump of spinifex. I don't fall but a couple of painful pricks leave my hand stinging. A thorn then works through the side of my shoe, and as I stop to remove it, I realize that these ancient rocks are fast losing their appeal.

Returning to Alice Springs, we replenish our supplies, then drive to Trephina Gorge in the East MacDonnell ranges. As it's only an hour away, we stop and check out two other gaps, where dry riverbeds cut through the hills. We also drive into a dolomite outcropping known as Corroboree Rock, which is said to have come from a formation laid down in a salty lake 800 million years before. Dolomite is similar to limestone, and the ridge-shaped column is maybe a hundred feet high.

As we clamber over weathered rubble surrounding the base, Dave notices a hole in the middle of the formation through which he sees daylight. Scrambling up the backside of the column, we crawl through the opening onto a protected ledge, where the temperature drops ten degrees and the flies disappear. Sheltered by the smooth, cool walls and floor of that shady stage, we stand and look out over the timelessness of the desert landscape. Then, all too soon, we're moving on.

At Trephina Gorge, we find a secluded campsite up a shallow canyon, then spend an hour climbing the Panorama Trail. We stop frequently to enjoy the views, with towering quartzite ridges to the south, and large red river gums scattered along the edges of a dry riverbed to the north. Below us, in a corner of the gorge's sandy bottom, a waterhole lies at the base of a vertical wall.

We avoid the flies that night by not preparing our meal until after sunset. But the temperature then drops quickly, and Dave disappears into the tent as soon as we've eaten. After cleaning up by starlight, I sit for a while, enjoying the solitude. The night is beautiful, with the moon hiding behind the canyon wall and bright, sparkling stars.

Next morning, we're at the Ridge Top Walk trailhead at 0800. The air is chilly and the wind brisk as we start up a steep path that climbs over rock and through spinifex for forty minutes. The grade then eases, and an hour later, the trail abruptly ends at the edge of a bluff, where a shear wall drops down 1,000 feet to the desert floor. I've been admiring panoramic views as we walk, but the distant spaces now before us are mesmerizing and we sit for an hour. When the flies reappear, I pull the netting on my hat over my face and we start down the back trail, returning via the gorge and the sandy bottom of the riverbed. Unaccustomed to so much exercise, we collapse into chairs on our return.

By 1600, the flies are driving me batty, and I'm constantly swatting them away from my face, or brushing them off my arms and legs. When I put on my hat and pull down the netting, a few crawl through and walk on my face, while others buzz around and sit on my ears.

After a half hour, I grab my camera and walk to the Panorama Trail, leaving most of them behind.

After supper, we walk through the darkness to the park shelter, where Ranger Paul is to give a talk. He has a campfire burning when we arrive and makes billy tea for the six people who show up. Occasionally, he pokes at the fire with a stick and, in the flare of the flames, pours tea for those who want it. As he speaks, the moon rises over the horizon; it's now starting to wane, but is still bright enough to dim the stars.

Paul begins by explaining local weather patterns, including the recent winter rains. Waving his hand at our surroundings, he exclaims, "This is as green as the desert ever gets, and right now there are lots of insects and birdlife."

He then continues, "Australia has many introduced species that are crowding out native plants. Wild melon is a camel feed and thought to have arrived via the saddle padding of Afghan camel drivers. Rosy dock grows wherever the ground has been disturbed, and a new type of bunch grass provides a fire load in two years instead of the normal ten of native grasses."

He then passes around a thick piece of cork-tree bark, which does look like cork on the inside, and explains that the heavy insulation protects it from fire, as well as extremes in temperature. We also examine a *bush coconut*, so called because it has a white center when cut open. The apple-sized ball comes from the bloodwood tree, which secretes a substance around the larva of a grub that affixes itself to the branches. The larva lives inside the ball as it develops into a grub. Claiming that it is bush tucker, he warns, "The grub is the best part, but you don't want to eat it if it's dead."

When asked how the local aborigines survived, he explains, "The people traditionally lived on roots and grubs gathered by women, as the men's efforts to hunt emu and kangaroo weren't very successful. But the old ones were knowledgeable about fire, and used it to clear areas of travel, scare out game, and provide heat."

I now ask about spinifex, and he responds, "I don't know of any animal that grazes on it, but insects eat the seed grasses, while snakes and lizards find safe haven in the hummocks." Another camper asks about the calicivirus, and he explains, "It was used by the government in an attempt to control the rabbit population. They are another introduced species with no natural predators and have caused significant environmental damage. And yes, in arid conditions it did work."

The fire is now dying down, and Paul douses the flames while we straggle off to our beds. Next morning, the flies are up almost as early as we are, and I pull my head net over my face as soon as I've finished breakfast. Although we'd planned a relaxed morning, we pack up and drive into Alice Springs, where we replenish our supplies.

CHAPTER 19
Kings Canyon and Ayers Rock

From Alice Springs, we drive 200 km south to Erldunda and the turnoff to Ayers Rock. Scattered clumps of green bush are blooming across the desert floor, most have small yellow flowers, but a few clusters are decked out in white or pale mauve. Rosy dock grows in the ditches, as do plants with yellow, mauve, and deep violet blossoms. Just to remind us where we are, tumbleweeds occasionally blow across the highway, and dust devils whirl farther out on the plain.

The flies in the 'van park at Erldunda are worse than anything I could have imagined. They drive me crazy as we're setting up the tent and are unbearable when I hang up the wash. As soon as my hands are busy, they attack. I try to blink them away but one crawls down my nose and another buzzes in my ear. I try working with one hand and waving them away with the other, but end up squeezing my eyes shut. Before long, I want only to escape into the tent. I have to say my sympathies are now with the two young girls who wouldn't peg the towels, just threw them at the fence.

That night is the coldest of our trip, and I wake up about 0500 with ice cubes for feet. I spend the next two hours curled up in a tight little ball, then find the flies waiting when I step from the tent. We eat quickly, pack up, and after filling the gas tank, invest in new hats with finer mesh nets, hoping they will provide better protection.

The landscape is strikingly beautiful during the 275-km drive west to Kings Canyon. Scattered clumps of dark green bush with bright yellow flowers are framed by burnt-red earth and a deep, blue sky. Wedgetail eagles soar overhead and others sit on branches of roadside trees, looking like stuffed images of themselves. Trees are more numerous as we draw near our destination, where Desert Oak is the primary species. The large trees have broad, shady crowns and rugged trunks, while younger trees march across the desert behind one another, like a row of wooden soldiers, with branches held close, seemingly wrapped around themselves.

Kings Canyon is a major tourist attraction and is situated at the intersection of the Simpson Desert, the Great Western Desert, and the Central Ranges. We spend over two hours hiking the six-km trail, and for once I'm not disturbed by the busloads of visitors who share it.

We first climb a steep, 350-foot-high rock staircase up a ridge, then skirt the edge of a canyon, cross a gorge, and descend on the far side. It's a world of red rock and green bush, with shear canyon walls and beehive-shaped sandstone formations. We climb natural stairs up and around domed outcroppings, then descend through narrow, rocky ravines. At one point, the view of the Great Western Desert stretching away to the southwest is breathtaking.

We marvel at a tropical oasis hidden deep in the heart of the gorge, where ferns and cycads grow around a pool. I'm awed when I see ripple marks etched onto a stone ledge, created millennia before when it was a sandbar at the edge of the sea. As we walk, Dave spots the bobbing backside of a kangaroo, a Euro we think. We trace it to a cave, where it crouches for a while, then lies down and is barely visible.

While returning to the campsite at Kings Creek, we see camels grazing in a field of flowers and are able to walk closer and take pictures. A woman at the roadhouse nearby tells us that they used to offer camel rides, but these animals are feral. She adds, "They are one of the purist breeds in the world, and occasionally are rounded up with motor bikes and shipped to Saudi Arabia."

The campsite that night is a delight; *there are no flies*! I feel as if I've died and gone to heaven. We set the tent near a small Desert Oak, amidst thick bush covered in small, yellow flowers, and occasionally, a faint fragrance wafts by on a light puff of wind. Later, we track a caterpillar humping its way across the fine red soil on an open patch of ground, and with the sun low on the horizon, rocks on a nearby ridge glow a deep red.

It doesn't get nearly as cold that night, and next morning the flies are back. As it's impossible to sit and read, even wearing our new head nets, we pack up and retrace our route for 130 km, then turn west and drive 175 km to Yulara. The desert is again colorful, with red sand dunes, green bush, and a few violet and magenta blooms sprinkled in a carpet of yellow flowers. When we glimpse a large shadow on the horizon, I think it's *the Rock*, but as we draw closer, I can see that it has a skirt. It turns out to be Mt Conner, a flat-topped sandstone monolith (a single great rock); it rises 1,000 feet above the surrounding plain and the lower slopes have eroded.

Yulara is the access point to Australia's most famous landmark, Ayres Rock (Uluru), and with shady trees and green grass, the campground is a big improvement over Alice Springs. After organizing our gear, we buy national park passes and drive 18 km to Uluru. We don't stop though, but continue on for 50 km to where the many heads of The Olgas (Kata Tjuta) rise above the horizon. Thought to have once been a single dome, it now consists of 36 formations, the highest of which is 1,800 feet.

After pulling on our boots in the parking lot, we set off on the 8.4-km Valley of Winds trail. Busloads of tourists also climb this trail, and soon, we're pushing at the heels of a group of people climbing up a steep, narrow rocky ravine. They walk just fast enough to make it difficult to get by, and when we do, another group blocks the trail ahead. After 1.5 km, we reach a high point between the formations, where strong winds occasionally close the trail, but in the heat that afternoon, the gusty wind is simply refreshing. The bus tours turn back here, leaving us to enjoy the trail at our own pace, and it now descends steeply and winds back across the desert floor.

Near the end of the trail, a Japanese couple stop Dave, and the young man wants to take his picture. Gesturing for him to pull the bug net on his hat down, he shoves the camera within three feet of his face and quickly snaps several. A few minutes later, we're sitting in the car, with Dave still grinning as he thinks about the incident. I'm more aware of a weak feeling in my knees and know that we pushed the pace, having spent less than two hours on route.

Stopping at a viewpoint on the way back, we study the brooding mass of dull, reddish rock that is Uluru. Framed against a dark, overcast sky, the monolith is 1,142 feet high and bare of vegetation. As we watch, the late afternoon sun finds a window through the clouds, and the surface brightens to a warm, reddish-gold, while shadows of clouds flit up and down its length. When the sunlight disappears and the color fades, I glimpse a path worn into the steep shoulder and laugh in disbelief; a person would have to be crazy to want to climb that!

Next morning we're up at first light because Dave wants to climb Uluru. The temperature is pleasant, as it rained a bit overnight and the sky is still overcast. As we approach *the Rock*, I see a line of human bodies stretching up its steep side. I'm instantly reminded of pictures taken at Chilkoot Pass one hundred years earlier, showing a long, dark line of men, outlined against the snow, climbing the steep mountainside. Those men were driven by gold fever, but I suspect the current crop of climbers is driven by the marketing prowess of some Australian entrepreneur, who came up with a plan to convince tourists from around the world to travel thousands of kilometers into the desert to see a large, bare rock.

Incredulous, I watch the bodies toiling up the sixty-degree slope that is Chicken Hill. Arms straining to cling to a chain, bent almost double, the climbers haul themselves upward. I still can't believe that Dave wants to climb it, but soon we're standing in the parking lot, warming up our muscles. One bloke tells us that the resort can handle 5,000 visitors a day, and that up to 1,000 people a day make the climb. A park ranger then tells us, "You're lucky, normally there's a queue."

The rock is dry, the footing good, and we quickly climb up 100 feet to the point where the chain starts. Metal posts about thirty inches high and twelve feet apart have been driven into the rock, and the attached heavy chain hangs near the ground in between. I quickly determine that the chain is more for comfort than necessity but keep my hand on it, just in case my boots slip on the smooth surface.

As we climb the next 800 feet, we cautiously leave the chain four times, joining other climbers for a brief rest. I actually lean on the chain twice; first, on a 25-foot section that is almost vertical, and then a ten-foot section near the top. Here, I wait politely for my turn, as people are also coming down, but could have waited all day and end up having to push my way in.

We're now about halfway, and from here, the route to the summit is marked by painted, white footprints that lead along narrow ridge lines around deep holes in the bare, pockmarked rock. We then climb out of the lee of the western slope and are hit by a strong, cold southeasterly wind. Clothes flutter around arms and legs, and everyone grabs for their hats. I tie a neckerchief over mine, as my ears start to ache. The wind then funnels through a gap, becoming stronger, and I have trouble getting my breath. Concerned that I could lose my balance, I brace myself carefully with each step.

We reach the top in just under an hour, then walk around taking pictures. The Olga's lie to the west, the salt flat that is Lake Amadeus is barely visible to the north, and distant ranges blend into one another to the south. After a half hour, we start back down, and I'm thankful that the rock is dry because it's now easier to see how steep the ten-to-twelve-foot-high ridges really are. Stopping frequently, we take more pictures, but are soon back at the top of the chain. With my boots slipping on the steep sections, I now hang on, and we're down at the bottom in under forty minutes.

My legs, which felt pretty good after the climb up, are feeling the strain, so I suggest that we walk for a bit. We start down a wide, level track that runs around the base of Uluru and discuss the people we saw. The Japanese tourists in several bus tours all wore a single, white glove, and most slid down the steeper sections on their bums. Then there had been a dark-haired boy, maybe six-years old, who pointed up *the Rock*, urging his parents to go farther; he really wanted to go to the top, but they shook their heads and said no.

Once on top, some people chatted excitedly, others just sat and absorbed the view. We escaped the wind for a while by joining a family in the shelter of a large hole; the couple were from Sydney and made the climb with their two daughters, ages eight and ten.

A light breeze cools the air as we walk, and I now study the dull, red surface of Uluru. The top is smooth and rounded, with black lines marking the routes followed by rainwater; the upper walls have eroded in places, creating almost mystical designs. Occasionally, the sun breaks through the clouds, brightening the dark rock, which is then in sharp contrast with the dark green of the trees around the base. At ground level, the shear walls are broken by numerous large caverns, most of which are signed as *Aboriginal Sacred Sites*. These signs include warnings not to take pictures, threatening fines of up to $5,000.

The walk is truly delightful and yet we see hardly anyone. Flowers are in bloom across the desert floor, bird songs float from bushy ravines, and the delicate perfume of silver cassia lingers in quiet corners. After an hour and fifty minutes, we're back where we started, having completed the 9.4 km circuit around the base of Uluru.

At the Cultural Center, we watch a video clip about the local tribe's recent history. The arrival of white men disrupted their lives and people moved away, but eventually, a reserve was established that included Uluru. Now the tribe owns the park, controls its use, and shares in its management.

I'm up to watch the sunrise next morning, and then it's time to move on. We retrace our route to Erldunda, where we turn south on the Stuart highway. An hour later, we stop at Kulgera, a roadhouse about 20 km short of the border with South Australia. The 'van park here is pleasant, with a bit of grass and a few trees, but flies are a nuisance. Shortly after we arrive, the sun disappears into a cloudbank sitting high in the southern sky. The forecast is for rain, with high temperatures of only 15-16 degrees C.

A vehicle pulling a trailer with a tinny (rowboat) on top pulls in beside us. The occupants, a family with two small children, have just crossed the Simpson Desert in a Toyota land cruiser. They left from Birdsville, which is 335 km south of Boulia by air, and probably the most remote community in outback Australia. They then followed a rough track west for 700 km through even more isolated country. Vehicles traveling the route would be counted in units/season, not units/day.

The girls are maybe two and five, and the youngest, a little towhead, runs around on bare feet. I wince as she races down the gravel road but she flies over the sharp rocks, seeming not to notice. While the dad labors over their vehicle, I talk to the mom, who confides, "We could drive only 10 km/hour, as the rough track was really hard on the trailer, but even the truck couldn't take 20. At best, we traveled 80 km/day."

"Worse yet," she reveals, "the alternator packed it in and then we couldn't start the truck or charge the battery. That meant we had no refrigerator, so had no cold water for the girls. Thankfully, another vehicle came along and the men got ours running again. We then pushed through and drove the last 250 km in two days."

She goes on to explain that they're from Sydney and quit their jobs in order to travel for twelve months; they expect to resettle on the north coast. But I'm in shock and barely listening. I've already learned that adults die from heat when vehicles break down in Australian deserts, and these girls would have been at far greater risk.

When I first saw families on cruising boats, I wondered how safe it was for the kids. But I knew that passages could be made safely and concluded that they were at no more risk than the adults. That wasn't the case here. The risk of dehydration was far greater for the girls due to their small bodies and lower reserves of water. I'm sure the parents did their best to mitigate the risks, but wonder whether they'd really understood the harsh nature of the land. Only chance saved them and that knowledge should have been terrifying.

CHAPTER 20
Opals, Rockets, and Wilpena Pound

The temperature drops overnight, and by morning, a cold wind is blowing from a dull, grey sky. Small puddles of water dot the edge of the road as we drive south, and two hours later, when we stop for gas in Marla, South Australia, bigger puddles spot the dirt parking lot. Red tire tracks lead in all directions, and the attendant tells us that it's drizzled for most of the last 24 hours.

As we drive the next 250 km, ground cover varies between grass, low bush, and small trees. The dark green clumps of bush are still blooming, and in addition to yellow blossoms, I see patches with pink, white, and occasionally magenta flowers. We stop when I spot the rich, deep-red petals and velvety black center of Sturt's desert pea growing on the verge of the road. The flower is remarkable and quite large compared to the small, dusty leaves.

The great salt basin that is Lake Eyre now lies 250 km to the east. It is 144 km long, 77 km wide, and drains one-sixth of the continent. The lowest elevation is nearly 50 feet below sea level, and the salt crust is reportedly 16 feet deep in places. Unknowingly, we've also crossed the 5,300-km-long dog fence, which protects the sheep flocks of southeast Australia from the dingo population. When it was built in the 1880s, the fence was meant to stop the spread of rabbits but didn't work. It now occurs to me that *the Brisbane Line* was designed to protect much the same area, which I find interesting.

The land flattens out as we approach Coober Pedy (pop. 3,500), and I see what looks like sand dunes on the horizon. As we draw closer, they turn into mounds of white dirt that separate into thousands of cone-shaped piles. Signs posted along the highway warn of open shafts in the surrounding plain and caution against running or walking backwards.

The story of Coober Pedy began 150 million years earlier, when an inland sea covered much of central Australia. When the seawater receded, the water table dropped, and solutions of silica were deposited in underground faults and fractures. Over time, they hardened into opals. In 1915, a small group of men camped in the area, prospecting for gold. One of their members, a fourteen-year-old boy, found the first opal. Today, the town and two other sites in northern SA produce over 85% of the world's opals.

The country is extremely harsh and inhospitable, and early miners packed in water as well as provisions. Soldiers coming home from the trenches of WW I are credited with introducing dugout living, and about fifty percent of the population now live underground. Many of the early underground homes were worked out mines. The town's name comes from the aborigine words *kupa piti*, meaning *white man in a hole.*

Reportedly, only five percent of local miners earn enough to cover their expenses. Dave now tells me that he had a mate in Mount Isa, who tried mining for opals. According to him, "Pete set off for Coober Pedy with a pickaxe and a gallon of wine. I think he lasted about as long as the wine did!"

But the town has a dark side, and hundreds of thousands of dollars' worth of mining equipment had been blown up in the past ten years. As well, the courthouse and a restaurant were bombed, and the police station was bombed twice.

A chilly southwest breeze blows about our ears as we set up the tent on a patch of gravel at a 'van park on the edge of town. The blustery wind then whips up dust as we walk downtown. Taking refuge in an opal shop, we study the gems on display and learn that the value of an opal is determined by its color and clarity. The color is produced when light is split and reflected by silica molecules. (Turns out, we have expensive tastes.)

We continue on to the Desert Cave Hotel, where we enter the lobby and descend a wide staircase to a magnificent underground hallway. The swirling tool marks of a tunneling machine are etched on the red and pink sandstone walls, which have also been glazed. I stare in stunned surprise, as it's unexpectedly beautiful.

A small room off the hallway features a Telstra display that answers a question we had while crossing *the top*. Repeater towers, located 50 km apart and powered by solar panels, can extend telephone service up to 600 km from an exchange. We also view a short video about the paving of the Stuart Highway. In it, an old-timer talks about driving the road, "You couldn't see the potholes or ridges because of bull dust, and as the truck jolted down the road, thick clouds of dust rolled up behind. If it happened to rain, you could be bogged down for weeks."

The wind has a real bite by the time we walk back to the campground, and without any shelter, we're not looking forward to supper. When we see a pizza sign in the window of a small restaurant, we don't think twice. The food turns out to be barely edible, but at least we're out of the cold.

We're now spending nearly twelve hours a night in the tent and listen to the radio a lot, but reception has been poor for a couple of days. That night, Dave is able to tune in a local station and hears that police have charged a 36-year-old man with *driving a camel while drunk*. He wonders if there really is such a charge. Weeks later, we hear that the man appears before a magistrate and gets off. Apparently, he did jump onto a camel's back but had no means of controlling it.

Before leaving next day, we tour through the town. From a store parking lot, we look down on a barren landscape of mounds and gullies. The few patches of green bush look unnatural, as do the entrances to underground businesses and residences that line the sides of ravines.

One of the entrances leads into the Old Timers Mine, which was hand dug about 1916. The mine was rediscovered in 1968, when a family living in a dugout were digging out a room for a new baby. They broke into an old shaft that was filled with mullock, waste material previously excavated from the mine. A miner commonly did this before going south for a break, as he'd immediately see whether anyone had been messing with his claim when he returned. This miner never came back. It was completely dug out in 1987 and provides a fascinating window into the past.

We enter the mine at a large *ballroom* at the base of the shaft, then walk over and peer up toward the surface. The shaft was custom-built to the size of the man doing the digging, with hand and foot holds dug into the walls so he could climb up and down. Upon reaching opal-bearing rock, the miner dug horizontal tunnels using pickaxe and shovel. In really hard rock, he'd sometimes use homemade explosives.

Tunnels lead off in several directions, some breaking through into those of other mines, and as we walk across the rocky, uneven floor, I'm glad to be wearing a hardhat, as the ceiling is low and jagged. Small holes and caverns pit the walls where the miner followed a seam, sometimes crawling on his belly, and three seams of opal have been uncovered and left in place, as have some opalized seashells.

Above the old mine, display rooms provide a window into underground living. One room was hand dug and furnished circa 1918; it's rough and dark and very much a cave. The other three rooms were dug with a tunneling machine, and I can almost imagine living there. With square corners and rock shelves, they're furnished with modern appliances, rugs, and pictures. The sandstone walls are a light pink, streaked with red, and not glazed. That's only necessary if the surface of the rock can dry out.

In an adjacent room, we learn about present-day mining practices. After digging down through 100 feet of overburden, miners use small tunneling machines to dig through the opal-bearing rock, but still use pick or knife in a good spot. Drilling rigs currently work at some sites and blowers at others. Blowers are trucks that vacuum mullock up out of a shaft and into a hopper, which drops it into a cone-shaped pile (mullock heap).

Curious about the mullock heaps we saw on the way into town, Dave asks the young attendant at the front desk, "Why don't the miners fill in the shafts when they finish at a site?"

The young woman happily explains, "If a tunneling machine digs into a backfilled shaft, the resulting fall of dirt and dust can kill the driver. As the whole field is still active, with more than 250,000 shafts, the decision was made to leave the mullock heaps on the surface. But the old mines still present a hazard because waste dirt was also stored in other drives. Only dirt that couldn't be stored elsewhere was hauled to the surface."

I now ask her if she lives underground, and nodding her head, she responds, "I share an underground flat with a mate." Seeing my curiosity, she goes on, "It's really very comfortable, as the inside temperature varies only five degrees throughout the year. We have a thirty-foot porch out front, and in summer the thermometer has read 52 degrees C (126 F) in the shade. In winter, it occasionally drops below freezing."

We learn that their water comes from a 200-foot bore and runs through a reverse osmosis desalination plant; their power comes from a diesel generator. "It's very expensive," she complains, "costs us $400 every two months, and we can't have a garden and can wash the car only once in that time." "But," she ends, "living here really isn't that bad, as long as you get out occasionally!"

Noticing pictures on the wall showing a flood in Coober Pedy in 1987, Dave now asks, "Did the town really flood?" Again smiling, she responds, "Oh yes. Shafts filled up with water, knocking equipment over, so it really was a mess!"

As other visitors enter the lobby, we say our goodbyes, return to the car, and start the drive south. A few miles from town, a young kangaroo hops out onto the road, then stops and stares at us. Dave slows the car to a crawl, and when it finally decides to move, the animal's feet slip and it falls forward onto its chin. As we laugh in disbelief, it scrambles up and hops away.

The 400-km drive that afternoon is monotonous, with long stretches of flat, treeless plain covered by low bush and patches of red gravel. When we meet a road train, we see the top half of the tractor and trailers for miles. Woomera (pop. 1,000) is a veritable oasis when it comes into view, with trees, green grass, and a large, grassy playing field, the likes of which we haven't seen in weeks. The 'van park is pleasant, the bugs not too bad, and the temperature comfortable until sundown. We're then in our sleeping bags at 1930 and only crawl out when the sun warms up the tent twelve hours later.

We spend the morning at the local heritage center, where several British rockets and Aussie planes are displayed in the yard. We now learn that the town was established in 1947 to cater to people developing and testing rockets. The British conducted missile and atomic tests in the area during the 1950s and 60s, and the town was closed to visitors until they left in 1982. The site is said to be perfect for launching polar orbits and watching deep space, so both NASA and the US Air Force have used the facilities. Plans for the future include launching commercial satellites.

The town's original water supply came from nearby salt lakes, but wasn't sufficient, so the Murray River pipeline was extended. The town now has an abundant supply of good water. A huge uranium, gold, silver, and copper mine called Olympic Dam is located 100 km to the north.

We now drive 200 km south to Port Augusta, following a tongue of flat, treeless desert down the west side of the Flinders Ranges. Scattered clumps of low, blue-green bush stretch to the horizon, and I'm mystified by how evenly spaced they are. After checking into a 'van park, we visit the Arid Lands Botanical Garden, where I satisfy my curiosity.

The plants are chenopods, which grow in arid, saline soils, and include saltbush, bluebush, and samphire. Because of the spread of their root systems, they are evenly spaced across the desert floor and are the ones I've seen for the past few days. The only trees that grow in this type of soil are Western Myall, and it's an acacia with long, needle-like leaves that show a lighter side when the wind blows. These small, slender, twisted plants can live up to 600 years.

As I leave the visitors' center, I'm fascinated to see a piece of brown coal, maybe six inches in length, with an exquisitely detailed fern fossilized on the surface. I then wander through rows of shrubs, including ruby saltbush, bluebush, and spotted emubush. (In the wind, its long leaves do look like ruffled feathers.) The blooms on

Sturt's desert peas are in their last days, their magnificent blood-red color fading, as are those of native fuchsias and hibiscus.

That night, while enjoying a warm, pleasant evening in the 'van park, we make plans to visit Wilpena Pound in Flinders Range National Park, a two-hour drive to the northeast. According to my guidebook, the geological history of the area dates back 700 million years, and a photograph shows Wilpena Wall soaring upwards almost vertically for 1,600 feet above the surrounding plain, with bush-filled gullies carved into the lower slopes. The land inside the pound slopes relatively gently away from the peaks, forming a large, natural basin containing about 80 sq km.

The temperature drops overnight, the tent is soaked by a heavy dew, and we get up to a clear, bright sky next morning. After breaking camp, we follow a winding road through the hills, where a very long snake slithers across the highway in front of us. I doubt that the vehicle in the adjacent lane was able to avoid it. By midday, we're driving through a flat, green valley, where a few sheep graze beside the crumbling remains of old stone buildings. Strong winds then buffet the car, bringing clouds and whipping up the dust. Not long after that, we're registering at the park entrance.

We now follow a narrow track beneath tall pine trees to a campground, where only a few sites are occupied. After quickly organizing our gear, we set off walking and quietly study the kangaroos grazing beneath scattered trees near the trail. After crossing a dry creek bed, we come to a second trail that leads to St Mary's Peak. According to a sign, the route is over 5 km long and rated as *difficult*.

We start up the wide, well-maintained path, which climbs steeply through the pine trees for 45 minutes, then ends at the base of a rock fall on the northeast face of the pound. We now follow trail markers as we clamber over the rocks, and I'm soon using both hands and feet. Dave quickly draws ahead, and I catch up with him 45 minutes later, when he waits for me at a fork in the trail high on the ridge. One path now descends into the pound, while the other continues over jagged rocks to the peak.

The light is fading quickly as we look out from our vantage point. Dark clouds hang over gloomy-looking ridges to the east and the wind is strong. The next kilometer is described as *a real scramble,* and rain could make the rocks treacherous, so we decide to turn back. The first shower hits us near the base of the rock fall, and rain then follows us down the back trail.

Showers persist through the evening, and by first light, rain is drumming on the tent fly. But the sky has started to clear when we get up, and the rays of the sun soon chase away the cool shadows beneath the trees. The previous day's exertions left us with aching leg muscles and stiff knees, so we take our time over breakfast and plan an easy day of hiking inside the pound.

Following an old road in through a narrow gorge, we pass huge, old river red gum trees, grasstrees, and twelve-foot-high spear grass. Bright yellow blooms decorate the wattle trees, and I recognize the sweet scent of yellow cassia flowers. A small, delicate white flower now catches my eye. I think it's a type of grass, and when I lift up its face, six petals form a perfect star, each with a slender gold line running down the center.

We soon arrive at an old stone building and stop to read the storyboards. Although stock was able to escape from the pound in only two places, life had not been easy for these early settlers. In the 1850s, they ran too many animals and overgrazed the land. The feed then failed during a drought in the 1860s, and many farmers lost everything. Those who survived faced drought again at the end of the century.

We climb a ridge behind the homestead for a view of the pound, then wander over trails through patchy grassland for the next four hours. Although the day heats up, a freshness in the breeze keeps us comfortable. We study unfamiliar three-toed tracks around the mudpuddles left by the rain, then see two emus in an open patch of grassland. The big birds are wary and move off whenever we head in their direction. Dave also stumbles across some scattered, well-gnawed bones hidden in the grass and finds a paw with five toes; all that's left of a kangaroo.

That night, the cold of the ground radiates through our air mattresses, and mine develops a slow leak. The sun is shining brightly in a clear blue sky when we pack up next morning, and we stop at the Visitor's Center on the way out. We now learn that St Mary's Peak is the highest in the range, with an elevation of 3,830 feet. As the campground sits at 1,800 feet, we figure we climbed up 1,500 feet the first day.

CHAPTER 21

Desert Sculptures and Zoos

With the forecast calling for cold, wet weather on the south coast, we now decide not to go to Melbourne. Instead, we drive east for 400 km to Broken Hill in New South Wales. This route takes us through the railway town of Peterborough, where three different rail gauges once met, then out into the desert.

We're soon playing tag with a long freight train that winds back and forth across the flat desert floor, looking like a toy with its load of colorfully painted containers. Another freight train then passes, heading west, and we catch sight of a third train waiting in a siding for the track to clear. This turns out to be the *Indian Pacific,* a passenger train on route from Perth to Sydney. The train has two engines, 25 passenger cars, and a small flatcar carrying two vehicles. It takes sixty-five hours to complete the 4,100-km trip, and when up to speed, we clock it at 110 km/hour.

Broken Hill (pop. 25,000) has been described as *lying beyond the Darling River, on the edge of sundown,* poetic words that ignore the reality of its location and its history. Silver was discovered here in 1885 and conditions in the early mines resulted in hundreds of miners suffering and dying from lead poisoning and lung disease. Four major strikes marred its beginnings and the last one in 1919-20 lasted for eighteen months. The settlement brought a 35-hour workweek and an end to dry drilling, which was responsible for the dust that afflicted so many.

We set up the tent on a patch of fine red dirt in the 'van park, and I find myself hoping that it doesn't rain. As it happens, the evening is very pleasant, and we sit out after supper, enjoying the clear desert air as we watch the sunset.

The next day is warm and sunny, and we stay over in order to visit a tourist attraction called *the Living Desert*. With only one mine still operating in the area, the town has been trying to attract artists. They brought in twelve sculpturers from Russia, Mexico, Syria, and Australia, and they worked on their creations at a site a few miles outside of town.

Leaving the car in a parking area, we follow a track up a low knoll overlooking the desert. Rocks of unusual shapes jut out of the ground on either side and I find them interesting in their own right. Clumps of green bush growing amongst them have small red and green leaves that look like paper wings. The track then levels off, bringing us to the first of twelve sandstone sculptures. Each is unique, beautiful, and mystifying, but for me, they can't compete with the surrounding landscape. Finding a place to sit where I can look out across the desert, I listen to the silence, feel the light movement of air on my face, and seem to glimpse eternity.

Much to Dave's annoyance, I insist on returning late that afternoon, when the sun is low in the sky and warms the colors of the rocks. But the morning's tranquility is gone, broken by chattering tourists who've also come to see the colors. While I find the noise distracting, it doesn't bother a large Euro feeding quietly at the base of the slope.

Dave's ill temper simmers while he waits in the car, and he drives much too fast on the narrow, single-lane gravel road back to town. When I warn him that he's coming very close to small posts marking the ditch on my side, he takes a devilish delight in coming even closer. He then hits one, breaking the side mirror off a few inches from my arm, and I damn near shit myself.

Clouds move in overnight, and we hurriedly break camp in light rain next morning. A steady drizzle sets in while we're downtown buying a new air mattress, and low cloud obscures the ridgelines as we follow the winding highway east through low hills. The rain eases when we start across a flat, saltbush plain, but the windshield wipers can't keep up as we near the next range of hills. When we stop for gas, the young attendant tells us that the Darling River peaked the day before and probably will peak again, then exclaims, "Normally, this country is just red dirt and saltbush! I was born here and I've never seen it this green."

A picture on a sign near the crossing of the Darling River shows steep banks beneath the bridge, but now there are no banks, just a lake. The river, peaking at thirty-five feet, has breached both banks and flooded back into the bush and into a 'van park. Water has also accumulated in numerous ponds and small lakes as we cross the eleven-km-wide flood plain.

The sky begins to brighten near Cobar, and the countryside becomes greener, almost lush, with flowers lining the roadway. We stop here for the night, having traveled 460 km. I counted 47 emus on the way, the largest group having 16 birds.

It rains heavily overnight, and we wait for a lull in the storm before making breakfast, then eat in the car. We break camp during the next lull. Sheets of driving rain then follow us across the plains. The Bogan River is in flood, with water pouring over the riverbank, through the trees, and under a railroad bridge.

At a nearby roadhouse, we learn that the area has had two months of rain and more is in the forecast. Farmers worry that wheat will rot in the fields and the cotton crop may go unplanted. When we drive on, pools of water fill the ditches alongside the road, overflowing into the surrounding countryside, and we see with our own eyes the waterlogged wheat fields.

When the sky beings to lighten, the views change. Flowers with purple and yellow blossoms grow taller on the roadside, and the orange-red mud of rutted sideroads glows vibrantly against the emerald green fields of grass and lush fields of wheat. By the time we've driven 300 km to Dubbo, the afternoon has turned quite pleasant. But as we check into a 'van park, we're told that two inches of rain is expected overnight.

The rain is over when we get up next morning, and while we were dry inside the tent, the grass is sopping. My shoes are quickly soaked through, and I pull on dry socks and boots. As the day is expected to be cool and overcast, with no rain, we set off for the Western Plains Zoo. Neither of us are zoo fans, not caring to see animals in cages, but this facility is renowned for housing animals in large open exhibits, simulating their natural habitat. It also maintains breeding programs for endangered species, including cheetahs, Przewalski's horse, and black rhinoceros.

Soon after starting the 15-km trek through the grounds, I'm wishing I'd brought binoculars. Scimitar oryx and others like them crowd into shadows at the rear of their paddocks. I can make out the dark front quarters and necks and light-colored bodies, but see no sign of the horn that is said to be as long as the animal is tall. Cheetahs, tigers, and Cape hunting dogs also hide in the tall grass, so only the tops of their heads are visible.

The black rhinos stand at a manger eating, while other animals stand quietly, seemingly asleep. Only the lemurs move about normally; they're housed on small islands and climb on ropes extending out over the water. They seem oblivious to the onlookers, as is a coal black pai with a baby (native to Malaysia). Her overdeveloped arms remind me of an orangutan.

It is now that I understand what bothers me about zoos. When I was small, my mother had pointed out the car window and exclaimed, "Arlene, look! A deer!" I was often disappointed as the animal would disappear before I saw it, and she responded, "Well, they're wild, nobody controls them, so you have to be faster." That disappointment led me to feel elated, privileged even, when I did see one, and that had never changed.

That essence, that wildness, is destroyed in a zoo, where the animals are totally dependent on humans. Whatever the barrier around them, they are no longer free. I even question the value of breeding programs, gloomily thinking, *are these creatures destined to exist only in zoos?* Because I don't see how they will ever be returned to the wild, even in the unlikely circumstance that new habitat was found.

The following day, we drive 400 km to Newcastle on the east coast, passing through huge fields containing flocks of newly shorn sheep, and others that are crowded with yellow-headed plants that I think are mustard. After entering a range of hills, we pass several large coalmines and two power generation plants, one coal and one nuclear. Clouds now settle on the higher peaks and showers follow us through the Hunter Valley, renowned for its wineries, and out onto the coastal plain.

We check into a 'van park close to the narrow mouth of the Hunter River, which serves as the entrance to Newcastle harbor. The wind is strong and I have doubts that the tent will survive the night, but it eases before we go to bed. The booming of the surf then keeps me awake, and for the first time in weeks, the sun hits the tent at 0600 next morning.

We spend a few hours exploring the harbor, which sits in a small basin sheltered by low hills, with low-rise buildings lining the waterfront. We then return to the river mouth and walk out to the end of the north breakwater, where a low swell crashes against the rocks. A large sandbar north of the river mouth has taken many casualties over the years, and so much wreckage has been incorporated into the breakwater that it's called *Shipwreck Walk*. We now watch a pilot boat going out the river mouth to meet a freighter, while three large tugs take positions at the entrance until it's safely inside.

The clouds have grown heavy by the time we return to the car and start the 775-km drive up the coast to Brisbane. Traffic is a nightmare, as much of the highway is under construction, and we spend that night in Port Macquarie, where the campground is crowded with families on school break.

Picking up a local newspaper, Dave reads that tons of rain have fallen on the Great Dividing Range since mid-July. All west-flowing rivers have overflowed, some peaking five times. Helicopters are ferrying supplies into stations that have been cut off, and a few could be isolated for two or three months. As the land is flat, the water moves at only 2 km/hour, and the schedule for flooding downstream covers weeks.

Next day, we move on to Coffs Harbor, where we tuck into a very comfortable 'van park behind sand dunes at the ocean's edge. Although the surf booms through the grounds at times, it's much to our liking and we stay four nights. The days are sunny, with high temperatures of 27 C, and we spend hours on the beach, enjoying the cool afternoon breezes.

Two kookaburras distract us each morning, sitting on the same bare branch and laughing crazily. A large goanna with a two-foot-long tail rests beneath our car one afternoon, and a neighbor tells us that he saw a brown snake on one of the trails. Ten large yellow-tailed black cockatoos move into the banksia trees the last morning. Gripping a nut in one claw, the birds eagerly strip off seeds with their beaks and then move on.

We walk across a breakwater to Muttonbird Island one afternoon, then follow a path to the rocky seaward edge, where we stand and study the restless waters of the Tasman Sea. The island is a reserve, as it's a nesting ground for wedge-tailed shearwaters. The birds are currently pairing off and digging burrows, flinging fresh dirt over the low foliage. They will start laying eggs near the end of October.

After following the Clarence River through sugarcane fields to Ballina, we check into a 'van park at Lennox Head for two nights. The campground here overflows with graceful palms, rubber trees, and flowering bottlebrush. Dave seems to have an allergy to something, however, and sleeps all the time we're here. I climb the trail up to the head, then watch enviously as three hang gliders, soaring in the updrafts, are etched against a brilliant blue sky.

CHAPTER 22

Once More to Sea

We arrive back at the Moreton Bay Boat Club on October 3, having spent four of the last eleven months on the road. With the approach of summer, the weather turns hot, humid, and wet, and in early December, Dave tracks down and installs a transformer, which allows us to plug the boat into shore power. He then turns on the refrigeration unit for the first time since leaving Canada, giving us cold water, and we start using the big fans.

The marina proves to be a busy place that summer, with lots of comings and goings at the clubhouse, and loud music on the weekends. For me, the novelty of having a bar so close quickly wears off, but Dave enjoys visiting with the Peyton-Place-like cast of characters that frequent it.

I'm now printing maps off my weather fax and studying the low-pressure systems that regularly move from west to east across the southern half of the continent. Just before Christmas, I see the tight circle of a low appear off the southern coast and am happy that we're not at sea.

The Sidney-Hobart yacht race is scheduled to start on Boxing Day, however, and organizers don't cancel it. While I can't believe that any sane person would willingly leave harbor, only 50 out of 113 entries have the good sense to withdraw. Within 24 hours, the leaders are being pounded by large ocean swells that push up on a shelf off the NSW coast. It's a disaster and rescue helicopters are dispatched. At one point, twenty sailors are missing, and in the end, five boats are lost, along with six crewmembers.

As we start into the new year, monsoonal rains set in. By the end of the first week in January, floodwaters have cut off northern and western parts of Queensland. On February 9, the Brisbane area is hit with 150 road closures; two days later, a Category 3 cyclone develops near Cairns.

The humidity turns the dust on the inside of the hull into a web-like layer that I think is some kind of algae or mold, so I spend hours scrubbing out lockers. Cockroaches take over the cupboards, and I'm cleaning up droppings every day. The ripstop nylon in the galley wind scoop rots after four months use, and chafing spots appear in the sunbrella in both deck canopy and wind vane cover.

On February 23, Dave has the boat permit extended to the end of June. If we haven't left the country by then, he'll have to pay import duty on the boat, or at least put up a bond. He's not about to do that and vows, "I've paid all the taxes that I'm going to pay on this boat. I'm not going to cough up another $7,500!"

Digging out guidebooks, pilots, and charts, we look at our options. Our preferred route is to go north to the Philippines and then on to Hong Kong. The problem is that we would be following a cyclone track for 1,200 nm, and cyclones could and did develop at any time of the year. As pirates are also active in that area of the Philippines, we shelve that plan.

An around-the world route through the Red Sea would have us home in 2003, but news reports out of East Timor are unsettling, with riots and beheadings occurring in several locations. We consider skirting along the western edge of Indonesia, making our first landfall in Thailand, but decide that wouldn't be very satisfactory. We'd prefer to do that passage when we can visit some of the islands.

Some cruisers talk about sailing from Darwin to Bali to Singapore, keeping on the move and seeking safety in numbers. Others discuss sailing to Vanuatu or the Solomon Islands, then fret about malaria, dengue fever, and other health issues. Preferring our challenges at sea, we decide to return to Fiji, which means sailing into prevailing winds for over 1,600 nm. There's a good chance we won't reach Suva, but we're confident that we can make New Caledonia.

We spend the month of May working on the boat and buying provisions. Preparing for this crossing is no less hectic than for our previous crossings, and our *to-do list* is a mile long. This time, we scrape a few barnacles off the side of the hull when we have the boat hauled, then have to hammer them off the narrow bottom of the keel, where we haven't been able to paint in the past.

Dave now scrubs the bottom with a long-handled scouring pad and finds fifteen small blisters on the port side, forward of the propeller. Apparently, blisters come with tropical waters. After grinding them out, he arranges for an on-site shop to apply an epoxy filling. After two days of non-stop effort, we're ready to go back in the water at the scheduled time.

Friends on another yacht depart for New Caledonia that same day, and we follow their progress on HF radio. They make good time until the seventh day, when they're only 100 nm from the passage through the reef. They are then hit by 20–25 kt headwinds and pushed north into the path of a small, developing low. When they don't keep a scheduled radio call next day, we have real concerns for their safety. We then learn that Abie was up earlier on another net. She'd said they were worried about the low, and trying to decide whether to run for it or put out the sea anchor.

The next day, we're relieved to hear Abie's excited voice on the radio. "We've been to hell and back!" she screams, adding emphatically, "I'm flying back to Australia and we're going to sell the boat! Mark will have to find someone else to help him bring it back." She then more calmly reports, "Winds are now down to 17 kt and we're about to pull in the sea anchor." We continue to monitor their progress and are very relieved when, late on Day 11, they arrive safely in port.

When we learn the details of their experience, I have no doubt the situation was dire. Early on, two windows in the spray dodger blew out, dumping seawater down the companionway into the cabin; everything below was soaked, including their new laptop computer. Winds were over 50 kt for three hours, peaking at 58 kt, and deck fittings started to leak as rough seas pounded the boat. The headsail furler was trashed, three front stanchions were bent when Mark deployed the sea anchor, and he came close to going overboard.

Unable to hold my tongue, I turn to Dave and murmur softly, "You know that old adage about not starting a voyage on a Friday? Well, they left on a Friday, so maybe there's some truth to it."

We continued with our preparations while monitoring events at sea, including home canning 34 jars of meat and vegetables. When every nook and cranny on the boat is full, Dave puts a *For Sale* sign in the car window. When that produces no results by the end of May, he buys a cell phone, places an ad in the paper, and reduces the price from $3,900 to $2,500.

One warm, sunny morning, we take *Windy Lady* out into the bay and check that all systems are working. We replace the genoa with the working jib because I'm adamant that we're not going to sea with the large sail up. We also clear with Customs, which gives us a week to finish our repairs, otherwise we'll have to check back in.

Dave now has an appointment with an endodontist in downtown Brisbane. He has an infection in the roots of two teeth, one of which has a root canal and crown. An hour later and $750 lighter, he emerges with ten stitches around the base of his gum. He finally receives an offer of $2,000 for the car, which he reluctantly accepts, only to have the young fellow withdraw the offer after test-driving it. Getting desperate, he has the car serviced and renews the registration for six months.

On a day with no wind, we check out our new MPS, a large light-wind sail that we'd recently acquired. It's encased in a long, sausage-shaped sock, with the top sticking out one end and the bottom out the other. Dave ties the bottom two corners of the sail to the deck and hoists the top up the mast with a spare halyard. Using an attached line, he pulls the sock up, which frees the sail and it billows out in a slight puff of wind. The sock pulls down easily, compressing the sail as he lowers it.

The last three days are spent selling the car. After getting an offer one day, he spends half the next day meeting with a woman and filling in forms, then all of the last day trying to get his money. At 1520, the buyer phones and tells him, "I'll have to give you a cheque because the bank won't give me cash."

Dave responds, "It has to be cash because we don't have a bank account!"

"Well, we're borrowing the money from the bank and they are issuing a cheque to you for $3,000. Oh, by the way, you'll have to give me $500 back, in cash."

The extra $500 is for insurance, but at this point, Dave doesn't care; he just wants to be rid of the car. He agrees, saying, "Okay, I'll open up an account at the ANZ Bank at the shopping center. Can you meet me there?" Ten minutes later, the buyer calls back and says, "Look, I'm stuck in traffic; I'm gonna be late."

Thirty minutes before the bank closes, Dave is opening an account, then withdraws $500 from his bank account in Canada. The buyer shows up just as the branch is about to lock the doors. What an ending to our stay!

CHAPTER 23
The MPS (Multi Purpose Sail)

The sky is bright and sunny when we untie next morning, and not a ripple mars the glassy surface of Moreton Bay as we motor across it. With the autopilot doing the steering, we relax in the cockpit, happy to have the turmoil of the last month behind us. I'm elated at the prospect of the voyage ahead, although we have no idea how long we'll be at sea. Normally, we would expect the crossing to take sixteen days, as it's roughly 1,600 nm, but we'll be sailing into prevailing winds, so it could take longer.

Windy Lady starts to roll in a slight swell as we near Moreton Island, and the rolling gets worse as we follow the shoreline around to the NE Passage. The tide is low, and I suspect that ocean swells are pushing across the shallow bar on the outside. Watching the masthead sway down toward the water, I feel for our friends in *Legacy*, the boat just ahead. They are bound for New Caledonia, and Paul gets seasick for the first three or four days of every crossing.

We're through the passage by 1230, with open sea in front of us, but a brooding mass of dark cloud is moving down from the northwest. Two hours later, the sky opens up and the rain pours down. We start our regular watch schedule at 1600, by which time we're clear of the shallow water off Moreton Island. I take the first shift, while Dave goes below to rest.

Half an hour later, the wind rises out of the south and I go below to wake Dave, so we can raise the mainsail. As I step down into the dimness of the cabin, I notice a trail of water on the floor (the sole) and smell something odd. Next thing, I'm yelling urgently, "David, get up! We've got smoke out here!" As he scrambles from his berth, I open the furnace locker door and realize that it is steam, not smoke.

He runs to the inside steering station, pulls back the throttle, then heads for the cockpit. I follow along behind and together we peer over the stern, listening to the reassuring sound of water spurting from the engine cooling system. Looking at the dark sea around us, he shrugs his shoulders, and grumbles, "It's almost dark, so I can't do anything now. It'll have to wait until morning. Let's go raise the mainsail."

He shuts down the engine on the way to his berth, and when I pull out the headsail, *Windy Lady* surges forward. While I have some misgivings about heading out to sea with a sick engine, I have faith he can deal with it. With winds at 10–20 knots (kt) from the south, *Windy Lady* is soon cutting smoothly through five-foot seas at 5 kt. We're steering due east, which puts her on a beam reach, our fastest point of sail.

Otto, our wind-powered self-steering system, is working well, leaving me free to sit and watch the stars appear, and I am soon entranced by the magic of the night sky. At 0800 next morning, we've been at sea 24 hours and log 126 nm for Day 1. (Rule of thumb: double knots or nautical miles to get kilometers.)

I usually don't sleep much for the first three-four days at sea. I seem to be filled with an inner excitement that won't let me rest until I'm exhausted. It also takes time to adjust to the boat movements, to say nothing of the watch schedule, which has us getting up and going to bed three times a day. My shifts run from 0800 until noon, 1600 to 2000, and midnight to 0400.

When I enter the cockpit that morning, a brilliant, sunny sky soars over restless blue waters. Falling into familiar routines, I turn in a full circle, scanning the horizon for ships, while studying sea and sky for signs of what the day might bring. I then tweak sails and adjust Otto's settings, looking for the best combination to keep *Windy Lady* moving in the right direction at the highest speed.

Within an hour, Dave has tied back the sole over the engine compartment and is lying on his belly, leaning down over the floor supports as he works on the engine. He's told me that the alternator belt failed, which caused the water pump to quit working, then the heat exchanger overheated, producing the steam and smell of glycol. He now discovers that the spare belt, which was on the boat when we bought it, is half an inch too short. In order to put it on, he has to remove the alternator from its bracket, and to do that, he has to remove the belt on the water pump.

As if that isn't enough, the wind eases, and seas pushing on the port quarter turn the bow, knocking the wind from the sails. *Windy Lady* then wallows in five-foot seas, and as she rolls, his ribs are scraped raw. They're sore for weeks.

Winds remain light for the next 20 hours, and we log 81 nm for Day 2. An hour later, I'm standing at the helm, hand steering, and see Dave wrestle the MPS up the companionway. He pulls the sausage up the mast, pulls up the sock, and the large, light sail billows out to port, looking good. When boat speed increases by a knot, Otto is able to steer again.

An hour after that, the breeze begins to strengthen. When it reaches 10 kt, Otto is overpowered. At 15 kt, it's all I can do to hold the bow on course. When Dave tries to pull the sock down, it doesn't move. He finally wraps the light line around a winch, then slowly pulls the sock down, compressing the sail, which he then lowers.

By mid-afternoon, south winds are gusting from 12–18 kt; by nightfall, they're up to 25 kt. With waves now seven-feet high, the sea is very rough. During my midnight watch, a solitary light pierces the darkness as a ship crosses in front of us. I turn on the radar, which usually picks up a ship at 6-8 nm. It doesn't find this one. A second light then appears, followed by several more, so I turn on our running lights, although I doubt that they can be seen in the high swells. I watch the lights for an hour, but the radar only sees the ship at 3 nm.

At the start of my watch next morning, winds are steady at 10–15 kt from the SW. By noon, Dave is worried that the combination of wind and swell on the starboard quarter will push us southward. I'm able to tell him that won't be a problem for long, as I've just taken off a weather fax showing strong westerly winds in an approaching system. Within a few hours, the sky clouds over, and by dark, winds have veered to the WSW. By midnight, they're gusting at 15–30 kt from the NW. We log 106 nm and 120 nm for Days 3 and 4.

Winds are gusting from 20–35 kt when I start my morning watch, and we have two reefs in the mainsail, four in the headsail, and I'm hand steering. Ten-foot swells are breaking on the port side, dumping water onto the deck and cabin roof, and the front window on that side is leaking badly, as are both hatches. The two dorads (air vents) also leak; they were left open and now can't be closed.

The seas then grow to twelve feet, and I can't stop the stronger gusts from turning *Windy Lady* beam on to the swell. I get clobbered hard a few times and end up with a cockpit full of water more than once, but make 30 nm during my watch, which is something of a record.

We put another reef in each sail when Dave takes the watch at noon, and a few hours later, a front moving in from the WNW brings gusts of 43 kt. Thankfully, after dumping a couple of heavy showers, it moves on. But it's midnight before winds drop below 30 kt, and seas then grow higher. Exhausted, we're both late reporting for the next two shifts, as we let each other sleep until we wake up on our own. We log 154 nm for Day 5, another record for us.

With winds at 20–25 kt from the west and six-foot swells, conditions seem to be easing that morning, but by noon, *Windy Lady* is surfing down ten-foot waves, and 30-kt winds from the WSW are again turning her broadside. With winds over the stern, we drop the mainsail, reef the headsail a bit more, and her speed increases by a knot. She's pretty uncomfortable, heaving and twisting while rolling from side to side, but Otto starts working again.

When dishing up at suppertime, Dave places our dog bowls on the gimbaled stove in the galley, which is supposed to swing with the boat movement. A sudden, vicious twist sends the bowls flying and he saves only one, so has to scrape the food off the floor for the other. I have a similar problem when cleaning up afterward, as twice water and dishes go flying.

When I come on watch at midnight, the sky is filled with a million brilliant stars. As we're heading east, I pick a constellation as it rises above the horizon in front of us, then use it to steer by. When the stars climb too high, I return to using the compass. Overnight, Otto works well in 10–20 kt winds, but we don't sleep well with all the rocking and rolling.

WSW winds are steady at 10–15 kt next morning in 8-foot seas, and we're making 5.5 kt. Twelve hours later, with 15–25 kt winds from the west and ten-foot seas, we're still making 5.5 kt. Clouds bring a few showers overnight, and lightning occasionally flares on the horizon. It's not forked or sheet like we're used to, but ball-shaped with a very white light. We log 120 nm and 125 nm for Days 6 and 7.

After a full week at sea, we've sailed 841 nm and are north of Norfolk Island. We're less than 1.5 degrees (90 nm) south of our starting point, so have pretty much followed the 27th parallel east. When the winds drop to 7–15 kt that afternoon, Dave runs the engine for two hours as the batteries need charging.

It's now time to start thinking about steering northeast, so when winds drop below 10 kt and back to the SE at sunset, we pole out the headsail and turn the bow to a new heading of 060 degrees. As the sea calms, the boat rolls less and that night we sleep like babies. Next morning, we log 101 nm for Day 8, and with winds down to 5 kt, we're making 2.6 kt in flat seas.

Dave brings out the MPS again, and we raise the mainsail and furl the headsail before he pulls it up the mast. As soon as he pulls the sock free, a squall comes out of nowhere, hitting us with 20-kt winds. The boat instantly heels over, dragging a foot of our brand-new sail through the sea. As I fight the helm, trying to level the deck, I turn the bow toward the wind, and Dave waves me back; he's afraid the MPS will wrap around the rigging. But when I turn back, the boat heels over and the sail is back in the water. I'm now hanging on to keep from sliding across the cockpit, and all I can think about is that we're a thousand miles from anywhere.

I then realize that the MPS isn't the problem; it's the bloody mainsail! Leaving the helm momentarily, I duck under the dodger roof to release the sheet brake, then return and ease out the mainsail. The boat is soon back under control, at which point a cold rain shower wets us down. Deciding we've had enough nonsense for the day, Dave tries to pull down the sock. Although the MPS is sheltered by the mainsail, it's still a struggle; then, the instant the sail is bagged, the squall moves on and the wind dies.

Winds are up and down all day as more squalls blow through, and we do a lot of hand steering. At midday, we turn our clocks ahead two hours, as the sun had been setting fifteen minutes earlier every day. The previous day it went down at 1600. The wind then dies at sunset and we sit for an hour in absolutely still air and flat seas.

Overnight, ESE winds are under 7 kt and we drift along at 3 kt. We log 69 nm for Day 9.

With the morning clear, quiet and sunny, Dave optimistically brings out the MPS once more. This time the sail fills with no drama, and the boat speed picks up. Then the wind dies, and with a great rustling of material, the sail collapses against the side of the boat. It continues to fill and collapse for the rest of the morning, and I doubt that we gain an extra mile before taking it down at noon.

We now motor for five hours, charging batteries, and with the autopilot doing the steering, Dave spends his watch making bread. I spend a couple of hours doing housekeeping chores, then try to figure out how to use the starfinder. I'd like to know which stars are in the constellations that fill the night skies. We then go back to drifting along in light and variable winds.

About midnight, the wind rises in the NNE at 10–15 kt, and for the first time in the voyage, we're sailing into wind (beating) and have difficulty making our course. When I come on watch at 0800, winds are gusting up to 20 kt, and the sea is very lumpy. I then get clobbered by a squall that I thought was going to miss us. It brings 35-kt winds, and even with three reefs in the main, *Windy Lady* heels over and turns into wind with sails flogging and sheets banging.

I watch another storm approach during my 1600 watch, with dark clouds stretching in a long curving line to the southwest. A black shadow of heavy rain lies beneath, but as it draws closer, the area in the mid-section grows lighter, as if a heavy curtain has been drawn back. The storm looks more threatening than it is and drops only a bit of rain.

The winds ease before the end of that watch, and we drift into the night at less than 3 kt, with a half-moon peeking through clouds, lighting up a ruffled sea. The winds return with the dawn, but we log only 89 nm and 94 nm for Days 10 and 11.

We make better time that morning, but a few squalls race through during the afternoon, bringing gusty winds and taking them when they move on. *Windy Lady* then wallows in three-foot seas with sails flogging, and we struggle to keep her moving forward. Just before nightfall, the wind settles at 10 kt from the SW. With winds now abaft the beam, we pole out the headsail and she makes 5 kt for the next twelve hours. She still rolls uncomfortably and neither of us get much sleep, but we log 124 nm for Day 12.

When I come on watch that morning, Dave is studying the chart on which we plot our daily progress. "Look here," he says, "this is where we are and here's the Vava'u Islands in Tonga; it's a good angle and we could probably make it. Do you want to try?"

We've now sailed over 1,300 nm, and the change will add an extra three days to our voyage. But the route looks doable and I respond, "Sure, let's go for it." We then adjust our heading by 30 degrees.

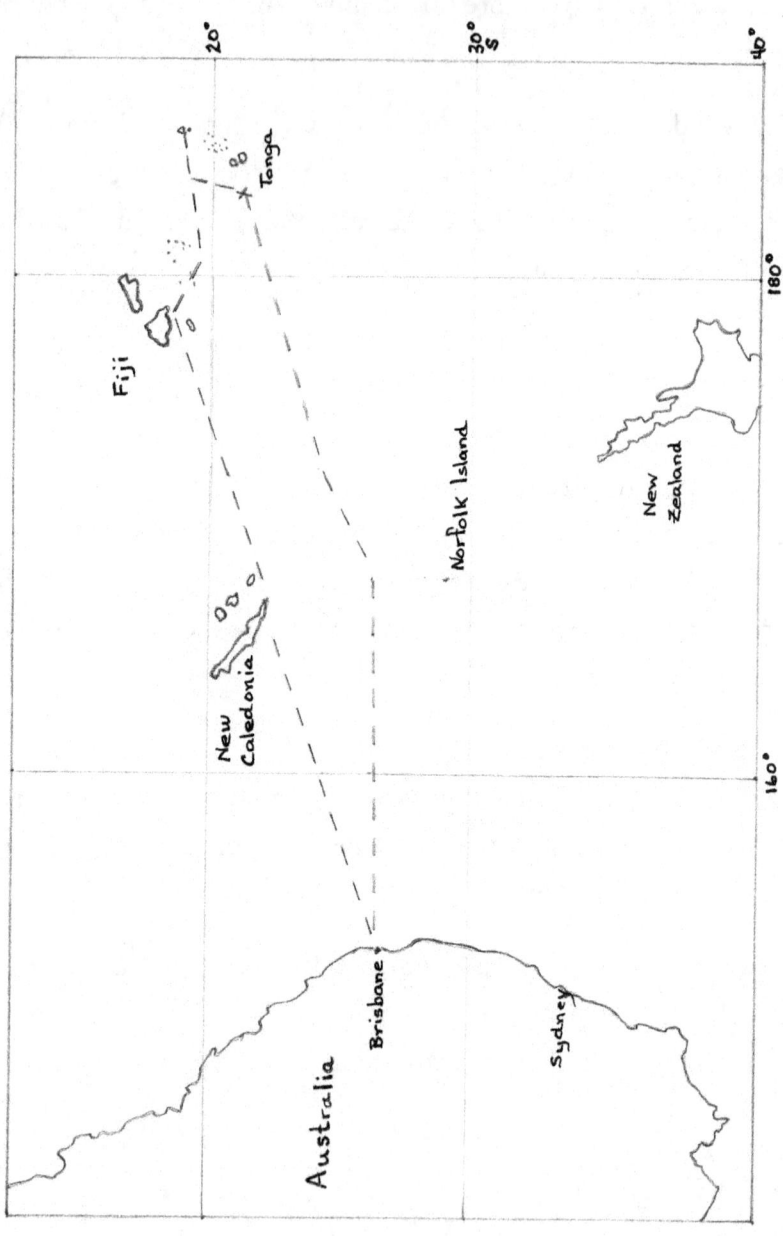

Round trip to Tonga-8,500 km

CHAPTER 24

An Unreported Low

With south winds of 10–15 kt, *Windy Lady* makes over 5 kt during my morning watch. They then veer to SSW early in the afternoon and begin to ease. By midnight, they are light and variable, and we drift along in a gentle southerly swell for the next two days. The water is so flat that it looks oily, and afternoon temperatures are uncomfortably hot. But what I most notice is the silence; there's no creaking of rigging, no murmur of water against the hull.

The weather fax has now packed it in, so I listen to forecasts on HF radio, taking down notes in shorthand. Each night, I check in with Des at Russell Radio, who also gives me updates. But I don't know where the isobars are located, or the shape of the weather systems, and feel like I'm getting only half of the information I need.

I take sunshots daily, trying to keep busy, then check my results against the GPS. Usually, I'm within a few miles of latitude, but longitude is more difficult. At night, I study the stars and identify Rigel Kent and Hadar in the constellation Centaurus. They point to the Southern Cross, and two of its stars, Acrux and Gacrux, lead to the South Pole. Regulus in the constellation Leo appears in the western sky just after sunset, and is so bright that even when cloudy, I can frequently spot it.

One night, during my midnight watch, a large fishing boat appears to starboard. I keep a close eye on it but it comes no closer than 4 nm. The following night, when I get up at midnight, I hear loud snoring and Dave confesses, "Yeah, I probably slept for three hours!" We log 89 nm, 57 nm, and 61 nm for Days 13, 14 and 15, including 40 nm under motor. After running the engine, we have hot water, so luxuriate in cockpit baths and I wash out a few clothes.

The winds return as we go into Day 16, gusting at 5–20 kt from the NE. As they're right on the bow, *Windy Lady* is pushed eastward. Rough, five-foot swells then keep us from making our course during the afternoon, when winds settle at 15–20 kt from the north. Only after nightfall, when they back to the NNW, are we able to steer in the direction we want to go. Cloudy skies bring a few showers overnight but visibility is generally good, and just before daybreak, a rotating beacon lights up the sky to the north for an hour.

Day 17 is cloudy and cool with a ruffled sea, and we drift along at 2-3 kt all day. Dave has a run-in with a belligerent booby on his evening watch; it wants to roost on the pulpit and he doesn't think it should. After a surly outburst, he needs the help of a winch handle to convince it to leave. Clouds are backlit by a waxing moon overnight, and visibility is again good.

A small pod of whales surface about 150 feet off the stern as we go into Day 18. Dave tells me he heard them blowing during the night. We haven't seen much in the way of life out here, not even flying fish. A trough passes over about noon, bringing some rain and a bit of wind, cooling the air. At dusk, the clouds break up and a big, full moon rises over the horizon. As it climbs up into the sky, its light forms a path across rippled waters and the night that follows is quite beautiful.

Later, after checking in with Russell Radio, we receive a call from our friends on *Legacy*. Diane explains that they've been in New Caledonia for eleven days and asks, "We were just wondering, how long are you going to stay at sea?"

We log 99 nm, 67 nm, and 55 nm for Day 16, 17, and 18, averaging only 12 nm per watch over the last six days. I know Dave is getting bored because he plays a practical joke that he thinks is quite funny. I don't! This is how he recorded events in his journal:

Lene was late getting up at midnight, and when she did, I hid myself in the starboard berth. She got up, had a look around, then went to the companionway to look for me in the cockpit. She called, "David!!! David???", with a hint of panic on the second David. I responded, "Yeass," to which she said, "You f-----g asshole!" and our new day started.

At 1030 on Day 19, I pass through the same position that Dave logged at 0800 and realize we're drifting south. A two-foot swell then ripples across the ocean, and as the boat rolls, the boom sways back and forth, squeaking loudly. Minutes later, a whale breaks the surface fifty feet to port; we hear it blowing and turn to see the broad, dark back and dorsal fin disappearing into the water. I wonder whether the squeaking boom brought it.

Just before noon, the air stirs and I turn *Windy Lady* slowly through 360 degrees to get back on course. Any forward movement seems a blessing compared to sitting and rocking in the slight swell. Soon, we're making 4 kt in a 9-kt breeze from the SE. The wind quickly increases to 15–20 kt, and we make 5.5 and 6 kt during the afternoon and evening watches. Our progress slows overnight, as a misty rain falls, then the clouds break up about 0400, revealing the moon. We log 101 nm for Day 19.

A high-pressure center building to the south now brings the promise of a south-easterly flow with stronger winds, and by mid-afternoon, winds are up to 25 kt and seas are building. A small conical hill then peeps above the horizon for a few hours as we pass 22 nm north of Vanyua Island, one of Fiji's southerly possessions.

A thunderstorm rumbles down on us during my midnight watch, and I get a closer look at several white balls of lightning. The flashes are like explosions, much brighter than a flashbulb; one is accompanied by a loud crash of thunder, and I see the outline of the dodger against a white sky before shutting my eyes tightly. I am quite happy when the storm moves on.

At 0800, we log 115 nm for Day 20 and have 220 nm left to go. Winds are now from the ESE at 20–25 kt, and we're making 4.5 kt. During the afternoon, they back to the east, putting *Windy Lady* on a beat, and ten-foot seas push us north. Waves wash over the foredeck and cabin roof, and water leaks in both hatches and the window over the chart table. As conditions deteriorate, Dave goes forward and puts a second reef in the main, hanging on with one hand and working with the other.

Winds gust from 25–30 kt during my sunset watch, and before long, I'm wishing they would ease a bit (20 would be nice). Then, when I return to the cockpit at midnight, we are tracking straight north. I record our positions for the next two hours and decide that we'd be better off on a port tack. I furl in the headsail, center the mainsail, and re-position them on the other side of the deck. When the captain takes the watch at 0400, he returns them to their original configuration.

I sleep for a couple of hours, then wake to flogging sails and banging sheets. I go out to the cockpit, and Dave tells me that we've lost the wind. The sky is overcast, leaden, reflected in oily-looking, eight-foot swells that have no order. With two hours to go before my next watch, I return to my berth but am wide-eyed and strangely restless. I get up minutes later. At 0630, Dave starts the engine, saying that the batteries were due to be charged the previous day. He then sets the autopilot and prepares breakfast.

A few minutes later, we hear wind in the sails, so he ducks outside and reports that the wind has come up out of the SE at 6kt. Thirty minutes later, the wind has increased to 20 kt. At 0730, a much stronger gust hits *Windy Lady*, heeling her over sharply. We rush up to the cockpit, where the wind gauge reads 40 kt. Our first thoughts are for the sails, and we put a third reef in the main, easing it out as far as it will go, then furl the headsail. When I look at the wind gauge now, my heart sinks; it reads 50 kt.

Soaked through and in shock, we hover under the dodger roof and watch the storm develop around us. Heavy rain accompanies the wind, and within seconds, visibility is down to fifty feet. The wind drives the rain horizontally across the water, whipping spray from the tops of swells, and it sounds like pellets are striking the side of the hull. Dave now adjusts the autopilot to head us into the storm, then braves the open end of the cockpit to feather the wind vane. He doesn't try to remove the sail, afraid of dropping it overboard.

It's July 1 and as we start Day 22, we don't know what hit us. I sit in the cockpit, my feet braced against the opposite seat, shivering from a combination of cold and fear, staring first at the wind gauge, which hovers between 45 and 50 kt, and then at the building seas. At 0915, I force myself to go below and listen to the weather forecast. The cabin is unbelievably rough and I'm flung in all directions as I cling to a grabrail at the chart table with one hand, and try to hold my notebook and write with the other. I use earphones, or wouldn't have been able to hear the broadcast over the noise of the engine and the storm. Unbelievably, the report provides no clue as to what is happening, just identifies a trough in the area with winds of 20–25 kt.

Returning to my seat in the cockpit, I again brace myself and resume studying the wind gauge and the sea. Although this is my watch, Dave makes no attempt to go below, for which I'm thankful. *Windy Lady* now pushes into the storm with a forward speed of 1.5 kt, and the autopilot is working 100%.

We've never been in such a violent storm before, so constantly check the boat for signs of equipment failure. At one point, Dave reluctantly crawls forward to secure the canopy poles, which have come loose on the foredeck. When he returns, his clothes dripping with salt water, he yells, "I saw something orange in the sea but it disappeared so quickly that I couldn't identify it. It could have been a life jacket."

Violent seas twelve feet high now roll the boat over onto its port side, and I feel my weight shift onto my feet, which are braced against the bench on that side. A huge wave then breaks on top the cabin and dodger roofs, and Dave and I both flinch at the force of the blow. He's standing at the chart table and sees it approach through the window. I'm braced in the companionway, looking out over the stern, and to my horror, the rear of the boat is pushed down into the sea and blue water runs in over the coaming. I know then that we would never be able to launch the life raft in such conditions, let alone get in safely.

At noon, the wind is still blowing at 40–50 kt and seas continue to grow. I think by then we've accepted the situation, and our confidence in *Windy Lady* has returned. Neither of us had the stomach for breakfast, but now we eat. Seas increase to sixteen feet as we punch into the storm that afternoon, and we have a wild, wet ride. The compass shows a heading of 050 degrees, although the autopilot is set on 090 degrees. I go below for a while, but water seeps in everywhere I look and it's impossible to rest.

Shortly after I take the watch at 1600, the wind drops below 40 kt for the first time in over eight hours. I know that seas will get bigger as the wind eases, but heave a sigh of relief, feeling that surely, the end is in sight. As I relax, I'm able to study the violence of the waves, and without fear, can see the beauty of the sea. Huge waves rush toward us, white water crowning their tops; they then break in a crashing roar, with a mass of white foam running out in front and a swirl of ice blue water running down the backside. The waves rise about fifteen feet above the swells, are maybe fifty feet long, and come charging across the sea from different directions.

When I check in with Russell Radio at 2000, Des tells me that we were hit by a small low-pressure center that raced down through Fiji the previous night. Defensively, he explains that they didn't report it, and he only saw it on the weather prognosis hours after the storm hit us. With a center pressure of 1008 mb, the winds were made worse by a 1034-mb high just to the south. After ensuring that we suffered no damage, he tells me, "There's another boat between you and Tonga, and they lost their boom."

The winds stay at 30–35 kt until 0200, then back to the east and drop down to 20 kt. I keep busy during my midnight watch by wiping off the layer of salt coating the ceiling of the dodger, then scrub the cockpit and sole. By the time Dave takes the watch at 0400, seas are down to eight feet, and I'm able to get a few hours sleep. I wake to a brilliant blue sky, 20 kt of wind on the nose, and lumpy seas. When I move, my body aches all over; my arms are especially sore, from hanging onto grabrails, I expect.

We're now 73 nm from the Vava'u Islands in Tonga and really want to make port that night, so motor sail. When Dave inspects the wind vane, he finds that a 3/8-inch stainless steel bolt has sheared off, and the pin locking the rudder in place is bent. Salt crystals have also immobilized the wind arrow at the top of the mast. We logged 95 nm on Day 21, which took us into the storm, and 81 nm on Day 22, which took us through it.

At 1600 on Day 23, we're still 20 nm out, but Dave pushes on, asserting, "We've been here before and know the way in, and we'll have bright moonlight to guide us." I'm not too keen, as we're both really tired and the moon won't be up until well after sunset.

The islands disappear into the night when we're still 10 nm out, so I dig out a chart and come up with several GPS waypoints to take us in. We turn on the radar as we approach the entrance channel, and I stay on deck, keeping watch, while Dave monitors the instruments down in the cabin. Before long, I see the dim outlines of two islands that don't fit with my memory of the route. I alert the captain, who only now reviews the GPS waypoints and finds the error; I misread the scale so the latitude readings are wrong.

Dave now recalls a small anchorage just outside of Neiafu harbor and decides to stop there, rather than tempting fate by going through the narrows. Slowing the boat, he cautiously turns into the small bay, then keeps a close eye on the depth gauge. I'm up at the bow and see only blackness in front of us. There are no lights anywhere. I cannot see the shoreline, and as we proceed, I make out the tops of a dark mass of tall trees outlined against a slightly lighter sky.

It's been a while since we anchored and we're tired, so of course we have problems. On our first attempt, the anchor pulls loose when Dave backs up the boat. The second time, we end up in shallow water and I can actually see coral heads rising up off the bottom. The depth gauge reads five feet, but *Windy Lady* draws six. I hold my breath, half expecting the chain to snag, but somehow, we make it back out to deeper water.

The third time, the anchor is well and truly hooked, and Dave then goes below, preparing to shut down the engine. I stay at the bow for a few minutes, soaking in the calmness of the night, and when I turn to go below, I notice that the chain has pulled back beneath the boat.

We're still in forward gear! Although the anchor has pulled loose, we're able to reset it without pulling it up.

I am now so tired that I'm beyond caring; I don't want to think about the boat. What I want is a good stiff drink and a good night's sleep. It was 2130 when we entered the bay and it's midnight when we go to bed. I sleep solidly for 6.5 hours and awake to calm water, a clear sky, and the sounds of birds chirping in the trees. The boat isn't moving, and when I get up, I don't have to hang on to stay in place, and the plates don't slide as we eat our pancakes. Simple pleasures!

We were at sea for 22.5 days and sailed 2,217 nm. Winds varied from zero to 50 kt and occasionally stopped at 20. Dave points out that the wind probably averaged 15 kt, which is what the pilot chart indicates for this route at this season, but what a wealth of experience lies behind that figure.

CHAPTER 25
A Delightful Surprise

We arrive in Neiafu late on a Friday and spend the weekend quietly in self-imposed quarantine. It's not really a hardship, given the passage we've had. An occasional shower passes overhead, but the air is warm, a light breeze ruffles the surface of the water, and bird songs drift from the soft green foliage along the shoreline. On Sunday morning, the breeze also carries the faint sounds of a church choir.

Dave calls out to the skipper of a yacht leaving the anchorage and manages to obtain the time and frequency of the cruisers' net on VHF radio. He then confirms what we suspected; today is the King's Birthday. That means tomorrow is a public holiday, so we'll be spending another day in quarantine.

We raise our yellow quarantine flag about midday on Monday, then motor the last two miles into Neiafu. Dave tours through the anchorage, looking for familiar boats, and homes in on a Canadian flag. As we draw nearer, he sees that the homeport is Victoria and exclaims, "That's Brian's boat!"

"No, it's not," I declare, "they can't possibly be here."

Reading the name on the bow of the boat, he states emphatically, "Yes, that's *Moonshadow!*"

I still don't believe him because such a coincidence beggars the imagination. The previous year, Dave's younger brother and his wife sailed their boat down the west coast from Victoria, Canada, to La Pas, Mexico. We'd heard four months earlier that they'd set sail for Tahiti and Fiji, but intended to bypass Tonga. Only when I read the boat name myself do I acknowledge that he is right. Excitedly, I run up to the bow shouting, "*Ahoy, Moonshadow! Ahoy, Moonshadow!*"

It takes a stentorian roar from Dave, however, before Brian pokes his head out of the companionway. Truly amazed and totally delighted, the four of us yell questions at each other while Dave maneuvers the boat to keep us a safe distance apart. They arrived the day before us and none of us can believe it; we couldn't have done better if we'd tried. When our initial excitement passes, we anchor *Windy Lady* down the harbor and Brian and Rita row across in their dinghy. We spend the afternoon catching up on their adventures, and then Dave cooks up a big pot of spaghetti, using fresh tomatoes and onions that Brian brings over.

Next morning, we motor over to the new container wharf to check in, and Brian and Rita wait to take our lines. I'm happy to have their help, as the new dock is no friendlier to cruising boats than the old one. During last week's storm, a yacht had suffered a fair amount of damage while tied up to it. The wind had pinned it against the cement wall while waves bounced it around.

Three Tongan officials climb over our lifelines, and the Customs Officer, a husky, dark-skinned man, seats himself in the center of the settee in the cabin. Arrogantly, he spreads his papers across the coffee table and demands answers from *David* in a thick accent that neither of us understand. The Immigration Officer squeezes in at one end of the settee and quietly fills in his forms, while a third man wanders about the boat, picking up items and looking in lockers. I keep an eye on him, hoping that he replaces everything, and after 45 minutes, we're free to go.

We do a lot of walking over the next few days, feeling the need for exercise after being confined to the boat for so long. The small, dark shops lining Neiafu's narrow main street carry the same limited variety of goods as before, but there are some obvious changes. Huge storm-drain pipes litter the length of the short street and a deep excavation, half the width of the road, runs for two blocks, with large piles of red dirt blocking access to the weather-beaten buildings. The people also look different. Women wear flowered print dresses rather than the long, dark skirts and tunic tops that I'd seen before. The men no longer have a woven mat tied around their middles, and some wear shorts instead of long pants.

Friday is still market day, however, and in the early morning, small powerboats chug into the harbor, loaded to the gunnels with people and produce. Later, the plaza in front of the wet market is filled with roots, leaves and coconuts. Dave stops to examine a pile of woven, palm-leaf baskets holding fruit and pays $3 for one that contains thirteen large papayas. We then pay $12 for a tray of thirty eggs.

We search out a new bakery and find it located in a rust-streaked, sheet-metal-walled shed in a vacant lot. After hesitantly stepping through the wide doorway, we're greeted by the aroma of freshly baked bread and see golden loaves resting on wire shelves in the dimly lit interior.

We now carefully inspect *Windy Lady* for storm damage. The leading edge of the dodger roof looks like it was smashed by a rock. When we check the sails, we find the metal sail guide missing from the furler, so figure it was the culprit. It had no longer locked in place, and the last time I saw it was whipping back and forth on the end of a short piece of cable.

Loose thread hangs off a three-foot section of the headsail, and we take it down, roll it up, and carry it below. The material is much too thick for my sewing machine, so I sit with thread and needle and repair it with the help of a leather palm. I'm just relieved that I'm able to re-use existing holes. I then climb the mast and check out the wind arrow, hearing a grating sound when I push it around. Assuming it's full of salt crystals, I keep pushing it until it moves freely. We're unable to find anyone to repair the weather fax, so will be without it until Suva.

When Dave services the engine, he is stunned to find the glass bowl beneath the Racor fuel filter is half-full of black gunk that came off the bottom of the fuel tanks. It's so thick that he has to scoop it out. This occurred once before in rough seas and killed the engine. I don't want to even think about how we would have coped, if that had happened during this storm.

He finds a perfect match for the broken bolt on the wind vane at a local boatyard and replaces it. But when we go back to sea, Otto still doesn't work. (The weight at the bottom of the sail binds against the lower part of the vane, and he discovers that a spacer is missing. By subtly applying a little brute strength, he gets it more-or-less working.)

With the weather still rainy, we regularly meet Brian and Rita ashore and spend a lot of time visiting with other cruisers. I'm soon bored with this routine, and when the sun comes out convince Dave to move to the anchorage at Vaka Eitu. I'm hoping to do some snorkeling, but the water over the reef is too deep when we arrive, and the following morning, low clouds bring more wind and rain.

When Brian and Rita anchor *Moonshadow* nearby, we take them to dinner at the eco resort overlooking the bay. Wind waves batter the small resort raft when we approach, and Dave cautiously maneuvers the dinghy around anchor ropes that lead off in all directions. Trying to avoid the salt spray, we then jump from the raft to the base of the catwalk and climb up several steps. This narrow, rickety structure, which leads across a 200-foot expanse of tidal mudflat, is not in very good shape, with only a single handrail and boards missing underfoot.

Once ashore, a wide path leads up the hill to the Lighthouse Café and beautiful views of the sea and nearby islands. We take our seats on benches at a roughly hewn table in a thatched-roof shelter with open walls, earthen floor, and well-stocked bar. As dusk is upon us, a young woman brings a candle to the table. When she later reappears out of the shadows, she serves a meal of local foods: tomatoes cut up in vinegar, marlin, wild yams, and papaya custard. The experience is unique and we enjoy ourselves immensely, although prices are twice what they were two years before.

We've brought a flashlight for the return journey down the hill in the dark. The tide is higher now, and wind pushes swirling waters up around the wooden supports of the walkway as we cross. It's a bit hairy as we leap onto the heaving raft and clamber into tossing dinghies, but we're away safely and stay reasonably dry on the way home.

When strong winds show no sign of abating, we decide to return to Neiafu. After four days of drifting back and forth with the tide, we carefully follow the chain as we pick it up, not wanting to snag it on the bottom. I'm at the helm and Dave stands at the bow, using a foot switch to operate the windlass and pointing in the direction he wants me to steer. The switch then sticks and the motor grinds on and on, taking us straight towards *Moonshadow*. I'm soon wondering if the other boat is sitting over top of our anchor.

Dave runs below to the electrical panel and shuts off the master switch, then flips it on and off a few times and the windlass switch starts working again. The anchor comes free well before we reach the other boat, but we now have a major equipment failure to add to our *to-do list*.

The rainy weather continues after we return to Neiafu, and we're now somewhat snarky with each other. I know that equipment failures are nagging at Dave, and we're tired of the rain, but I am also strangely restless and can't settle to anything. I should be placing a phone call to my dad in Canada, but keep postponing it. I finally have to force myself to walk down to the telephone exchange and place the call, then the connection is poor and the conversation disappointing.

Only later does it occur to me that the circumstances were eerily similar to our visit two years earlier. I'd received a message over

HF radio that my mom was very ill, and I needed to come home immediately to say goodbye. I had had to phone my dad and tell him that wasn't possible.

When the weather clears, we spend three nights at Port Morelle, joining a dozen other yachts in the quiet, sheltered bay. I spend hours paddling through the blue-green waters on a second-hand yak board that I bought in Australia, and my spirits start to lift. Sprinting across the bay against a light wind, I follow the shoreline back while admiring the coral formations through crystal clear water. One morning, I'm in maybe two feet of water and the surface is like glass, when a fish suddenly darts away in front of me. It looks like a reflection in a mirror, and I'm enchanted.

Our last evening is warm and balmy and a little more private, with only six yachts in the anchorage. Relaxing with drinks, we watch the sun slip down behind the palm trees and count the stars as they appear overhead. The quiet chirping of cicadas then breaks the silence, quickly building to a high-pitched hum that is broken now and again by the cooing of doves.

Low cloud and rain send us back to Neiafu next day, where we learn that *Moonshadow* is leaving for Suva on Thursday. We now do what we've accused others of doing, just mindlessly following along behind. We haven't made any preparations, not even checked the weather, and really haven't recovered from the last passage.

We clear with Customs, then prepare to move *Windy Lady* to a small bay outside the harbor, where we won't be delayed by a low tide in the morning. Dave is at the bow, raising the anchor, when the chain bunches up in the windlass, bringing it to a grinding halt. The chain stripper that dislodges the links from the gypsy has come adrift. (The gypsy is a rotating wheel that pulls the chain in.) As he struggles to remove the bolts that hold it, a squall brings wind and rain. Half an hour later, he returns to the cockpit and disgustedly reports, "The bolts are all frozen and one just broke off, so I'll have to pull the anchor up by hand."

He takes another look at the windlass after we've re-anchored in the smaller bay, but is not able to fix the chain stripper. This is sobering news, as it's not much fun pulling in 100 feet of chain, or lifting up a 45-pound anchor in 60–100 feet of water. Silently, we proceed to check the boat, ensuring that all is ready to go to sea in the morning.

CHAPTER 26
Contrary Winds

Next morning, I'm up early, walking about the deck. The sky is overcast, the water clear and calm, and a large patch of coral is visible thirty feet down. Several schools of fairly large fish drift nearby, and a native man carrying a small net quietly wades through the water along the shoreline. Every now and again, he stops and shakes out the net, then casts it and carefully pulls it in; once he removes a fish.

At 0800, Dave pulls up the anchor, then we motor out into open water. Winds are light when we turn the bow WSW, and we continue motoring, as we've had enough of sitting around going nowhere. We expect the 450-nm crossing to Suva to take five days. (We actually carry enough fuel to motor all the way.)

Moonshadow is away before us, and two hours out, Dave notices that Brian has raised his large, light-wind sail. After checking the winds a time or two, he raises our MPS and shuts down the engine. I've lost all confidence in the sail, so keep it under tight control during my morning watch. When he takes over at noon, however, he eases the sheet, allowing the sail to sit more toward the bow, and boat speed picks up by a knot. Now happy, he sits back and picks up a book. Half an hour later, the MPS is wrapped around the headstay, not once but countless times, and it is knotted tight.

It's impossible to just unwind the sail, and we now spend the next hour and a half freeing it. The only way we can do so is for Dave to untie a corner of the sail at the base of the mast, take it forward and pass it around the headstay, then return to the mast and retie it. He repeats this procedure with the second corner and does this over and over again.

The problem is that a light wind fills the sail as soon as he unties it. He then tries to run toward the bow, so he can pass the line around the headstay. But the deck rolls in a low swell, and occasionally, the wind catches him off balance and drags him toward the lifelines. A stronger gust then hurls him across the narrow keel of the dinghy, which is tied in the center of the foredeck. He lies there a moment, winded, but hangs onto the line, then gathers his strength and makes a dash for the bow.

With the engine running, I watch all this from my post at the helm and half expect him to go overboard. I try my best to keep the deck steady, but my stomach is in knots and all I want to do is climb the mast and cut the halyard. Then, when the sail is finally free, he triumphantly turns toward me and orders, "Okay, let's get this boat sailing and back on course!"

For the first time in five years, he faces mutiny. I shake my head emphatically and shriek, "*No bloody way! Take it down!*"

Giving me a strange look, only then realizing how perturbed I am, he shrugs his shoulders and tries to pull the sock down. It doesn't move. He tugs a little harder, but it still won't budge. Looking up, he sees that the lines for the sock are also wrapped around the headstay.

It takes another half hour to untangle them, by which time, he too has had enough. When he puts the sail away, I hear him mutter, "I will never again raise this sail during a passage!"

We're still motoring in light winds when I come on watch at 0800 next morning. Dave now points to the wind arrow on the masthead and notes sourly, "It's stuck!" When we first moved onto the boat, I insisted that I would do the mast work, but hadn't fixed this problem when I had the chance. I glance repeatedly at the top of the mast as the morning progresses, each time growing more annoyed. When Dave takes the watch at noon, I decide to try again.

Putting on shoes and gloves, I wedge a can of RP7 into a pocket and start climbing. I'm about thirty feet above the deck, when the mast starts swaying from side to side as a series of large swells rock the boat. Feeling the strain on my arms as my body swings out over the water, I hug the mast, wondering whether this had been such a good idea. As the rocking continues, I scan the empty ocean around us, and it occurs to me that I may have bitten off more than I can chew.

But when the swaying eases, I look down and see the spreader below me. Getting around it is the most difficult part of the climb, so there really is no reason not to continue. I climb up another fifteen feet and then hang off the masthead, outside the protection of cables and halyards. I work quickly, pushing the arrow around and spraying it with lubricant. Soon I'm back on deck, my arms aching, but at least the arrow is turning.

A storm brings wind and heavy rain that afternoon, and we're able to sail for four hours. It then moves on, taking the wind with it. We start the engine and are still motoring next morning, only winds are now on the nose at 5 kt, with a two-foot swell.

Dave is totally exasperated, and when he hears me stirring below calls out, "Lene, come have a look." As I enter the cockpit, he points behind us and grumbles, "I saw that sail at daybreak and the boat is catching up fast." By 0800, the boat is within half a mile and appears to be under sail.

Studying it through binoculars, Dave now reports, "It's about 45 feet long and has twin headstays; I can see the flutter of sails being raised and lowered." Becoming more incensed as the boat draws closer, he fumes, "They make a sail change as easily as shifting gears!"

His frustration then boils over, and he turns his fury on *Windy Lady*, complaining bitterly, "This good-for-nothing old tub is just too bloody slow!" He then lets fly with a stream of pent-up venom, citing a long list of design flaws as he rants on and on. When I can't listen any more, I scream back, "*If you don't like her, then sell her!*"

Glaring at me, he goes below and calls the boat on VHF radio. During their short conversation, the skipper tells him, "Yeah, the boat's called Shaman and we're out of Australia, on route from Raratonga to Suva. By the way, we've just caught two tuna."

Shortly after this conversation, the wind increases to 10 kt and shifts from WSW to SW, allowing us to set the sails again. But it's still on the bow and pushes us northward, toward a small chain of islands. The captain now groans, "First, no wind, then wind on the nose. Why can't we ever have decent winds?"

The high, looming shapes of two islands appear out of the clouds just before dark. They're uncomfortably close and I can't believe that I didn't see them earlier. Winds then gust from 10–20 kt overnight and seas are rough. When a third island appears just before midnight, Dave is forced to tack south for an hour. He loses a mile to the waypoint, which further annoys him.

When we reach the next waypoint at 0420, we're able to turn back on course. By 0800, we're making 5.5 kt in 10–15 kt winds. Two hours later, the breeze backs to the SE, and the mainsail starts blanketing the headsail. We lose steerage and *Windy Lady* wallows in a five-foot easterly swell. At noon, we drop the mainsail and pole out the headsail, then make 4 kt for the next 20 hours.

A big 3/4 moon lights up the sky that night, and with only a few clouds, it's incredibly beautiful, but the temperature drops. At midnight, the high profile of Totoya Island, 10 nm away, appears on the horizon. Two hours later, I hear metal clanging and turn to see a piece of the life-ring hanger lying on the cockpit sole. The metal has completely corroded through. Fortunately, we keep a safety line on the life ring, or might have lost it.

By morning, east winds are up to 15 kt, with a six-foot SE swell. We take down the whisker pole and reset the headsail, and soon *Windy Lady* is making a comfortable 5 kt. After estimating the distance to Suva, Dave decides to enter the harbor after dark, so we plot a series of waypoints, each checking the other's work.

At 2300, when we're 20 nm out, visibility drops to zero in heavy rain. Using GPS and radar, we sail for two hours, then motor for two more. When 9 nm out, a few lights are visible on shore, then all is dark. The clouds lift as we near the harbor entrance, and we're able to find the leads and follow them in through the reef. Once inside, we look for sailboats, then drop the anchor at 0300.

After a late breakfast next morning, Dave contacts Port Control and arranges to take *Windy Lady* to King's Wharf at 1400. A dinghy then comes alongside carrying the skipper of *Shaman*, the boat that passed us at sea. We anchored beside it last night, and even in the dark, I'd recognized the profile. He informs us, "Hey, one of us is going to have to move because my boat swings differently than most boats; there's nothing underneath it!"

Dave assures him that we'll be moving once we've cleared Customs and then asks about the boat. The skipper happily tells him, "She's 88 feet long, carries 15,000 sq. ft. of sail, and can do 12 knots in 15 knots of breeze." I think he starts to feel a little better about having it race past us.

The quarantine anchorage is sixty feet deep, and Dave now pulls in 180 feet of chain as well as the 45-pound anchor. The tide is extremely low as we motor over to King's Wharf, and he repeatedly circles through shallow water at the south end, trying to bring *Windy Lady* alongside. With the chart showing rocks on the bottom on one side, and a cement wall on the other, I work myself into quite a tizzy before he succeeds. We then anchor at the Royal Suva Yacht Club (RSYC), and end up too close to another boat and have to re-anchor.

It would be nice to report that our time in Suva is an improvement over Neiafu, but it isn't. The rain never stops. We walk downtown for groceries when we can, but mostly take taxis and wait out downpours at the RSYC, along with other cruisers. The city is much as I remember it, the traffic hectic, the wet market a favorite spot for shopping, and native Fijians still call out "Boolah" as we walk by.

We don't notice any racial tension, as Indo-Fijians quietly pursue their business and Fijians confidently go about theirs. The coup d'état that overthrew the government twelve years earlier has had a price, however, and cruise ships have stopped visiting the city. Dozens of small stalls in the handicraft complex at the waterfront are piled high with woodcarvings, woven baskets, and shell jewelry brought in from outlying villages. The venders are desperate for cash, and one young man practically gives jewelry away in order to make a sale.

Within days of our arrival, I've collected four large buckets of water off the dodger roof, and when there's a break in the weather, I sit out in the cockpit and wash clothes with a bucket and toilet plunger. A SW wind is gusting up to 20 kt, so I keep an eye on nearby boats and am astonished to see the bow of a green sailboat rear high in the air as it lunges back about ten feet. When it happens again, I call Dave, who watches for a moment, then climbs into the dinghy and motors over to collect his brother. *Moonshadow* is then anchored a few boat lengths away.

The two men chase after the boat and climb aboard, only to find the cabin locked. Unable to access the engine, they go up to the bow and let out a little more chain (all that there is). It's not much, but it settles the boat. They're still onboard when the owner returns, and he gets a little excited upon seeing them, but soon recognizes that the boat is not where he left it. The brothers then help him re-anchor.

We take the weather fax into an electronics shop, but never hear from them. Dave starts phoning in every couple of days and is finally told that it's ready, that water had seeped inside. It still doesn't work when we bring it back to the boat, so Dave checks it with a multi-meter and discovers a blown fuse, which he replaces. After re-programing the frequencies, I pick up a weak HF signal, which is normal for Suva. We never get a bill, so doubt that anything else was wrong.

Dave orders replacement parts for Otto from England, and a new foot switch for the windlass from New Zealand. While we wait, he buys some tools and spends a morning working on the windlass. With the foredeck rolling and bobbing, it's not a good day. He breaks his new extractor trying to remove the broken bolt, and the side of the housing breaks off when he attempts to drill out the hole.

The two orders arrive within two days of each other, so we take the boat papers down to the Post Office to collect them, then proceed to the King's Wharf office of the Boarding Officer. When Dave steps up and places his two small parcels on the counter, the officer takes one look and says, "Oh no, now I've got a problem. I am required to place these articles on your boat!"

Seeing Dave's look of protest, he hastily explains, "I can't let you carry these parcels out through the gate. I've already been in trouble for doing that." Recalling that Customs Officers chased us down the street when we picked up the weather fax, I have no problem believing his story. Still, Dave tries to reason with him, explaining, "I need the switch in that New Zealand package in order to raise the anchor."

The officer has heard it all before and responds, "You can get a Customs Officer to deliver them for a fee of $160, or you can get an engineer's certificate to confirm the boat can't be moved."

"But the two parcels together aren't worth $160!"

Shrugging his shoulders, the man replies, "I agree, but these are the procedures and I have to follow them."

When we continue standing there, looking like we've taken root, he relents and asks, "Do you have a dinghy?" As we really don't want to bring the boat back over to the wharf, Dave seizes on the suggestion and agrees to return in the dinghy.

As the days go by, clouds descend on the hills and rain obscures the city, isolating us in a small circle of yachts. The water in the harbor turns a chocolate brown, with a strong ebb current, and the radio reports that one part of the city is under four feet of water. Brian bakes a cake for Dave's 60th birthday, but is unable to deliver it.

After eleven miserable days, the sun shines for one day, then it rains so hard for three days that we're bailing out the dinghy twice a day. A few days later, a front passes over top of us and the heavens open up. It's the worst weather we've seen since the cyclones in New Zealand. Rain seeps in the masthead and runs down onto the galley floor, and also comes in around the window over the chart table. With winds gusting up to 25 kt, boats are dragging all over the anchorage. High waves now cause the dinghy to start bucking, with the bow leaping higher than the toe rail, so during the next respite from the wind, we bring the engine aboard.

With all the water coming from the sky, the outside of the boat should have been washed clean, but isn't. The wind carries dust and ash from a nearby landfill, and the rain brings down diesel and exhaust fumes from the air. When I scrub the teak on the cockpit floor, I brush up a layer of mud. I also notice a black, oily film in the clear plastic hoses that run from the dodger roof drains to my buckets; every week, the bottom foot of each one needs to be cleaned. Large iridescent pools of fuel drift about the harbor too, bringing the heavy smell of diesel into the cabin, and we're told that the mud on the bottom is so toxic that the galvanizing on the anchor will be gone in three weeks.

Although we try to maintain some normalcy in our days, I feel like a prisoner confined to quarters. I spend hours sitting in the cockpit, staring at the rain, counting the boats in the anchorage (from 24 to 42), and studying the assorted weather gear worn by people passing in their dinghies. If anyone anchors nearby, I watch critically, as a few boats drag in every squall that has winds over 20 kt.

One morning, Brian stops by and tells us that they're leaving; they've had all the rain they can take. Dave tells him that our chores are nearly complete, and we won't be far behind. A few days later, a plume of grey smoke rises from two fish boats rafted up to a mooring buoy at the edge of the anchorage. A work crew had been stripping their interiors. The smoke gets thicker and darker, and soon tongues of flame are visible. The flames pose no threat to nearby boats, but a thick cloud of toxic black smoke drifts over a few that are downwind. Eventually, a tug arrives and pumps a single column of water and foam onto the fire; when it's under control, they attach a line and tow it away.

We check out on a Friday afternoon and find six people crowded into the small Customs office at the dock. By the time the lone agent gets to us, it's 1545, fifteen minutes after closing. The officer doesn't even look at the two sets of forms Dave has completed in triplicate, just hands over our clearance. Looking a little bewildered, Dave protests, "Don't you have to enter us into your log?"

The officer responds impatiently, "Get! Get! We'll do it Monday!" Waving us out with his hands, he follows us through the door and locks it behind him.

CHAPTER 27

A Challenging Season Comes to an End

The sky is dark and overcast when we prepare the boat next morning. I have no idea what weather to expect during the 800-nm crossing to Noumea, as the HF signal has been too weak to pick up any forecasts. But when we exit from the channel through the reef, *Windy Lady* is pummeled by east winds of 25–30 kt and tossed in all directions by eight-foot seas.

An Australian warship, the *Fremantle*, comes out behind us, climbing up onto waves and dropping down into troughs. She looks most uncomfortable and I feel sorry for the crew, wondering how many sailors will miss dinner that night.

With winds on the stern, we set the headsail, but continue to motor and charge batteries. Seas are extremely rough, and two hours out, I hear a metallic clanging and turn to see a stainless-steel bolt lying on the cockpit floor. I look at it suspiciously, knowing it means trouble, then call down to the captain.

Dave quickly homes in on the radar-dome platform that hangs off the backstay; he can see two holes where bolts are missing. As I watch nervously, he climbs up on the coaming to take a closer look, but can't quite reach it. Stepping down and thinking aloud, he murmurs, "We can't leave it like that, but I'll have to stand on the railing to replace them."

I immediately freak out and screech, "Look at the way we're bouncing around. "You'll be so busy hanging on, you won't be able to work. If you try, you'll end up overboard!" As we stand glaring at each other, I see an island behind him and desperately plead, "At least, let's pull into the lee of the island!"

When he agrees, I turn the boat toward the channel leading into Beqa Lagoon. We've been here before, and as soon as we find calm water, he climbs up onto the stern railing and replaces the bolts; two hours later, we're back on course.

A light rain falls just before sunset, then the sky clears, the stars come out, and a big, almost full moon rises over the horizon. It's a beautiful night, the first we've seen in weeks. At 2130, with batteries charged, Dave shuts down the engine and sets the headsail. Otto now does the steering, working much better with new parts, and we make 5 kt for the next 15 hours, although the boat rolls uncomfortably.

The sky is overcast come morning, and at 0800, we log 115 nm. As the day progresses, the winds ease and clouds grow darker. Heavy rain falls during the afternoon and the wind then dies, leaving *Windy Lady* rocking uncomfortably in seven-foot swells. By sunset, the swells are down to three feet, but hit us broadside and the rocking continues.

Overnight, winds are light and variable and we drift along at 2 kt. When Dave doesn't appear at 0400 for his watch, I let him sleep, doubting that I'll be able to get any. He appears an hour later and starts the engine. With a steady forward movement, the ride is much smoother, and surprisingly, I sleep soundly for three hours. When

I return to the cockpit at 0800, the morning is grey and quiet, with light winds and four-foot seas. Static on the HF frequency still makes it impossible to hear or print a weather report. We log 73 nm for Day 2.

We shut the engine down at 1400, when SSE winds increase to 10 kt. Two hours later, winds are steady at 20–25 kt, gusting to 35, and Otto is overpowered by eight-foot swells. The winds hit 40 kt during the night, and the sea dumps buckets of water onto the rear seats, where I sit. A light rain then falls for a while, but not enough to wash away the layer of salt that coats the cockpit floor. It is enough, however, to lift the dirt out of the teak boards and turn it into mud. At 0800, we log 147 nm for Day 3.

With winds at 20–30 kt from the SE, we now have three reefs in the main and four in the headsail. Nine-foot-high waves that sound like freight trains are roaring up on the port quarter, breaking at the stern or amidships, and keeping the deck awash. *Windy Lady* makes 7 kt for the next twelve hours, by which time, the head hatch is leaking and seawater seeps in at the bottom of the mast. The winds then ease a bit and we average 6 kt for the following twelve hours. At 0800, we log 155 nm for Day 4.

Winds are now gusting from 15–30 kt from the ESE, so we drop the mainsail and run with two reefs in the headsail. The sea continues to dump buckets of water into the cockpit, and I reluctantly move from a rear seat to a side bench, as my wet weather gear isn't keeping me dry. I then sit with my back to the wind, and brace my feet against the opposite seat for support.

At some point, I move back to adjust Otto's settings and notice that the nut is loose on the bolt that Dave replaced in Suva. Astonishingly, I make no attempt to tighten it myself, just call the captain. Crawling from his berth, he digs out a crescent wrench, gives the nut a twist, and with a murderous look in his eyes, disappears below.

That afternoon, winds veer to the SE, still gusting from 15–30 kt. Waves are now over ten feet high and incredibly rough, so we put two more reefs in the headsail. Overnight, a few stars appear between rain showers, and by daybreak, winds are from the east at 15–25 kt. At 0800, we log 141 nm for Day 5.

We are now within striking distance of Havannah Pass and need to slow the boat. I furl in most of the headsail at the start of my morning watch, leaving out just enough to maintain steerage. During the afternoon, we backwind both sails, and basically hove to, *Windy Lady* turns broadside to the swells, rolling easily, and we drift for two hours. While we relax, a bit of sun pokes through the clouds. By sunset, the sky has cleared, seas have eased some, and the temperature is almost pleasant.

Winds gust up to 30 kt overnight, but at daybreak are down to 10–15 kt from the east, and low cloud sits over the island. We enter the pass with the tide, under sail, but have the engine running on standby. We are barely through the reef when a grey, misty rain sets in, hiding the islands and calming the sea. We furl the sail and continue motoring through the winding channel that leads to Noumea.

Dave talks to Brian on VHF radio and learns that *Moonshadow* is at anchor 15 nm ahead, in a bay that is really just a widening of the channel. As it's September 4, Brian's birthday, he bakes a date loaf on the way in. We raft up beside them and he produces it at dinner that night. As we can't check in on the weekend, we stay over a day, relaxing and visiting. We learn that both our passages were rough and fast; we logged 755 nm in six days.

I put my yak board in the water and paddle around the bay that afternoon, noticing extensive erosion in the low hills nearby. Steep gullies with six-foot banks end at the high-water mark, and the sea bottom is littered with rubble, mostly boulders from what I can see. A few birds twitter in the undergrowth, and a sweet smell drifts down on a light breeze, coming from somewhere upslope of the mangos that line the shore.

We check into the marina in Noumea on Monday and spend most of the afternoon dealing with officials. The next morning, the dock crew pushes an Aussie boat in beside us; I'd heard the skipper talking to Des on the radio the night we arrived. He now tells us that they waited out strong winds in the Loyalty Islands, then their engine wouldn't start and they had to be towed in.

Another morning, we see a small, wooden boat tied up across the dock; the top half of its mast is lashed to the deck. The skipper says that he ran into an island, explaining, "I was under sail and went below about 2300 to make a cut of tea; soon after, the mast struck a rock face that sloped out over the water."

The weather in Noumea is a big improvement over Suva, with lots of blue sky and sunshine, but it's not that warm and the city is expensive. Dave and I continue to disagree about everything, getting angry over nothing, and now that we're in port have the luxury of not speaking for days. We then learn about people with real problems.

The skipper of an Australian boat, *Moody Blue*, goes missing and is located in hospital, unconscious, with no ID. Reportedly, he was drinking at the Yacht Club Bar, then wandered off downtown late at night. He was found in an alley, having been mugged, although police are quick to point out that he could have fallen on his own. He lasts barely 48 hours, and his parents arrive from France just in time to say goodbye. The young couple crewing on the boat are part owners, but novice sailors, and Noumea was their first port of call on a round-the-world cruise.

I now start studying weather faxes, looking for wind to take us the 800 nm to Brisbane, Australia. I don't want a repeat of our previous crossing, when the boat had rolled uncomfortably in high waves and light winds for days. After only two weeks in port, we set off for the pass through the reef. Strong currents then overpower the autopilot and we hand steer for four hours. I have to wonder, *could strong winds at sea be responsible?*

It's raining heavily when we exit through the passage, and *Windy Lady* is immediately hit by 20–30 kt winds from the SE, and ten-foot-high waves. We hang onto whatever's handy until she settles down, then pull out the headsail, put in two reefs, and shut down the engine. After turning the bow WSW, winds are abaft the beam on the port side, and conditions remain much the same for the next two days.

At 0800 the first morning, we log 136 nm for Day 1. When I start my watch, Dave cheerfully tells me, "I saw a large bird just after daybreak; I think it was an albatross."

I respond, "They're supposed to be good luck for sailors, aren't they?" and he nods his head in agreement.

But as I settle into my watch, ESE winds are gusting from 15–25 kt and rain is pouring down. Ten-foot-high swells continue to dump water onto the rear seats in the cockpit, so I sit on a side bench, my feet braced against the seat on the lower side. I steer using reciprocal numbers on the compass, and I'm bored because the only view is down into the ocean depths behind us.

By noon, the wind gauge is regularly reading into the mid-thirties, seas are well over ten feet, and Otto needs constant attention. Dave sees gusts of 48 kt that afternoon, and during my sunset watch, 43-kt gusts have *Windy Lady* rolling heavily. When my weight starts to transfer onto my feet, I recall the previous owner claiming that he'd never been able to put the toe rail in the water. A few minutes, I'm horrified at the sight of blue-green seawater pouring over the side of the boat into the cockpit.

Before I can react, *Windy Lady* is upright and several inches of water sloshing around the cockpit floor are draining out through the scuppers. I know I should close the companionway to keep water from going below but can't bring myself to move. (I later estimate that the toe rail must have been a foot under water for the sea to run in around the rear winch.)

At 0800 next morning, we log 128 nm for Day 2. SE winds are now down to 15–20 kt and seas are under seven feet. The rear seats are dry when I start my watch, and I happily reclaim my seat. Sitting under the dodger roof may have kept me dry, but I'd felt isolated from the action, a spectator. Now, with open sea and a big sky spread out before me, I contentedly study the sails, the clouds, the waves, and occasionally a bird or two.

The winds ease during the afternoon, and it's really very pleasant, with the sun peeping through the clouds and seas down to five feet. The rain washed much of the salt from the cockpit, and it's no longer grimy, although some did track down into the cabin. At sunset, fluffy trade-wind clouds are scattered across the sky, and *Windy Lady* is making 6 kt, with 15 kt of breeze and a following sea. A big, full moon now rises in the east, its rays lighting a pathway across the water, then lighting up the night sky. We make good time, and at 0800 log 133 nm for Day 3.

The morning is sunny and warm, and I'm feeling well rested when I start my watch. Overnight, my berth had been more like a cradle that a threshing machine. About midday, SE winds increase to 15–20 kt, and we raise the mainsail for the first time on this crossing. Otto requires constant assistance, but we make better time. A big, full moon lights up the sky again that night, and it isn't as cold.

The morning that follows is gorgeous, with gently rolling blue waters and skies so clear, it seems that I can see into eternity. Conditions remain the same for most of the next 40 hours, and we log 126, 120, and 132 nm on Days 4, 5, and 6.

The sky is overcast and the air cool as we approach the north end of Moreton Island. Currents are strong as we follow GPS waypoints around Flinders Reef to the NE passage, and half a dozen dolphins lead us in, small graceful creatures that ride the bow wave. A huge expanse of aquamarine water extends over sandbars to the lighthouse, and I marvel at how shallow the water is. The tide is out and the depth gauge reads twenty feet at the first marker buoy.

We motor sail for seven hours as we cross Moreton Bay to Scarborough Marina. The day remains cool, but we have hot water with the engine running and luxuriate in baths in the cockpit. Customs officers are gone when we arrive, so we're locked behind the gate on the Customs' dock overnight. *Moonshadow* is three hours behind us, and Dave calls Brian on VHF radio and gives him waypoints to the marina. He then guides him to the berth with a flashlight and takes the lines as he rafts up beside us.

We were at sea 6.5 days on this crossing, so lopped 2.5 days off our previous time. In all, we were away 110 days, spent 40 of them at sea, and sailed 4,272 nm.

CHAPTER 28
Finding a New Direction

When we return to the Moreton Bay Boat Club at the end of September, 1999, *Windy Lady* needs a lot of work. We don't rush into it, instead spend our time visiting with cruisers on the dock, having buffet dinners at the RSL Club, and working out at the gym. There's lots to talk about, as the news that summer is worrisome.

In mid-November, an Aussie sailboat, *Aphrodite*, is attacked off the coast of Yemen. We know the family, as they spent time here in the marina. The youngest, a tow-headed, five-year-old boy named Martin, spent all his time catching minnows and was a fixture on the dock. He would approach anyone who came by, saying, "Excuse me, excuse me, do you want to see my fish?"

The father had built the boat himself and was taking it to Europe to sell. His wife and two children were with him. Five men pumped over 100 bullets through the hull and portholes during the attack, terrorizing the family. Thankfully, no one was physically injured, but the boat was badly damaged and had to be towed into port.

Before Christmas, a terrifying incident occurs to a family camped on Moreton Island. The father wakes to find a python curled around his six-year-old-son, trying to swallow him; he successfully fights it off. Our friends on Limbo, who are anchored in Cairns, then have an electrical fire onboard, which pretty much destroys the inside of the boat.

Over Christmas, we hear from cruisers who've just sailed up the Red Sea; one boat took two months and was sandblasted all the way. None of the boats make the trip sound interesting. On January 1, 2000, the Y2K bug fizzles out and is never again mentioned. For weeks, if not months, news reports had predicted that it would cause financial markets to collapse, electricity grids to fail, and airplanes to fall from the sky. Another Aussie yacht is then attacked by pirates off Yemen and a woman is shot.

It's now apparent that Dave and I have lost our way. I'm spending two-three hours in the early mornings walking on the beach, while he finds companionship at the club, even spending New Year's Eve there on his own. We clearly no longer share the motivation that took us across the Pacific Ocean to Australia, and without a definite plan, we just drift.

One morning, as I stop to watch the sun rise over Moreton Island, I seriously consider returning to Canada. But going to sea has changed my life, and I can't imagine going back. *Windy Lady* is now my home, and as long as I am here, there is always the hope of making another crossing.

We eventually get around to discussing options for the upcoming cruising season, and perhaps to humor me, Dave seems interested in sailing to the Philippines. I spend weeks with charts, pilots, cruising guides, and inventory lists, but when it's time to start preparing the boat, he reneges.

He now learns that his daughter is getting married in Cancun at the end of March and plans a trip back to Canada, with a stop in Mexico. It's not easy to get there from Brisbane, and the travel agent recommends going around the world. We opt to stop off in Hong Kong, Istanbul, Jersey, and Cancun, and when we arrive in Vancouver, we separate and visit our respective families.

The first week of May is gone when we return to Scarborough, and most cruising boats are ready to leave for the season. We have the boat hauled, antifoul the bottom, and have the windlass and dodger roof repaired. Although Dave says nothing, his leg, groin, and hip are bothering him. (He has hip surgery in India in 2007.)

Ten days after we return, another coup d'état takes place in Fiji, with reports of rioting and looting in the streets of Suva. Hostages are held for eight weeks and the army eventually declares martial law. In early June, a coup takes place in the Solomon Islands, with armed men take over the government in Honiara. Four days later, the Australian Navy is evacuating nationals from Guadalcanal. Cruising boats in the area buddy up for safety, and Dave now isn't interested in sailing anywhere.

Given all the unrest in this part of the world, he decides that a berth at the Moreton Bay Boat Club would be a good investment. As soon as he buys one, however, another cruising couple who own a berth come to talk to him. They've studied the club documents and financial statements and are worried about the organization's solvency, and whether they could be liable for its debts. There's also the matter of recently implemented live-aboard fees, which we all now pay.

Dave's interest immediately turns to the club's operations, which include poker machines, bar, and marina. As a member, he questions the information provided, and because he's an accountant, he's soon meeting with club directors. Work on the boat comes to a halt, and we're nowhere near ready to leave when the boat permit expires on June 30, 2000. After a one-month extension, we still aren't ready. We meet with Customs and renew the permit for a year; if we're not gone then, a bond will have to be posted or taxes paid.

As Dave becomes more involved with the club, I'm drawn into the process too. It's quickly clear that staff are untrained and that controls over cash receipts and bar inventory need to be tightened up. But club politics get in the way of operational accountability, and the board of directors split, people are fired, and even less competent ones hired. I don't understand these Aussies, so wash my hands of the whole affair, but he continues to be involved.

By December, we're talking about sailing *Windy Lady* back to Canada. We could continue on a round-the-world trajectory by going to Thailand and through the Red Sea, or by crossing the Indian Ocean to South Africa. The fastest route would be north to Japan and east across the Pacific. I put together some information on this route, but when Dave sees how often the area is hit by typhoons, he's not interested.

Instead, he suggests visiting my brother in Chile, and our focus shifts. We plan a second around-the-world airplane trip, this time stopping in Bangkok, Athens, Lisbon, Rio de Janeiro, and La Paz, then going overland through Bolivia, Peru, and Chile. (These stories are in my third book.)

We're away four months and return in mid-May of 2001. As Dave is still unwilling to pay the taxes on the boat, we have to be out of the country by the end of July. Deciding that we'll sail up to Thailand, we haul the boat and antifoul the bottom. I then keep busy provisioning the boat and poring through reference material. It's 4,500 nm from Brisbane to Phuket, and 1,400 nm of that is through the Great Barrier Reef.

Dave is still more interested in the sailing club than the boat, and it occurs to me that, given the right circumstances, he'd say in Australia. But, a few days before our scheduled departure date, he arranges for Keith, the Car Doctor, to curb the car. (He's to keep 10% of the proceeds and deposit the rest into our bank account.) He also sells the berth at the boat club to the couple in the slip beside us.

On the morning of July 22, 2001, we untie the boat and motor away from the marina for the last time. Dave still shows no enthusiasm, but I'm more than ready to move on. We don't even make it out of Moreton Bay before the engine overheats. We raise the sails while Dave checks it out, and he assures me, "Not to worry, the lid on the header tank wasn't on properly, so I've added water."

With winds steady at 10–15 kt from the SE and a three-foot easterly swell, we sail about 10 nm off Fraser Island as we head north. Overnight, a few squalls bring 25-kt gusts and rain showers, but by 0730, we're becalmed. When Dave now starts the engine, it again overheats. This time, he doesn't know what's wrong. We've then been out 24 hours and are 120 nm from the marina.

After studying our charts, we decide that Mooloolaba, 80 nm to the south, would be the easiest harbor to enter under sail. With light winds, the overnight trip is long and slow, and when we're 11 nm out, the breeze dies. When the engine won't start, Dave calls the Mooloolaba Coast Guard on VHF radio. *Windy Lady* is taken under tow at 1030, and two hours later, she's tied up to a dock at the yacht club. A Coast Guard crew member comes aboard and demands a *donation* of $200, which we happily pay.

Dave phones a diesel mechanic from the marina office, and while we wait, he manually cranks the engine, satisfying himself that it's not seized up. Ian arrives at 1800 and checks the fan belts, saying they're likely the problem. He also inspects the starter motor and finds a dirty, loose terminal, so starts the engine by doing *a dead start.*

Expecting him to return next morning, Dave is up early and removes the two v-belts. Ian doesn't appear until noon the following day. After discussing a course of action, he then goes off to lunch. He later drops off two new belts, but work doesn't begin until the third day.

The two men systematically go through the engine, replacing fan belts, freshwater pump, thermostat—and still it overheats. They finally disconnect the heat exchanger and find a wad of tape trailing from the exit port down into the hose. They figure the tape was used to join hoses of different sizes and are confident that it's the problem.

The heat exchanger is sent off for an overnight acid bath, and when re-installed next day, water temperature readings are normal. They now replace sensors and gauges for water and oil temperatures, but can't get the gauges at the inside steering station and cockpit to work at the same time. Dave finally installs a switch, so readings can be directed one way or the other.

There's not much I can do while this is going on, so spend my time walking. It's only fifteen minutes to the store downtown and I go every day. There's also a pleasant trail leading across a boardwalk under the trees near the ocean. When I wander farther afield, I come across an attractive beach promenade that I don't recall seeing when here in 1997. Hotels and sidewalk cafes line a winding drive across from a wide beach where blue waters roll up and break on white sands.

After sixteen days in Mooloolaba, we again start the journey north. With winds from the SSE at 10–12 kt, we raise the sails and *Windy Lady* makes 4 kt all that day. Winds begin to ease as night falls, and by daylight, she's down to one knot. I then spend my morning watch staring at the same sand hills on Fraser Island, which are unusually clear and sharp in the still air.

We start the engine at noon and are soon rounding the top end of the island, where a strong, south-flowing current mixes in with the SE swell. We then alternate between sailing and motoring every twelve hours for the next two days. One night, we see the lights of container ships anchored in 200 feet of water, and the next morning, two whales surface about 200 feet off the stern.

At noon on Day 4, Dave poles out the headsail when the winds ease and is able to keep on sailing. A fast-moving squall then hits the boat at sunset, blowing the bow off course and backwinding the sail. A pin is bent on the whisker pole in the process, and he spends an hour working on it. Forty minutes later, the darkness grows blacker and rain pummels the deck, then the sky clears.

For the next 36 hours, winds are steady at 10–15 kt from the E and ESE, and *Windy Lady* makes between 4 and 5 knots. With Otto working well, we concentrate on staying exactly on our route line, as there won't be much room to deviate from it in the narrow shipping channels farther north. We obviously need practice, as we're a mile off at one point.

At noon on Day 6, winds are gusting at 15–25 kt from the SE, and two hours later, they're over 30 kt. As we're not far from Hook Island in the Whitsundays, we head for a nearby anchorage. The sea is wild for the last four miles, with waves rolling *Windy Lady* far over onto her sides and washing over the dodger roof. After we're safely anchored, I spend half an hour wiping off the salt crystals that coat the windows, handrails, and cockpit surfaces.

We finish tidying the boat about 1630, and as we relax with drinks in the cockpit, a dinghy appears alongside. The two men in it tell us that they're roasting a leg of lamb in their motor sailor and invite us to dinner. Dave enthusiastically accepts. We're picked up in the dinghy at 1845, and once onboard, we meet the six blokes in residence.

The men are from Brisbane and, except for one man's son, are all over age sixty. Two of them are owners, and they're here for a week. We're told that the boat is brought up to the Whitsunday Islands for three months each year. We enjoy their company and the lamb, served with plenty of wine, is delicious. At the end of the meal, a huge block of Roquefort cheese is produced, bigger than anything I've ever seen.

Mostly, the men are curious about our lifestyle, and we really have to stop and think as they pepper us with questions. They don't understand how, at our age, we could just give up our lives and go sailing. Dave finally tells them, "We were just like you, no different, but we made the decision to go and never regretted it."

Someone then asks, "What will you do when you quit sailing?" When we tell them we've been out six years, they're even more curious. "Why do you keep going?" "Haven't you accomplished what you set out to do?"

I respond, "What's the alternative? Go home and get old?"

With the weather warm and sunny, we stay in the Whitsundays for eight nights. I put my yak board in the water most days and explore reef and shoreline. We hear a whale one morning and spot it about 150 feet from the boat. It then exhales three more times while rocking back and forth, revealing about ten feet of back from blow hole to dorsal fin. The back then curves, the tail flukes rise up out of the water, and it disappears. I sit and watch for an hour as it surfaces a few more times.

Other than a large school of eight-inch, yellow-tail tuna fingerlings sheltering beneath the boat, there aren't many fish about. We do see turtles, however, and one has a shell over three feet long. When I first see its beak poking out of the water, the curved, colored lines on the neck make me think of some strange prehistoric creature.

Occasionally, we hear squawking and see white cockatoos flying high up against the green shrubbery of Mount Hook, while kookaburras call at sunrise and sunset, their raucous laughter seeming out of place in a seascape. At 1700, the sun sets behind low hills to the west, the water frequently calms, and it's extraordinarily peaceful.

As we wait for a southeasterly flow to take us up the coast, Dave discovers that a bolt on the steering ram has sheared off, then the dinghy engine develops a fuel leak. We decide to do repairs in Townsville, 140 nm to the north, and not waiting for wind, we leave early on a calm, peaceful morning. Unfortunately, we leave at low tide, so have adverse currents for six hours.

After motoring for two hours, winds pick up from the NNE at 8—12 kt and we raise the sails. The sea is rough, with three-foot waves hitting *Windy Lady* on the beam, but we sail through the night. The winds die come morning and we motor for the last three hours, then see another whale as we round Cape Cleveland. Lazing on the surface, it blows and rolls forward and back, then disappears for a few seconds before re-surfacing. It hardly seems aware of us as we pass.

CHAPTER 29
Tropical Bodies

After finding our way into the fuel dock at Breakwater Marina, we settle *Windy Lady* into a temporary berth, then walk downtown for groceries. It's a pleasant fifteen-minute walk to Flinders Mall and five minutes more to the grocery store at Woolworths. We don't rush back. Next morning, after we've hosed down the deck and hull, Dave sets the dinghy motor up in the cockpit and drains out the fuel. Before he's finished, a bloke appears alongside and introduces himself. "Hi, I'm Philip. I was in the office yesterday and heard you asking about outboard repairs. Is there anything I can help you with?"

After a brief discussion, Dave gives him the job of repairing the engine, but he isn't able to finish as new parts are required. Two days later, on a Monday, Phillip picks up most of what he needs, but two seals have to be ordered. Meanwhile, Dave spends the morning removing the steering ram, which is picked up, repaired, and returned that afternoon. On Friday, we're told that the seals have been lost in the mail.

Conscious that time is slipping away and Thailand still a long way off, we wonder aloud about staying in Darwin over cyclone season. When the locals hear that, they shake their heads and tell us, "Bad idea!" They then explain, "During the wet, it rains for months in Darwin and the humidity causes mold to grow inside boats. Townsville is a lot drier, and a lot safer during cyclone season."

Philip has moved on by the time the seals show up the following week, but leaves a sketch of the engine for Dave to follow. He studies it and all the pieces, but ends up having to order another seal, and so another week goes by. We then wake up on September 12 to news of the attacks on the Twin Towers in New York City.

I think everyone knows instantly that the world has changed forever. People spend hours glued to television sets, and without one, we listen to radio reports. We then hear that cruising boats are returning to Australia from South East Asia. No one knows what is going to happen next, and after talking to Customs, we're allowed to remain in the country for another year. We start paying moorage by the month, and as cyclones do hit the area, we buy boat insurance for the first time.

The marina is really very pleasant, with Castle Hill just behind it and a man-made waterfall spilling down across the road. We are less than a block from Tebruk Pool, a beautiful 50-meter facility that we visit frequently. As it has no sunshade, we swim before 1000 or after 1600, as does everyone else. The lanes are busy and even in the slow lane, these Aussies pass me by; they really do like to swim.

When we walk downtown, we cross through Anzak Park, which is more tropical than we're used to, with green grass and huge banyan trees. We often see ibis, cockatoos, and parakeets, and one of the trees catches my eye, too, as roots grow from branches down to the ground, forming a six-foot-high wall. After leaving the park, we walk past *the strip*, where tourists spend their evenings in bars and restaurants. A nearby creek is used by boats to access a basin upstream, and the sight of a large boat drifting between buildings with no sign of water anywhere is a bit startling to say the least.

That brings us to the two-block-long Flinders Mall, which has many small stores and is full of trees, flowers, and fountains. The plumeria (frangipani) trees seem to bloom from October to February, so their fragrance drifts down the street for weeks. Here we find a good gym and a movie theater, but there are also many empty buildings, as businesses and government offices have moved out of the downtown area.

I don't think we miss a Sundy morning market at the mall while we're here. Strolling past stalls lining both sides of the street, we inspect glass butterflies, garden gnomes, didgeridoos, drums, wood carvings, t-shirts, cookies, fresh fruits, and vegetables. Dave's arms are then stretched to the limit as he packs home rock melons and pineapples.

We manage quite well without a car, but in early December, Dave buys two used bikes and helmets for $150. We don't do much riding initially, as the temperature hits 38 degrees over Christmas. The NE wind then dies at nightfall, the surface of the water turns glassy, and heat retained by the boat hull moves inward. Sometimes the low setting on the fans doesn't even stir the air, and sleep is impossible without them.

We start riding the bikes regularly in January, and one morning Dave passes the bike rack on his way to the ablution block and sees that my back wheel is missing. As a new wheel costs more than he paid for the bike, we strip off a few parts and consign it to the garbage bin. He then purchases a used one from a bike shop, I inherit his old one, and we're soon biking 20–25 km in the mornings.

My riding ability quickly improves, as unlike Dave, I didn't have a bike when I was young. As I gain confidence in dealing with city traffic, I come to thoroughly enjoy the rides. The terrain is generally flat with bike lanes on all major streets; motorists are usually courteous, and the worst hazard is a door being thrown open on a parked car. Before we leave, strangers recognize us as the bike riders. When a chap sees us at the Liquor Stop, he comments, "Oh, you're those fit people I see riding down Ingham!"

Of all the good experiences we have in Townsville, the gym is the best. We join Tropical Bodies soon after we arrive and are pleased with the facility and the staff. Sean and Sharyn Muir, the young owners, are courteous and likeable; he's a world class power lifter, having competed in Finland the year before.

At the beginning of November, we start counting calories, as we've both put on weight since arriving in Australia. We work out at the gym three days a week, spending 45 minutes on weight training and 35 minutes on cardio. Two months later, Dave has lost 22 kilos and I'm down 10. According to Sean's body fat analysis, however, all our weight loss is muscle; not an ounce is fat! We question him extensively, not believing the results, and he tells us that our experience is normal; we just have to work harder on weight training.

Although unconvinced, we work hard for another two months. Sean changes our training regime, so that we max out on the last set, and sometimes require assistance. My weights in the squat go up dramatically from 65 to 105 kilos. We take a closer look at diet, too, and monitor carbohydrates, protein and fats. I'm astonished at the protein I eat and adjust my diet accordingly. When we next weigh in, Dave has lost a total of 35 kilos and his body fat measures 18%. I've lost a total of 14 kilos, and my body fat reading is down by 5%.

While we never intended to stop in Townsville, the lifestyle agrees with us and we really enjoy our ten-month stay. We feel good, and even though we wear only tee shirts and gym shorts, we look good. One day, a woman comes up behind me at the mall and astonishes me by saying, "You got nice legs, lady!" Another woman sees me on the dock one morning and exclaims, "Are your eyes ever blue!" That sense of feeling good is reflected in our relationship, and we are well on our way to being best mates again.

As April turns into May, we work on the boat. Dave paints the top sides and has an arch mounted, then installs the radar dome and a new wind turbine on top of it. We haul the boat one day, and even though it rains sporadically, paint the bottom, polish the hull, and put it back in the water the next. I also clean lockers, looking for mold and mildew, and we restock the boat with provisions for four months.

CHAPTER 30

The Great Barrier Reef and Arafura Sea

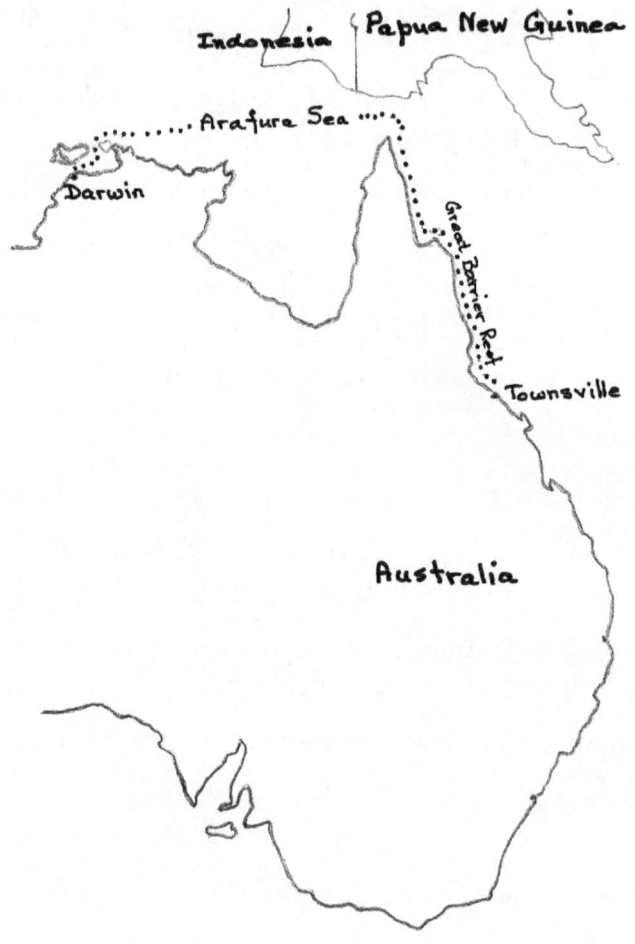

The Great Barrier Reef

We depart for Darwin on a quiet, sunny morning in late June. Although there is no wind, a deviant current in the marina causes us problems when we leave. It's strong enough that the helm doesn't respond when Dave backs *Windy Lady* from the berth. He eases the throttle forward a little, then a little more, and on the third attempt the helm responds, and the bow spins about and the stern does likewise.

Unfortunately, the boat has been creeping backwards, and because the channel between the two rows of boats is very narrow, the stern heads straight for a cement piling on the dock behind us. I just have time to fling a fender between it and the pushpit railing, and then, when the boat moves forward, the life ring and its holder are scraped off. To say Dave is annoyed is putting it mildly, and we leave the marina quickly, hoping no one has noticed.

I take the helm as we motor out past Magnetic Island, while he goes below to check on the navigation program that he recently installed on our laptop computer. He's already entered the waypoints needed to reach Cairns, and the GPS now feeds in our actual position, so the map on the screen shows both the route line ahead and the track behind. It's very reassuring to see our track appear just where it's supposed to be. The program will be particularly useful during the next six days, about 600 nm, while we're sailing through the coral reefs, shoals, and islets that lie inside the Great Barrier Reef.

We pull out the headsail when a light wind comes up, but continue motoring for six hours. We're then able to sail for 20 hours, with winds of 10–25 kt from the E and NE. We have to hand steer, however, as a five-foot swell pushing against the starboard quarter overpowers Otto.

As we near Cairns, SE winds gusting up to 30 kt push up a six-foot-high following sea. We drop the mainsail, but *Windy Lady* still surfs down the waves at 6 kt. The waves then sweep beneath the stern, turning the bow first one way then the other, and I spend my sunset watch turning the wheel from lock to lock, trying to stay on course.

At dusk, a large seabird circles around the boat, and I suspect that it's eyeing up the arch as a potential roost. Concerned that it will tangle with the wind turbine, I fling the end of a rope toward it, trying to scare it away. It ignores me. I don't see what happens next, but hear two thumps when the bird hits the arch and then the side deck. I can't see it and can't leave the helm, but ten minutes later, I hear a noise and see the bird groggily crouched beside the toe rail. Ten minutes after that I hear a splash and the bird is gone, leaving a spot of blood on the coaming and a little more on the side deck. The wind turbine is fine, so I never know what happened.

Hand steering with winds on the stern is exhausting, so we run the engine for ten hours overnight, which gives us both a chance to rest. We start sailing again at 0500, using only the headsail, with SE winds at 10–20 kt. We're now in the shipping channel, where the water is more protected, and *Windy Lady* moves along smoothly with Otto doing the steering. I have my doubts as to how well Otto will perform in its narrow confines and spend my morning watch running below to check the computer screen, confirming that we're still on course.

While in the channel, we will use the GPS to sail from waypoint to waypoint, sometimes changing direction up to three times during a watch. A few of the turns are almost ninety degrees, and there's a lot to do, so I work out a routine. When we're about .2 nm from a waypoint, I go below, bring up the next waypoint on the GPS, and determine the new heading. Rushing back to the cockpit, I adjust the sail, turn the wind vane into wind, and take control of the helm. After settling the boat on its new course, I reset the wind vane. If all goes well, the whole process takes about ten minutes, and brings a satisfying sense of accomplishment.

The weather is good as we make our way up the coast, with warm, sunny days, cool nights, and strong winds. In the late afternoon of Day 3, we're overflown by a Customs aircraft, and Dave responds to a few questions over VHF radio. Monitoring traffic in this area would seem to be an easy job. The temperature is noticeably warmer as we go into Day 4, with winds moving between south and east at 20–35 kt.

Occasionally, sea conditions overpower Otto and we have to hand steer. This happens during my midnight watch, and I'm hand steering as we approach the waypoint near the north entrance to Lizard Island. I'm about to change waypoints, when I spot navigation lights amongst the lighted buoys marking the narrow channel. Needing to look for traffic, I feel the need for help and turn on the autopilot, while softly whispering, "Sorry, Dave!" (We don't normally use the autopilot under sail because of the power it consumes. It's also very noisy, making sleep impossible.)

When we sail through Adolphus Channel on the fifth night, 35-kt winds from the ESE are pushing waves up against the starboard quarter, and Otto is again overwhelmed. Peering into a pitch-black night during my midnight watch, I try to keep the bow pointed toward a flashing light about ten miles ahead. With winds, waves, and currents turning the bow in all directions, the light bounces all over the place, and I spin the wheel from lock to lock for three hours. A sudden gust then backwinds the sail, and tired of fighting, I decide to tack. Lo and behold, Otto then comes back to life and steers us through to the next waypoint.

Dave has his own misadventure that night, coming within 100 yards of a naval vessel in the inky darkness. He explains that he misread the navigation lights and thought it was headed in the opposite direction. Two hours before dawn, we're approaching Blackwood Bay on Adolphus Island and still fighting currents. The navigation program takes us in safely, and we have no problem anchoring in the dark. We have a fast trip, taking five days to sail 632 nm. A catamaran follows us in about mid-morning and three sailboats arrive two days later.

We have a number of maintenance issues to check while we're here, as the icebox isn't working, we have no hot water, and the wind turbine is causing a vibration. The first three markers have rotted off the chain, too, and I couldn't tell how much I was letting out when we anchored. The bikes are another problem. We didn't want to leave them behind, so they're tied to the lifelines and the chains are already coated with rust.

While Dave unsuccessfully works on the icebox, I dig out the flagging tape and replace the missing markers on the chain. We then tighten up the lifelines, which seem to be the source of the vibration, and check the bolts in the new arch while we're at it.

Dave figures there's an airlock in the freshwater system, which is why we have no hot water. As the water circulates in the hoses of the heating system, he decides to start the furnace. When waves of smoke waft up the companionway, I think of *Limbo* and freak out, but he only shuts it off when it doesn't accomplish what he wants. He then recalls filling the cooling system in Townsville and checks his journal. He starts the engine and is able to add five liters of coolant, and the next time he runs the engine, we have hot water.

One morning, the skipper on the catamaran gets on the VHF radio and tells everyone that he saw a crocodile when he was up the mast. Later that day, Dave feels the need for some exercise and rows over to a small cove in the dinghy, where he sees a dark shape a foot wide and six feet long under the water; he doesn't stay to investigate. Meanwhile, a couple of Kiwis crewing on a boat swim several hundred meters to another boat and then return.

From Mt Adolphus, it is 770 nm to Darwin, and we leave at first light on July 6, heading northwest on an outgoing tide. We motor, as we have seven hours to transit through 35 nm of reefs in the Torres Strait before the tide changes direction. With SE winds at 10 kt, we also set the headsail. The tides here are large, with strong currents, and we average 7.7 kt over the first four hours. We exceed 10 kt for half an hour and hit a top speed of 10.8 kt off Hammond Rock in Prince of Wales Channel.

When we enter the broad waters of the Arafura Sea, winds are from the east at 10 kt, the water is flat, and we drift along using the headsail. We soon pass over a shallow section that is only fifty feet deep, which is a bit creepy. The wind strengthens early in the afternoon, but the sail flogs in five-foot-high seas, so Dave sets the whisker pole. At change of watch at midnight, we're out on the foredeck taking the pole down as winds gust to 25 kt. At 0800, we log 138 nm for Day 1.

I'm delighted to be back in open water when I start my watch that morning, even though I've had only two hours sleep. Winds are steady at 15–25 kt from the SE and seas are a bit rough, but the day is gorgeous. Puffy clouds sail overhead, whitecaps dot the sea, and a freshness in the breeze offsets the heat of the sun. As the morning progresses, flying fish soar from waves near the bow, a black fin pokes up out of the water alongside, and occasionally a bird flies low in the troughs. Reportedly, there are lots of fish in these waters, which are shared by Australia and Indonesia.

I nap for a bit during Dave's afternoon watch, then am back in the cockpit as the day ends. As I watch the sun sink below the horizon, I feel a sense of peace, that all is right with the world. Jupiter is now visible high in the sky, and as darkness steals across the water, the heavens fill with stars. Overnight, winds drop to 10-15 kt and the sea isn't as rough. An orangey-green crescent moon rises above the horizon at 0400, and at 0800, we log 115 nm.

Wind speed remains about the same on Day 3, but it moves between SE and E, and seas are rougher. The temperature in the cabin reaches 30 C. During my evening watch, a good-sized seabird attempts to land on top of the mast. Starting low over the water, it flies straight up for fifty feet, then strains every muscle and feather to hover long enough to settle onto the swaying masthead. With flapping wings that resemble human arms bent at the elbows, each individual tail and wing feather is outlined against the dying evening light. It tries three times, but doesn't succeed.

The bird makes another pass over the cockpit after dark, and a few minutes later, I hear squawking overhead. Shining my flashlight beam upward, I see the bird clinging to the crossbar of the spreader, wings flapping desperately as it tries to remain upright. Two shrouds (cables supporting the mast) and a halyard are stretched nearby, and when I check five minutes later, it looks like a wing is draped around one of them. The bird soon gives up and flies away.

When seas drop to three feet during the night, Otto works better, and we get more sleep. Next morning, we log 104 nm. Dave now talks on VHF radio to the captains of two boats that left Adolphus Island the same day we did, but are sailing along the coast. Reception is terrible initially, but once we ensure that wind turbine, computer, inverter, and fluorescent cabin lights are turned off, the static disappears.

One skipper reports that he made 175 nm the day before, which causes Dave to foam at the mouth. He comes up on deck venting his spleen, enraged by how slow *Windy Lady* is. We then go through the exercise of raising the mainsail, but it blankets the headsail, which then flogs. The boat speed remains the same, but now Otto needs help with the steering.

Dave is obviously frustrated when we lower the mainsail, but our relationship has improved enough that I feel we can talk about it. I first observe, "You seem to think that the wind vane should work like the autopilot, that it should steer in a set direction regardless of wind and sea conditions." When he doesn't respond, I bring up another topic, one that we've been avoiding for two years.

"David, what are we doing out here? You're not happy and seem to be either completely frustrated or bored to death, all the time!" When he doesn't answer, I continue, "Look, if you really hate passage-making so much, maybe we should have *Windy Lady* trucked back to Brisbane when we get to Darwin."

He just turns and goes below, and I shrug, telling myself, w*ell, we're obviously going to sail to SE Asia, whether or not it drives you and me mad in the process*!

Next morning, the wind dies at 0630, and Dave starts the engine. He shuts it down a few minutes later because the alternator isn't working. As this could be serious, I leave my berth to give him a hand. He soon decides that the alternator belt is slipping and tightens it up; ten minutes later, we're underway. But now he fusses over the new wind turbine, which is not producing anywhere near the power he expected. At the end of Day 4, we log 102 nm.

Shortly after my watch starts at 0800, we run into currents. I first notice them when the boat speed drops by half a knot, then see that the bow is pointing off course ten degrees. I hand steer for thirty minutes, by which time we're through them. At 0930, the wind comes up at 10 kt from the south, and I pull out the headsail and shut down the engine. Before long, a number of dolphins stop by for a brief visit.

Just before noon, we're overflown by a big four-engine airplane, the kind used for reconnaissance. It's painted a light grey and the only marking I see is a faint outline of a circle on the fuselage. The plane passes in front of us, then pulls into a tight turn and comes up behind us, roaring overhead at 200 feet. No effort is made to contact us on VHF radio before it continues on its original easterly heading.

The winds grow lighter as the afternoon progresses, and we start the engine at 1900. The autopilot then suffers from some sort of malaise overnight, and *Windy Lady* keeps changing course and heading for Indonesia, but only during my watch! I then have nightmares about hand steering for 110 nm through the reefs into Darwin. At the end of Day 5, we log 107 nm.

We start sailing again at 0845 and are soon making over 4 kt in a SE breeze of 9 kt. The winds ease as the temperature rises, and we're now content to drift along, as we're not far from Cape Don and have hours to fill before leaving there on a rising tide. That night, my berth is so comfortable that I oversleep and am an hour late for my midnight watch.

When I rush up to the cockpit, *Windy Lady* is drifting silently through an eerie world. The stars are veiled, the horizon misty and ill-defined, and the cockpit seats wet with condensation. Dave has sheeted in the headsail as tightly as possible, and I hear an occasionally whump when air is knocked from it as the boat rocks in a slight swell. As air and sea become completely calm, we drift WSW at .5 kt and then at .1 kt. When I check the chart, I see we're headed for a shoal three nm away. We drift backwards, with the bow pointing N or ENE, and at our present rate of drift, it would take thirty hours to get there.

I now hear a dolphin cough and then hear others, so scan the water for twenty minutes, but see no sign of them. I imagine that a bit of phosphorescence here and there is caused by a fin breaking the water. I'm down in the cabin, checking the navigation program, when it suddenly shows the boat moving north. I rush outside to find a whisper of wind, just enough to change our direction of drift.

The wind slowly increases to 5 kt and I then have steerage, so bring the bow back on course. Sea conditions are now so smooth that I have only to touch the helm to correct our heading. A soft whisper of water on the hull is the first tangible evidence that we are sailing. By the time wind speed reaches 9 kt, I've set the wind vane and then the wind turbine starts turning, waking Dave. He takes the watch at 0600 and starts the engine; for Day 6, we log 72 nm.

I spend the morning checking the route into Darwin. We're expecting the tide to change direction four times on the way in, and using information in the cruising guide, I calculate the currents. I figure they'll be favorable for five hours (up to 2.0 kt), then adverse for three (up to 1.5 kt), favorable for five (up to 3.0 kt), and adverse for seven (up to 2.5 kt). As my calculations are rough, Dave and I agree that if we haven't reached a waypoint halfway through by 0200, we'll anchor behind Cape Hotham and wait for the next tide.

We arrive at Cape Don at 1600, right on schedule, then turn our watches back half an hour to Darwin time and start into the Van Diemen Gulf. I'm at the helm as we ride the current in, and Dave takes us through the first tide change at 2230. He then has a problem with the computer, has to shut it down and loses all the waypoints. With Abbot Shoals not far away, he's in a bit of a panic but manages to sort it out in time. He then runs into cross currents and has difficulty settling the boat on course.

When I come on duty at midnight, the wind is on the nose at 13 kt, the sky is full of stars, and a heavy dew coats the top sides. As the tide will change direction during my watch, and we've heard that Howard Channel can be a challenge, I warn Dave that I may need to call him early.

With a functioning autopilot and the navigation program, my watch turns out to be a piece of cake; we exceed 7 kt for two hours, and have a top speed of 8.1 kt. *Windy Lady* stays rights on course as I maneuver through the waypoints, but I keep an eagle eye on the autopilot, and adjust it by two degrees whenever it starts to deviate from the required course. When Dave appears for the next watch, we're an hour ahead of schedule, which isn't all good, as he then has a long, slow slog against the current for the last 25 nm.

We arrive in Fannie Bay at noon and end up anchoring in thirteen feet of water. As Darwin has twenty-three-foot tides, we go much farther out and try again; we're then in eighteen feet. With a refreshing offshore breeze, we relax in the cockpit and gaze at the distant shoreline. Dave would like some eggs for breakfast, but we have no desire to dinghy in. There's no place to tie up, and we'd have to drag the boat up a broad, flat expanse of sand.

CHAPTER 31
Putting Hatches in the Cabin Roof

Our *to-do list* is long when we arrive in Darwin on July 13 and making repairs at anchor not practical, so Dave gets on VHF radio next morning and calls Tipperary Waters Marina. They have a vacant berth, but the marina is two hours away and can't be accessed at low water. As the tide has started to ebb, we leave the cabin a-clutter, pull up anchor, and motor off. An American warship is tied up at the main wharf when we pass, and a police patrol boat stationed 100 feet off keeps pace with us as go by, not letting us come anywhere near it.

Ninety minutes later, we're near the end of Stokes Hill Wharf and I call Peter, the lockmaster, on the radio. He guides us up a narrow channel near shore, and when we're only feet away from a stone breakwater, he instructs Dave to turn hard aport. The entrance to the lock then comes into view fifty feet ahead. He's already told me where to place the lines and fenders, and soon I'm passing the lines up to him. After securing *Windy Lady*, he closes the gate and lets in seven feet of water. Dave then motors out into a small basin containing the marina and we're directed to a slip.

As we need transportation, our first challenge is getting the bikes working. In the seventeen days since leaving Townsville, they've rusted badly and the links in the chains are frozen solid. After copious amounts of WD 40 and elbow grease, the chains again move freely around the sprockets, but there's still a lot of banging and clanging as we ride downtown for groceries. Within a few days, Dave drops his front wheel off a curb and breaks five spokes. When I later check my rear tire, seven spokes are broken. Before they're replaced, I have a flat tire, so also need a new tube.

In spite of the effort needed to maintain the bikes, they serve us well while we're in Darwin. We can frequently be seen riding around town, whether it's downtown for groceries, over to the chandlery at Fannie Bay for boat parts, or making occasional sight-seeing trips. In due course, I clean my gear selector with WD 40, and it works better than ever. The next time we have the bikes out, I get mine into high gear and go flying past Dave, which I've never done before. He lays on the muscle and gets up to 39 km/hour but can't catch me.

After eight years of living on *Windy Lady*, we need to replace the icebox and perhaps the toilet, which is leaking around the base. Given the uncertainty of how long we'll be in the tropics, Dave also wants to put two small hatches in the cabin roof, hoping to improve air flow.

He looks to a motley crew hanging out at nearby Dinah Beach for assistance. At one time, pearl luggers were careened on the sands here, but now makeshift shelters surround numerous boats in various stages of repair. Before long, we will find out that the NT for Northern Territory also stands for *Not Today, Not Tomorrow,* or *Not Thursday*—take your pick!

Dave first hires the friendly neighborhood electrician to connect the wind turbine to the energy monitor (Emon), so we know how many amps it produces. Wally's a slim fellow in his late thirties, a very earnest sort who seems to want to do a good job, but he's intimidated by our electrical panel. He's back and forth four times the first morning, before deciding he doesn't have the right part for the job. We wait a week for a shunt to come in, and then Wally shows up late in the day and works by lamplight. He's constantly checking on himself, and I start to wonder if he knows what he's doing.

He also talks nonstop and tells Dave, "My folks settled in Papua New Guinea after the war, and my dad did quite well. I was born there but was sent to boarding school in Brisbane, as were my five siblings. When the country became independent in 1975, our property was confiscated." He then volunteers, "I'm trying to raise $20,000 to open a shipyard in Kupang, West Timor."

Early one morning a week later, Wally and Dave pore over wiring diagrams, as the amps are still not being recorded. Wally's now back and forth four times in twenty minutes, as something new occurs to him every time he leaves. The last time, he draws more diagrams and moves the shunt from one wire to another. Now happy, he promises to return and solder the wires after we've confirmed that it works. With the next strong breeze, it does, but we never see him again. We're told that he's gone prawn fishing for twelve weeks.

Another denizen of Dinah Beach is a shipwright named Jamie. He has a boat on the hard, a big, old, wooden-planked vessel riddled with worm holes. The boat is about the size of *Windy Lady* and is covered by a tarp and surrounded by piles of equipment and supplies. Jamie has removed several old planks and a new one, made from local hardwood, is clamped onto the ribs. He shows us the long, corrugated-iron steamer that he uses, explaining that a plank will begin to stiffen within minutes of being taken out; within twelve hours it will be fixed in its new shape. A few days later, I see the plank sitting beside the hull and have to admire the graceful arch in its length as well as the curve in the width.

On July 16, Dave talks to Jamie about putting hatches in the cabin roof. After a long discussion about how to proceed and where teak can be sourced, they reach an agreement. A week later, a teak log is delivered to Dinah Beach for which Dave pays $300. When we see it, Jamie has already cut off the pieces needed and there's a lot of wood left over. The two men then agree to meet in the morning to check out the cabin roof and decide where to cut the holes.

When Jamie doesn't show up, Dave and I go ahead without him. After removing the ceiling panels, it's obvious there's not a lot of choice, as there are light fixtures and cross-strips of teak on the inside, and deck organizers, ropes, and staysail track on the outside. He zeros in on two spots, measures them, and places an order at a chandlery.

While waiting for the hatches to arrive, Jamie works on the teak frames that are needed and Dave starts on the toilet. One morning, he bikes over to the chandlery at Fannie Bay three times looking for solutions. A new base for the existing electric toilet costs $460, but there isn't one in stock. A new manual toilet is priced at $540. While we see strange things packed on motorbikes in Asia, nothing is odder than him returning on his bicycle that day with a toilet sticking up out of his backpack.

The new toilet has a different footprint, and he needs a chunk of wood on which to set it, so he scrounges a piece of Indonesian mahogany, a hardwood, over at Dinah Beach. A neighbor walks by as he's struggling to cut it with a handsaw, and generously offers him the use of grinder, drill, bits, and extension cord. By the end of the afternoon, the block is shaped to fit the corner, holes have been drilled on top for the toilet and underneath to secure it to the floor. Next day, he epoxies it and then makes another trip to the chandlery for new hose.

Finally, everything is put back together, but when he tests the toilet, water pours from the top of the pump; two of the screws are stripped. When we take the pump back, the manager narrows his eyes suspiciously; clearly, he thinks Dave is responsible. He then goes through an exaggerated testing process, pumping water out of a bucket and checking each and every screw in the new pump. Personally, I suspect he could be the guilty party because he didn't hesitate to take the electric motor apart when showing us that model.

As the icebox isn't repairable, Dave orders a new refrigeration unit, and when it arrives, he turns to another resident of Dinah Beach for help. Mike is a diesel mechanic and says he'll be there next day to install it. He is, and we have a working icebox by 1300.

Red dust from a nearby construction site settles on the boat daily, and a heavy dew leaves it looking pretty grubby, so I wash the decks every morning. Then, when the temperature rises above thirty degrees, the humidity increases uncomfortably, and we put up the deck canopy and dig out a fan. The mossies and sandflies on the marina boardwalk now make my life miserable, so I leave Dave to attend social gatherings on his own. In late July, a smoky haze appears on the horizon as large areas of jungle are burnt off. The smoke soon covers most of the sky, and frequently I can smell it. It seems to adhere to the dust because now I have to scrub the decks.

In early August, Dave checks on Jamie's work on the teak frames. They need to be rounded on the bottom to fit the curve of the deck and flat on top to support the metal hatches; he's not impressed. I now wonder whether he'll actually let him cut the holes. Then the hatches arrive, and early on the morning of the sixth, the two men have a brief discussion and set to work. Jamie is soon drilling and sawing through the three-inch-thick fiberglass roof.

By noon, the inside of the boat is covered with dust and sawdust, and Dave is very quiet. I figure there's no need for both of us to stand around looking worried, so go downtown for groceries. When I return, light floods in through the holes, a fresh coat of epoxy covers the raw edges, and the cabin has been vacuumed. But an agitated Dave points to the ceiling and agonizes, "Those holes are too big! The hatches have rounded corners and he's cut them square!"

Jamie has now gone and doesn't appear as scheduled next day. By then, Dave is convinced that he'll have to order larger hatches, which could create all kinds of problems if electrical fixtures, teak trim, or deck fittings have to be moved. When Jamie eventually shows up, I again desert the ship. When I return, a new layer of dust circulates inside the cabin, and the men have left for Dinah Beach. Dave is in a happier frame of mind when he comes back, and Jamie later appears with the frames. They then work for an hour, screwing them in place.

When they're finished, Jamie announces, "I'm going to be away for ten days; I've agreed to take someone up to a festival in Arnhem Land." Upon seeing our looks of dismay, he goes on, "No need to worry, I've got a mate who's going to come round and finish the job; his name is Stu." I do worry though, because he says nothing about getting paid.

On August 12, a Monday, Stu phones and puts us off for a week. Dave is more than a little annoyed, and I'm beginning to wonder if we'll get away this season. Stu appears on the Friday and picks up a hatch, saying he'll build the liners in his workshop. He returns at 1700 and confesses, "I'm not really sure what's the best way to proceed with the lining." When pressed, he admits, "I'm having difficulty filling the corners; I would never have cut them square."

Seeing the look on Dave's face, he quickly reassures him, "Don't worry, I'll finish the job. Just don't expect it to be the same standard as the rest of the interior, and don't tell anyone who did the work!" Small comfort for us.

Two more weeks pass, during which we twiddle our thumbs and worry, then Stu returns with the liners. By the end of the day, the hatches are installed. However, more work is needed to finish them off inside the cabin, and Dave moans despairingly, "We're going to have to redo the whole job!" It is then August 26 and we've lost six weeks.

While this has been going on, we've been trying to support friends on another boat, whose tale of woe never stops. Everywhere they look they find problems, one of which is seemingly unsolvable. An airlock in the engine caused it to stall eight times the night they motored through the reefs into Darwin. Lloyd spends weeks trying to sort it out, talking to all the local diesel mechanics, but no one can help. After trying everything else, he re-plumbs the air vents for the fuel tanks. Turns out, they were plugged. It was never a problem when the boat was used for local sailing, as the engine ran for only short periods of time.

They are often at wits end, which brings on bouts of self-doubt, and all we can do is listen. I'm reminded of how dejected we were after the frustrations of our passage from Hawaii to Palmyra. If we hadn't been on a deserted atoll in the middle of the ocean, I wonder whether we'd have carried on. The folks on *Byjingo* helped us by listening, and I can only hope that we do the same for these folks.

But I also remember an old maritime adage that warns: *It's bad luck to change the name of a boat!* This couple did that when they bought it. I now think of the difficult passage other friends had when they ignored the maxim about starting a voyage on a Friday. I always claimed that I was not superstitious, but don't any more. Those adages came from somewhere and ignoring them doesn't seem worth the risk.

CHAPTER 32
An Uncertain Future

We soon discover that the marina in Darwin is a jumping off point for cruising boats going in all directions. Four sailors on a French boat are returning to Europe via the Red Sea and Suez Canal. Another boat is being prepared for a voyage across the Indian Ocean to Mauritius and South Africa. The skipper on a power boat tells us that he's going to the Philippines and describes the route as running straight north for 1800 miles, with SE winds and following seas. A couple on an American boat are looking for company on the passage to Indonesia, and a Tasmanian couple plan to leave their boat in Darwin and fly to Singapore, then spend four weeks traveling overland through Malaysia to Bangkok.

We initially share a slip with an Aussie boat that is taking part in the Matthew Flinders Bi-Centennial Circumnavigation of Australia. Their schedule has them in Perth in October and Sydney Harbor the following June, on the 200th anniversary of Flinders arrival. We're invited to join the group for dinner at the Darwin Sailing Club, which overlooks the yacht anchorage at Fannie Bay. The club is busy, with 200 people having dinner, all wanting to watch the large, red sun disappear into the Arafura Sea. People line up for two and a half hours to get in, just to take pictures.

The Aussie sailors pepper us with questions. Most don't understand why we would choose to stay out for seven nights when crossing the Arafura Sea, as safe anchorages were available most days. We do our best to answer them, but it's only as I'm writing this that the explanation comes to me. It's simply a state of mind.

When we left the west coast of Canada, I remember how jarring it was when I turned and saw that the mountains were no longer visible on the horizon. But the following year, when we left New Zealand, I barely noticed as the hills disappeared from view. In between, we'd spent weeks at sea and grown comfortable in that environment. For us, staying at sea overnight was as natural as breathing. Needing to find an anchorage meant you were still connected to the land.

The boats that left Mt Adolphus when we did and anchored along the way also took a full five days longer to reach Darwin. (Although some reportedly made much better time on a daily basis.) More practically, it takes about three days to adjust to our watch schedule. If we anchored, we'd have to start all over again.

I very much enjoy the dinner that night, but next morning brings a reality check. I recall doing a lot of talking and am embarrassed to think that I probably dominated the conversation. I never used to do that. Our talkative friend, Leo, blamed such behavior on spending too much time alone at sea. (*Too much time to think*?) Regardless, in the years to come, Dave tells strangers, "If you want to hear stories about our time at sea, just buy Lene a couple of beers."

On August 1, a soiree is held on the marina deck for a special guest. Eugenie is a Russian single-hander on his second circumnavigation. He was here first in 1995. Speaking a mixture of Russian, English, and Italian, he has three interpreters to help tell his story. What makes him so interesting is that his boat, *Said*, doesn't look safe enough to untie from the dock. It's twelve feet long, weighs 365 kg, and he built it on the balcony of an apartment in Moscow.

From Europe, he crossed the Atlantic Ocean to Rio, then sailed south and rounded the Horn. After spending 38 days in the Straits of Magellan, the Chilean Navy put his boat on a ship. When 45 km north of Puerto Montt, he was allowed back in the water. Sailing along the coast to the top of Chile, he then crossed the Pacific Ocean to Darwin. I find myself thinking, *now here is a sailor with stories to tell.*

A week later, we stand around and watch as Eugenie unties his boat and motors over to the lock; he's been kicked out of the country. Australian Immigration allowed him to stay only a week, as he carried an expired Soviet passport and the Soviet Union no longer existed. He's off to South Africa, which is the closest point on his route where he can have it replaced.

With the war in Afghanistan, and the rhetoric about weapons of mass destruction in Iraq, the events of 9-11 have cast a long shadow over the cruising community. When I borrow a book of map stencils from a woman on an American boat, she tells me, "It's not much fun being an American abroad these days. Some people will have nothing to do with us; others just harangue us about our foreign policy."

Recognizing the possibility of war in the Middle East, Dave suggests that we head for Africa, rather than follow the usual cruising routes through the Red Sea and Mediterranean. That's a non-starter, as I know that he's not keen on the long voyage across the Indian Ocean. In the end, we decide to continue up to Phuket in Thailand (2,500 nm), then hunker down there in the hope that things calm down in a year or two.

Facing an uncertain future, we have no enthusiasm for the upcoming passage. Things had been different when we left Canada eight years before; we'd been consumed by the idea of sailing across the Pacific Ocean to Australia. But we intend to continue traveling, as we both enjoyed touring in Australia, and the time spent in Townsville has renewed our relationship and our commitment to this lifestyle. It's just unclear as to how much of it will be done aboard *Windy Lady*.

Epilogue

Sailing from Darwin to SE Asia proves to be a very different sailing experience. We don't make it to Thailand, but stop at a new marina in Port Dickson, Malaysia, where we find people we like and conditions that suit us. We stay for eight years.

Buying a car, we drive all over Malaysia and Thailand, even venture into Myanmar. In between trips, we fly to Nepal and spend a month hiking in the Himalaya Mountains, climbing up to 18,000 feet. We're driving along the west coast of Thailand when the sea rises up, 50 km away. Some 225,000 people in fourteen countries lose their lives that day.

When we start traveling by air, we visit Hong Kong, Istanbul, Athens, and Lisbon. We spend three months in South America, arriving in Rio do Janeiro and traveling overland through Bolivia, Peru, and Chile. We then fly to Xian and follow the Silk Road through western China. Next, we visit Vietnam, where we peer down into Cuchi Tunnels, and Cambodia, where we stare with disbelief at the site of mass graves in the killing fields.

All the places we visit are far away in miles, but some of the most interesting are also far away in time, like the Delphi in Greece, Machu Picchu in Peru, and Angkor Wat in Cambodia. (*Exploring Far Away Places, Dreamers and Doers, Part III*)

GLOSSARY

At Mount Isa Mines

The Autoclave

The Road Train

The Great Southern Ocean

The Southwest Corner

Carnarvon Gorge

Kings Canyon

Ladder up to the Amphitheatre

The Devils Marbles

Mullock piles at Coober Pedy

Uluru (Ayres Rock)

Dave stands at the bow of Said, Eugenie in the cockpit

In 50-kt winds for 8 hours

An unreported Low

Arriving in Tonga

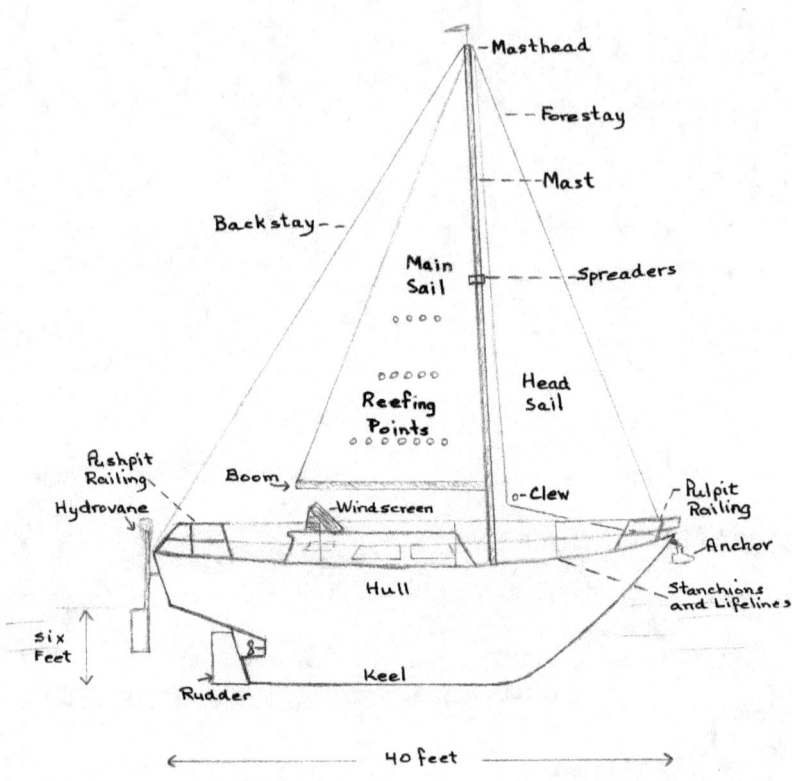

Masthead

Forestay

Mast

Backstay

Spreaders

Main Sail

Head Sail

Reefing Points

Pushpit Railing

Boom

Hydrovane

Windscreen

Clew

Pulpit Railing

Anchor

Hull

Stanchions and Lifelines

Six Feet

Keel

Rudder

40 feet

Boat Exterior

aft, abaft: near or toward the stern

autopilot: self-steering mechanism used under power

backwind: to deflect air onto the back of a sail

beam reach: fastest point of sail

binnacle: the stand in which a ship's compass is kept

blanket: to prevent the wind from filling a sail

chart datum: the water level used to identify depths on a chart

coaming: the raised edge around the cockpit that keeps water out

cockpit: an opening in the deck from which a boat is steered

companionway: stairs between cockpit and cabin

course: the direction in which a boat is steered

dodger, spray dodger: a canvas or fiberglass structure
   protecting the cockpit

fender: a cushioning object placed between boat and dock

to flog: for a sail to flap or flutter when no longer supported
   by the wind

foredeck: deck area between mast and bow

galley: kitchen area of boat

HF radio: high-frequency radio used for long distances

halyard: a rope used to raise or lower a sail

hatch: an opening in the deck that can be sealed off

head: a marine toilet, or the room in which it is located

heading: the direction in which the bow points at any given time

headsail: sail attached to the headstay

headsail furler: a system that rolls the sail around the headstay by
using a rope that runs back to the cockpit

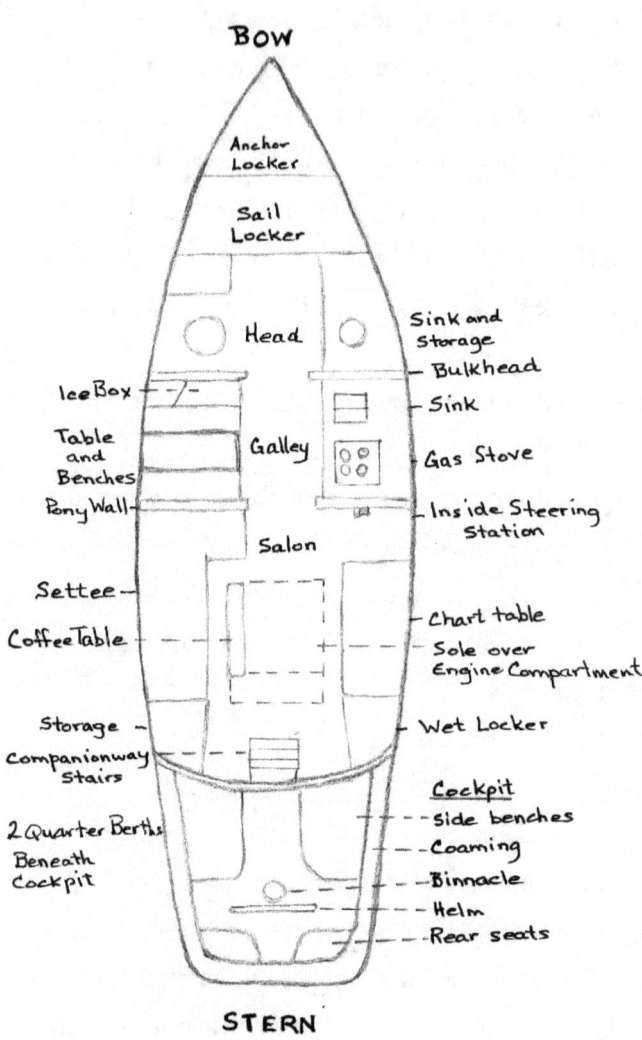

BOW

Anchor Locker

Sail Locker

Head

Sink and Storage
— Bulkhead
— Sink

IceBox

Table and Benches

Galley

Gas Stove

Pony Wall

— Inside Steering Station

Salon

Settee

Coffee Table

Chart table
Sole over Engine Compartment

Storage

Wet Locker

Companionway Stairs

Cockpit
side benches
Coaming
Binnacle
Helm
Rear seats

2 Quarter Berths Beneath Cockpit

STERN

Boat Interior

headstay, forestay: supporting cable running from
    upper mast to bow

heat exchanger: a device that transfers heat from engine water
    on one side of a barrier to cooling sea water on the other side

heel: the angle of the boat to the water

helm: the wheel controlling the rudder

heave-to: to have sails/helm positioned so that boat remains
    almost stationary

hull: the body of a boat, much of which is underwater

keel: an extension of the hull that goes deeper into the water

knot, kt: one nautical mile/hour, or 1.852 km/hour

mainsail: principal sail on the main mast

mast: a pole on a boat that supports the sails

nautical mile, nm: equal to one minute of latitude,
    or 1.852 kilometers

port: the left side of the boat when facing the bow

quarter: the side of a vessel near the stern

to reef: to reduce the area of a sail using pre-established reefing
    points on the mainsail or by furling in the headsail
    (three feet along the bottom equal one reef)

rigging: the system of ropes and cables used to support
    the mast and sails

rudder: an underwater vertical surface that steers the boat

scupper: a drain hole in the cockpit

sheet: a rope attached to the lower corner of a sail that
    allows it to be moved

snatch block: a pulley inside a metal casing that can be
    opened on one side to receive the looped part of a rope

stanchions: metal posts supporting the lifelines

starboard: the right side of a boat when facing the bow

stern: the back end of a boat

squall: a sudden violent windstorm that is brief and
   usually brings rain

tack: to turn a boat so that the bow passes through the eye
   of the wind

toe rail, rail: the outer edge of the deck, usually raised

VHF radio: very high frequency radio used for local
   communication

whisker pole: a pole used to hold out a sail in light winds

windlass: a winch used to raise the anchor

www.ingramcontent.com/pod-product-compliance
Lightning Source LLC
Chambersburg PA
CBHW071142130626
46553CB00004B/1480